NAPOLEON, KING OF ELBA

Staseli and Ray Titus

NAPOLEON AT FONTAINEBLEAU PREVIOUS TO HIS DEPARTURE FOR ELBA.
After the Picture by Paul Delaroche.

[*Frontispiece.*

NAPOLEON
KING OF ELBA

FROM THE FRENCH OF

PAUL GRUYER

With Thirty-eight Illustrations

PHILADELPHIA: J. B. LIPPINCOTT COMPANY
LONDON: WILLIAM HEINEMANN
1906

Richard Clay and Sons, Limited,
BREAD STREET HILL, E.C., AND
BUNGAY, SUFFOLK.

AUTHOR'S PREFACE

THE sovereignty of the Island of Elba was granted to the ex-Emperor of the French in Article III. of the Treaty signed at Paris, April 11, 1814, by the plenipotentiaries of the Allied Powers, and by Coulaincourt and Ney for Napoleon—who ratified it at Fontainebleau. "It is chosen by him as his residence, and will form a separate principality, which he will possess as sovereign and proprietor for the remainder of his life." He was entitled, moreover, to an "annual revenue of two millions of francs reserved from domains and rent charges in the great book of France." The King of Elba would hold the rank, title, and dignity of a crowned sovereign, but he must become a stranger to France. If the members of his suite did not return to their country within the period of three years, they would lose their qualification as French citizens (Article XVIII. of the Treaty). On April 20, after hastily putting his affairs in order, and embracing General Petit in the *Cour du Cheval Blanc*, Napoleon left Fontainebleau, between 11 and 12 in the morning, in a large travelling carriage, and set out for the Mediterranean coast. Thirteen other carriages and sixty post-horses accompanied him, with the following members of his suite and household: Grand Maréchal Bertrand and General Drouot, always his devoted attendants, the Major of the Polish Imperial Guard, Colonel Jerzmanowski, Pay-Master Peyrusse, a doctor, a chemist, secretary Rathéry, M. Colin, household steward, two pay-masters of the household, two chief farriers, half a dozen valets, lackeys, and grooms; and four foreign Commissioners with their aides-de-camp, *viz.*, the Austrian General, Field-Marshal Koller, the Russian General Schouvaloff, the Prussian General Waldbourg-Truchsess, and the English Colonel, Sir Neil Campbell, whose duty it was to watch over the fallen Emperor and defend him, if necessary, from any attack or insult, to accompany him as far as Saint-Tropez, where he could embark for the Island of Elba. From twelve to fifteen hundred troopers of the Guard were to serve as escort (Article XV. of the Treaty). But the chasseurs of Lefebvre-Desnoëttes went no further than Nevers, and after passing Roanne (from Nevers to Roanne the party travelled without escort) detachments of Austrian hussars and Cossacks escorted him the rest of the way.[1] The Emperor, on seeing the bad impression made on the population by this foreign guard, protested against its presence, declaring that he needed no troops to protect him, as he still possessed the affection of the French people. He was soon to

[1] Campbell, 9–29, 38–43; W.-Truchsess, 1–48; Peyrusse, 223–228; Fabry, 17–64; Pons de l'H., 18–25; Ile d'Elbe et Cent Jours, 1–10; Sellier Vincent, 229–234; Gl. Durand, 239–246.

be undeceived. After passing Lyons, the acclamations and respect of the populace came to an end, and as he approached the Southern provinces, the Emperor saw the white cockade appear on hats, and illuminations to celebrate the Restoration light up every town and village. Popular hostility increased, even threatening his personal safety. At Avignon he found the crowds gathered, armed to prevent his advance, and the foreign Commissioners were obliged to interfere and hurry on the changing of horses (as the journey was made day and night without rest), which was effected in the suburbs, to the shouts of "*À bas le tyran!*" "*À bas Nicolas!*" (Nicholas is the name given to the devil in the South), "*À bas la mort!*" At Orgon, he was hung in effigy when he arrived. A small lay figure, provided by a butcher, smeared with blood, swung on a tree in the public square. Round the neck was a placard with the word *Buonaparte.* The crowd, on hearing that the real Buonaparte was on the spot, broke the windows of his carriage with stones and sticks, and he was forced to descend and assist at the immolation of his effigy, which terminated the proceedings, accompanied by yells of applause.

The Emperor, to avoid being torn to pieces by the mob or left murdered in some roadside ditch, borrowed the livery of one of his outriders, and rode in his placc. Galloping on in front of his suite, he arrived alone at the inn at La Calade, near Aix, worn out, horribly bruised by the saddle, panting and half stifled by the *mistral*, which blew a hurricane and raised clouds of dust. The wife of the landlord, to whom he gave an order to get ready fresh horses for His Majesty, asked him if his master was close behind. "I seem to remember your face, my lad," she added with a savage expression. "I advise you to have nothing to do with him. We intend to give him a taste of salt water, him and all his gang. If we don't, he will be back again in three months." As she finished sharpening one of her kitchen knives, she invited him to feel the edge, sneering, "Look, that's very sharp; if anyone would like to make use of it presently, I shall be glad to lend it. It will be done all the sooner." As the rest of his suite joined him, they saw him dash the wine served him on to the ground, white with rage. During dinner, at which he ate nothing, either from loss of appetite or because he feared the dishes might be poisoned, the crowds collected outside the inn, talking excitedly. The Emperor examined the window of the room, which looked on the fields, but was protected by bars. It was impossible for him to mount a horse, bruised as he was, and suffering from an internal malady. He therefore asked General Koller to lend him one of his uniforms, in place of the livery he was wearing, put on General Schouvaloff's cap and cloak, and sent his aide-de-camp to occupy his place. He then got into the Austrian Commissioner's carriage. "Sing," he said. "Sire, I cannot sing," "Well, then, whistle."

Thus he left La Calade, towards midnight, this time escaping recognition.

Before arriving at Aix, the Commissioners wrote to the Mayor asking him to safeguard the Emperor through that town. Severe police regulations were enforced, and the hootings and disturbances kept at a safe distance. Saint Maximin was passed through at a gallop, twelve mounted gendarmes preceding the cortège. Luc was reached on April 26 at four in the afternoon. The Emperor spent the night at the château of Bouillidou, close by, where his sister Pauline, then much out of health, was being entertained. She was astonished beyond words at seeing her brother in an Austrian uniform, and refused, pouting, to kiss him until he had taken it off. She promised to join him at Elba.

On the 27th, at daybreak, he resumed his journey, and instead of going straight to Saint Tropez, diverged towards Fréjus, hearing that the road was in a better state. He found the country, however, full of allied troops, and in one place two squadrons of Austrian hussars lined the road. The Emperor was obliged to pass through them huddled up at the back of his carriage, trying to conceal his humiliation. At nine in the morning, seven days after leaving Fontainebleau, he came in sight of the sea.

It had been arranged that a sloop would be waiting for him, sent by the French Government, and after reaching Elba, to remain as his personal property. (Article XVI. of the Treaty.) But only an English frigate, the Undaunted, was waiting in the roadstead, which Colonel Campbell, at the Emperor's request, and in case of difficulties arising with the French authorities, had brought from Marseilles. He gave orders that his baggage and some of his carriages should be embarked at once on the Undaunted, Colonel Campbell and Captain Asher offering their services, and he himself would go on board later. He spent that day in looking over accounts and official papers with Bertrand, Drouot, and the foreign Commissioners.

During the evening, the French frigate Dryade, flying a fleur-de-lys flag, arrived from Toulon. She brought with her the brig Inconstant, for which she had been waiting at Saint Tropez, having received orders to escort the Emperor and the brig during the crossing to Elba, as it was rumoured that the Barbary pirates were preparing to capture him and take him a prisoner to Algiers. The Emperor refused to accept the Inconstant, saying that he had the right to a sloop, and not an old half rotten brig.[1] Captain Montcabrié then proposed to take him on the Dryade, but he replied that since he could not make the crossing on his own vessel, which was not forthcoming, he preferred to sail under a foreign flag, rather than as a humbled exile under that of the Bourbons. Captain Montcabrié promised in vain that, to please him, he would sail without a flag, but the Emperor was determined,

[1] In size, the sloop came between the frigate and the brig. She usually carried three masts as well as the bowsprit, and 14 to 32 guns; a brig had two masts and 12 to 20 guns.

saying that he had given his word to the English, and would not take it back.

Perhaps he had made up his mind beforehand, and feared, in trusting himself on a French vessel, to be the victim of some plot, or exiled to some distant place, or even perhaps to be assassinated, as threatened by the woman at La Calade.

He was ready to embark on the morning of the 28th, but the wind had dropped, and he remained on land, suffering from a bilious attack and sickness, to which he was often subject, caused partly by the fatigue and excitement of the hurried journey, and partly by some lobster he had eaten for lunch.[1]

In the afternoon he wrote to Marie Louise, and towards sunset he went on board the Undaunted in a small boat, the Austrian hussars lining the quay and the crew of the Undaunted showing him military honours. He took his departure from the little harbour of St. Raphael, where he had landed fifteen years before, on his return from Egypt, in the dawning of his glory. It was now at its setting, his day was nearly over.

General Koller and Colonel Campbell went on board with him; the other two Commissioners had taken their leave. Captain Usher gave up his cabin to the Emperor, who divided it into two by a curtain and shared it with Marshal Bertrand. On the 29th, at seven in the morning, the vessel

[1] Letter from Gen. Bertrand to Meneval (Meneval, II, 243); Fabry, 63.

sailed, in a fresh breeze. Two or three days' journey still separated the Emperor from his new dominion, where he was fated to remain only till February, 1815.

What manner of place was this Island of Elba, and what was the Emperor's life during his ten months of residence there? How did the man live, he who stood only yesterday on the summit of the Western World, and who now was merely the ruler of this infinitesimal corner of it? Hardly a thought has been given to this period, and from Napoleonic history it has almost disappeared; not, however, from lack of documents. These exist in plenty, in official papers and letters, written either by the Emperor's companions, or by persons employed by the different Governments to watch him during his stay. None of the documents are complete in themselves, and taken separately they give a confused impression—but it is by no means an impossible task to put them together, classify, and compare them one with another.

But public interest seems now, as it seemed then, to be aroused only by what happened in France. The great man is allowed to rest in his island, to be taken up again only when he leaves it, from the Hundred Days to Waterloo. If modern historians have noted this period of the Imperial life, they have taken only a cursory view of it as a mere prelude to the Fifth Act which is to come.

The Island of Elba is only a name. It conjures up no picture before the mind, as St. Helena and

Corsica recall Hudson Lowe, or the home at Ajaccio. Of the three islands which represent the birth, life, and death of the Emperor, Elba alone is unnoticed. It is scarcely known whether the country bearing this name is large or small, flat or mountainous, barren or fruitful; scarcely where it lies, except that it is somewhere in the Mediterranean.

When I landed at Elba, I vaguely imagined I should find some bare and arid rock; a foretaste of St. Helena—and my first surprise came in seeing a picturesque country, full of variety, well worth the trouble of the journey. Moreover, this little island, half forgotten in the sea, has remained almost precisely what it was a century ago. The modern life that has penetrated so far has not altered either its natural aspect nor its villages or towns. The Vandalism of modern improvement has spared the strange buildings and left the old walls intact. The very same houses, roads, even stones on the paths, have seen the Emperor pass. I find all the places spoken of in the memoirs of his time; every fact, every event, falls into its place in public functions and private life; there are the same names and the same families.

The history I read lives and breathes again—instead of dried phrases set in unknown scenes, the past is there, living before me. I can see them all as if they exist to-day; the Emperor, ageing a little, but always alert; inscrutable Madame Mère, the venerable Corsican; Pauline, the sweet and beautiful "Venus"; the fair Polish lady, Walewska; the old devoted but grumbling Bertrand, the wise Drouot, the watch-dog Cambronne, making up the little Court of a day, where, under the veil of comedy, is gathering the thunder-cloud of the Return.

These impressions, which I collected or experienced, I have put together in this book.

PAUL GRUYER.

TABLE OF CONTENTS

III

THE LAST IDYLL

IV

THE LION IN THE FOX'S SKIN

V

FROM THE EVASION TO OUR OWN DAY

LIST OF ILLUSTRATIONS

BIBLIOGRAPHY

Archives du Ministère des Affaires Étrangères. France, 675.

Bosworth (T.), *The Island Empire.* London, 1855.

Brunschvigg, *Cambronne.* Nantes, 1894.

Cambronne (Vie de) et son Procès. Paris, 1822.

Campbell, *Napoleon at Fontainebleau and Elba,* London, 1869, partially translated under title of *Napoléon à l'Ile d'Elbe,* by A. Pichot, Paris, 1873. The references, when not otherwise stated, are to this translation.

Catalogue du Musée Demidoff à San Martino. Florence, 1860.

Catalogue de la Vente San Donato. Paris, 1880.

Chautard, *L'Ile d'Elbe et les Cent Jours.* Paris, 1851.

Constant (Napoleon's valet de chambre), *Memoires.* Paris, 1830.

Correspondance Impériale. 1814—1815.

Durand (Mme., widow of the General), *Mémoires.* Paris, 1828.

Fabry, *Itinéraire de Buonaparte.* Paris, 1815.

Fieffé, *Napoléon et la Garde.* Paris, 1857.

Fleury de Chaboulon, *Mémoires.* London, 1819.

Foresi, *Napoleone I. all' Isola dell' Elba.* Florence, 1884.

Foresi, *L'Isola d'Elba.* Pitigliano, 1899.

Giunti (Benvenuto), *Appurti statisti ci del* 1806 *al* 1815. Bologne, 1902.

Giunti (Benvenuto), *Il V Maggio a Porto Ferraio.* Pisa, 1902.

Helfert, *Napoleon von Fontainebleau nach Elba.* Vienna, 1874.

Hyde de Neuville, *Mémoires.* Paris, 1888.

Ile (L') d'Elbe et les Cent Jours, Supplement to *Corresp. Imp.* (Ed. 1870).

Joseph (King), *Mémoires.* Paris, 1857.

Labadie, Larabit, Sellier Vincent, *Souvenirs,* Léon Pélissier. *Nouvelle Revue Rétrospective,* I and II. Paris, 1894—1895.

Laborde, *Napoléon et la Garde.* Paris, 1840.

Larrey, *Madame Mère.* Paris, 1892.

Livi (G.), *Napoleone I. all' Isola d'Elba.* Milan, 1888.

Marchand d'Huiles (Le), *Rapports à Mariotti*, pub. Marseilles.

Pellet, *Napoleon à l'Ile d'Elbe.* Paris, 1888.

Mémorial de Ste. Hélène.

Meneval, *Napoléon et Marie Louise.* Paris, 1844.

Monier (A. D. B. M***), *Une Anneé de le Vie de Napoléon.* Paris, 1815.

Montholon, *Captivite de Sainte Hélène.* Paris, 1847.

Ninci (Giuseppe), *Storia dell' Isola dell' Elba.* Porto Ferraio, 1815.

Peyrusse, *Memorial et Archives.* Carcassonne, 1869.

Peyrusse, *Lettres à son Frère.* L. G. Pélissier, Paris, 1894.

Pons de l'Hérault, *Souvenirs et Anecdotes de l'Ile d'Elbe.* Paris, 1897.

Pons de l'Hérault, *L'Ile d'Elbe au début du XIX. Siècle*, and *L'Ile d'Elbe pendant la Révolution et l'Empire* (*Bulletin de la Soc. Languedocienne de Géographie*, 1896—1897. *Miscellanée Napoleonica III.* Paris, 1897. (All pub. Léon G. Pélissier.) *Biographie.* Paris, 1848.

Registre de l'Ile d'Elbe. Paris, 1897.

Talleyrand, *Correspondance avec Louis XVIII.* Paris, 1881.

Thiébaut (Arrène), *Voyage à l'Ile d'Elbe.* Paris, 1888.

Vincent (Gen.), *Mémoires*, in *Mémoires de Tous.* III. Paris, 1835.

Vincent (Sellier). *See* Labadie.

Waldbourg-Truchsess, *Itinéraire de Napoléon de Fontainebleau à l'Ile d'Elbe.* Paris, 1815.

(Marchand, Napoleon's valet, left memoirs relating to this period of the Emperor's life which have not been published.)

I

THE ISLAND OF ELBA

Elba lies in the Mediterranean, between Corsica and Italy, and, with the other islands of Gorgona, Capraia, Pianosa, and Monte Cristo, forms part of the Tyrrhenian archipelago. It is a day and a half's journey from Paris by express, *via* Modane, Turin, Genoa, and Pisa, and only half a day distant from Rome. A branch line on the railway from Pisa to Rome, starting at Campeglia, crosses the Maremma marshes and terminates at the little port of Piombino.

Piombino is a typical old Italian town, with narrow streets, deep archways, and stone towers scorched by the sun. It offers no accommodation whatever to travellers, scarcely even for one night. Facing the sea, its houses and ramparts descend abruptly into the water. Opposite is the island of Elba, outlined in violet against the sky; rocky and mountainous, its summits almost always enveloped in cloud. The distance between the mainland and the nearest point of the island is seven miles: to Porto Ferraio it is twelve and a half miles. A steamer conveys passengers and the mails twice a day, but these are obliged to go on board in small boats, as the shallow water does not admit of a large vessel close to shore. It frequently happens that the steamer is unable to cast anchor at all, or the small boats to put off with their load of passengers and luggage, and some little neighbouring port, or perhaps Porto Vecchio, is the starting place. Another service leaves Leghorn, and the passage, calling at Gorgona and Capraia on the way, takes eight hours.

The journey is, after all, an easy one, and yet no one goes to Elba, even from Italy; and although the island is beautiful and healthy, and within such a short distance from Rome, it is only occupied by a few farms. Foreign tourists as a rule, and especially in Italy, keep to the well-known routes, and Elba shares the fate of most islands, in being neglected. They need a special journey, and travellers experience a vague feeling of uneasiness, as if they were in prison.

Elba has belonged many times to France; at present it is Italian—but by its physical formation, its climate, and the customs of its inhabitants it is essentially Corsican. Its port is Porto Ferraio, the ancient capital of the island, founded by Cosimo de' Medici in 1548, and still the principal town.

* * * * *

Try to imagine a Swiss lake, only more beautiful, under an Eastern sky; one of those enchant-

LIVOURNE
I. Gorgona
TOSCANE
Volterra
Sienne
les Maremmes
Campiglia
I. de Capraia
Cap Corse
Pto Vecchio
Piombino
Palmaiola
I. Cerboli
Pto Ferraio
G. de St Florent
Bastia
ILE D'ELBE
Grosseto
CORSE
I. Pianosa
Formiche di Grosseto
ARCHIPEL TOSCAN
I. del Giglio
Formica
I. Monte Cristo
Corte
ILE D'ELBE
C. delle Vite
C. d'Enfola
Scoglietto
PORTOFERRAIO
Cap S. Andrea
MARCIANA MARINA
Rio Marina
Rio Montagne
Marciana Alta
G. de Procchio
Mt Giove
Poggio
Procchio
Mt S. Martino
Mt Castello
C. Nera
Mt Capanne
S. Pietro in Campo
Pto Longone
Campo
G. de l'Acona
Capoliveri
G. de Campo
C. Stella
Mte Calamita
C. Calamita
V.H.

MAP OF ELBA.

ing Mediterranean bays of which Naples is the pattern. On a rocky promontory, crescent-shaped, and lapped by the waves, a town is perched, its flat roofs crowded one above the other. A wall surrounds it, climbing up and around the steep rocks, with a little tower at each angle, almost making one expect some Levantine sentry to start up and complete the effect. In the harbour below, enclosed by a jetty covered with houses, and terminating in an old Genoese town, are some tartans, painted bright green, their sails furled like the antennæ of some great beetle. They seem to be asleep on the blue-black water. The whole is a bewildering mass of colour, dazzling and radiant.

This is Porto Ferraio, as the steamer comes up alongside the quay, while the porters shout and gesticulate, taking possession of passengers and luggage. I asked for the *Albergo de l'Ape Elbana* (Hotel of the Bee of Elba), in memory of the Napoleonic bee. Here I found good service, food, and lodging. The only remarkable dish at dinner was one of raw peas served in their pods, and French beans, also uncooked, elegantly arranged on a vine leaf. The other guests seemed to enjoy this form of dessert.

I made inquiries as to the people to whom I had letters of introduction: Signor Emmanuel Comera de Ascarta, the temporary *Sous-Préfet*; Signor Tonietti, French Consular Agent; Signor Bigeschi, Syndic of Porto Ferraio; and the excellent Abbé

the streets. The paving and flagstones are unsullied by dirt or refuse of any kind, and hardly a piece of paper or orange-peel is to be seen. A perfect Dutch cleanliness reigns in this southern town. Four or five street sweepers are employed with a little donkey cart in clearing up any rubbish they can find, and taking it outside the town. This they continue from morning till night.

At the top of the steepest street, a house with red tiles and green shutters overlooks the town: this is Napoleon's house (*casa di Napoleone*), the imperial palace. Outside, it is like one of the simplest Italian villas seen at Genoa or Bordighera. Part of it is now occupied by the military government. Over the door are trophies of cannon-balls, fitting emblem for a conqueror. But the spirit of the god of war is absent; a feeling of peace and happiness seems to pervade the place, as across the myrtle bushes and flowers in the garden stretches the immense horizon of the Tyrrhenian sea, blue and white like a glimpse of Paradise, the headlands outlined against gold. The prospect is brilliant, profoundly peaceful. After so many struggles, so many crushing disasters on Russian plains, after the agony of abdication, the formidable conqueror must have felt something of this ineffable peace as he gazed on the horizon. Every human being is akin, and the same feelings exist in all, in spite of surface differences, and there must have been days, hours at least, when his iron brain relaxed its tension, and a vision of a rest he had never known

ing Mediterranean bays of which Naples is the pattern. On a rocky promontory, crescent-shaped, and lapped by the waves, a town is perched, its flat roofs crowded one above the other. A wall surrounds it, climbing up and around the steep rocks, with a little tower at each angle, almost making one expect some Levantine sentry to start up and complete the effect. In the harbour below, enclosed by a jetty covered with houses, and terminating in an old Genoese town, are some tartans, painted bright green, their sails furled like the antennæ of some great beetle. They seem to be asleep on the blue-black water. The whole is a bewildering mass of colour, dazzling and radiant.

This is Porto Ferraio, as the steamer comes up alongside the quay, while the porters shout and gesticulate, taking possession of passengers and luggage. I asked for the *Albergo de l'Ape Elbana* (Hotel of the Bee of Elba), in memory of the Napoleonic bee. Here I found good service, food, and lodging. The only remarkable dish at dinner was one of raw peas served in their pods, and French beans, also uncooked, elegantly arranged on a vine leaf. The other guests seemed to enjoy this form of dessert.

I made inquiries as to the people to whom I had letters of introduction: Signor Emmanuel Comera de Ascarta, the temporary *Sous-Préfet*; Signor Tonietti, French Consular Agent; Signor Bigeschi, Syndic of Porto Ferraio; and the excellent Abbé

B 2

the streets. The paving and flagstones are unsullied by dirt or refuse of any kind, and hardly a piece of paper or orange-peel is to be seen. A perfect Dutch cleanliness reigns in this southern town. Four or five street sweepers are employed with a little donkey cart in clearing up any rubbish they can find, and taking it outside the town. This they continue from morning till night.

At the top of the steepest street, a house with red tiles and green shutters overlooks the town: this is Napoleon's house (*casa di Napoleone*), the imperial palace. Outside, it is like one of the simplest Italian villas seen at Genoa or Bordighera. Part of it is now occupied by the military government. Over the door are trophies of cannon-balls, fitting emblem for a conqueror. But the spirit of the god of war is absent; a feeling of peace and happiness seems to pervade the place, as across the myrtle bushes and flowers in the garden stretches the immense horizon of the Tyrrhenian sea, blue and white like a glimpse of Paradise, the headlands outlined against gold. The prospect is brilliant, profoundly peaceful. After so many struggles, so many crushing disasters on Russian plains, after the agony of abdication, the formidable conqueror must have felt something of this ineffable peace as he gazed on the horizon. Every human being is akin, and the same feelings exist in all, in spite of surface differences, and there must have been days, hours at least, when his iron brain relaxed its tension, and a vision of a rest he had never known

ing Mediterranean bays of which Naples is the pattern. On a rocky promontory, crescent-shaped, and lapped by the waves, a town is perched, its flat roofs crowded one above the other. A wall surrounds it, climbing up and around the steep rocks, with a little tower at each angle, almost making one expect some Levantine sentry to start up and complete the effect. In the harbour below, enclosed by a jetty covered with houses, and terminating in an old Genoese town, are some tartans, painted bright green, their sails furled like the antennæ of some great beetle. They seem to be asleep on the blue-black water. The whole is a bewildering mass of colour, dazzling and radiant.

This is Porto Ferraio, as the steamer comes up alongside the quay, while the porters shout and gesticulate, taking possession of passengers and luggage. I asked for the *Albergo de l'Ape Elbana* (Hotel of the Bee of Elba), in memory of the Napoleonic bee. Here I found good service, food, and lodging. The only remarkable dish at dinner was one of raw peas served in their pods, and French beans, also uncooked, elegantly arranged on a vine leaf. The other guests seemed to enjoy this form of dessert.

I made inquiries as to the people to whom I had letters of introduction: Signor Emmanuel Comera de Ascarta, the temporary *Sous-Préfet*; Signor Tonietti, French Consular Agent; Signor Bigeschi, Syndic of Porto Ferraio; and the excellent Abbé

Soldani. My best thanks are due to Signor del Buono, the proprietor of San Martino; and I am also grateful to many others. I have seldom experienced in any country more kindness and eager desire to be of service. The people I met in the street were also very good in giving information, and seemed full of ready sympathy for the wandering *Francese.*

Porto Ferraio is an extraordinary town. Many streets are nothing but staircases, and the place is full of arches, tunnels, and ramparts covered with the sword-like aloe leaves and cactuses. Imagination takes one back to Carthage! Surely Salammbô's litter will appear on the steps, just at that corner flooded with sunlight, and up above, between those battlements outlined against the blue sky, there must be a mercenary stringing his bow and polishing his helmet.

But at this point a man, most unlike a Carthaginian, ran up to me crying, "*Signor, la teste di Napoleone.*" (The head of Napoleon.) "Come and see, Signor. The head with his coffin." "He takes me for a fool," I thought, "and thinks I do not know whether Napoleon died at Elba or St. Helena." I shook my head, and walked on quickly, to escape from his "*Nobilissime Signor*" and his excited gestures. But the Italian cicerone is not got rid of so easily, and the man followed me repeating, "*Si, si, la teste, l'empereur Napoleone,*" and as we passed a church he pointed to the door, "Here, Signor, here!" I felt curious, and went into the church, thinking that in any case I should be rid of him.

But he had already spoken to the sexton, and came to me with the sacristy key. There on entering I saw an ebony coffin, black and polished, with the initial N. Four candles in silver candlesticks burned at the corners. I stood wondering, when the sexton, opening the cover of the coffin, disclosed the head of the Emperor—rigid, the eyes shut. My cicerone hastened to explain that the head was of bronze, and tapped it lightly as he spoke. The impression was none the less striking, so little did I expect to see this tragic mask—a reproduction of the mould taken after his death at St. Helena by Dr. Antommarchi. In the dead silence of the church the bronze under the slight blow gave out a sound like a stifled sob, which echoed through the arches of the church, and gradually died away. I learnt later that, unable to possess the tomb of its short-lived king, Elba accorded all the honours to this false coffin ; and on the 5th of May, the anniversary of the Emperor's death, it was placed on a catafalque with lighted tapers round it, and a funeral mass was said in the presence of the official authorities.[1]

I got rid of my cicerone by a *pourboire*, and continued my wanderings about the town in almost tropical heat, up and down the steps, between white walls and closed shutters.

I noticed everywhere the extreme cleanliness of

[1] See p. 269 for the origin of this ceremony.

the streets. The paving and flagstones are unsullied by dirt or refuse of any kind, and hardly a piece of paper or orange-peel is to be seen. A perfect Dutch cleanliness reigns in this southern town. Four or five street sweepers are employed with a little donkey cart in clearing up any rubbish they can find, and taking it outside the town. This they continue from morning till night.

At the top of the steepest street, a house with red tiles and green shutters overlooks the town: this is Napoleon's house (*casa di Napoleone*), the imperial palace. Outside, it is like one of the simplest Italian villas seen at Genoa or Bordighera. Part of it is now occupied by the military government. Over the door are trophies of cannon-balls, fitting emblem for a conqueror. But the spirit of the god of war is absent; a feeling of peace and happiness seems to pervade the place, as across the myrtle bushes and flowers in the garden stretches the immense horizon of the Tyrrhenian sea, blue and white like a glimpse of Paradise, the headlands outlined against gold. The prospect is brilliant, profoundly peaceful. After so many struggles, so many crushing disasters on Russian plains, after the agony of abdication, the formidable conqueror must have felt something of this ineffable peace as he gazed on the horizon. Every human being is akin, and the same feelings exist in all, in spite of surface differences, and there must have been days, hours at least, when his iron brain relaxed its tension, and a vision of a rest he had never known

THE HEAD OF NAPOLEON.

(Testo di Napoleone.)

NAPOLEON'S BANNER IN THE ISLAND OF ELBA.

passed before his eyes. If it came, however, it passed rapidly out of his reach; fate impelled him on, to further battles and fresh disasters.

The exterior of the house has not changed. Inside, most of the rooms have fallen into decay, but the large *salon* on the first floor, with eight windows, four looking on the town and four on the sea, has remained intact. Its plaster walls are still decorated with the paintings the Emperor designed. They seem to be waiting for his return. The furniture was removed after Waterloo, and only two busts remain of the Dukes of Tuscany, Ferdinand III and Leopold II, sad and solitary on their pedestals.[1] The shutters were closed, but badly hung, and rays of light filtered through. On the dusty floor were scattered a few grains of maize; spiders had spun their webs across the corners. Did the master of the house leave it a year, or a century ago? I turned the gilded handles of one of the windows, and opening the shutters, looked out on the little garden, starred with thousands of daisies. The dazzling azure of the Tyrrhenian Sea seemed to fill the room, just as the Emperor saw it. Below the window on an asphalted path is the mark of a horse's shoe, made, they say, by the Emperor's horse while the cement was soft. This has grown already into legend, and Napoleon's horse has become as mythological as the paladin Roland's, whose hoof-marks on stones and rocks are shown all over Europe.

[1] These Dukes owned Elba after the fall of Napoleon.

As the evening closed in, I went down the hill to the town. Sunset is the hour when people of the South grow active after the heat of the day. The town, silent up till now, almost suddenly became active and noisy. On the public square near the harbour the townspeople walked up and down talking and exchanging greetings. Such places are the forum of Italian towns, where all affairs public and private are discussed. The shops were full of buyers. I read amongst the names: Andrea Borgia, Sweet Biscuits; Dante, Shoemaker; and farther on, Orestes and Son, Groceries and Macaroni. A decrepit old woman under an archway sold beans and baked almonds. Women drew water from the fountains in their hammered copper jugs. And as the evening wore on the noise increased. The people seemed to talk for the pleasure of talking, and children cried for the same reason. It was like Paris on some 14th July—guitars, flutes, and accordions joined in the concert. Every sound was musical. Even the street urchins shouted musically. The sounds floated to my windows, mingling in a joyous melody. In this theatrical setting they seemed like the music of an opera.

It lasted till eleven or twelve, and then, little by little, the sounds ceased. The waning moon rose, whitening the stones of the stairways and the battlemented walls, and on their terraces reappeared the shadowy form of Salammbô, mysteriously dancing and beckoning.

* * * * *

The next day I spent in exploring Porto Ferraio. At every turn I found the picturesque and unexpected. The Abbé Soldani, who acted as my guide, slapped me on the shoulder in a friendly way at intervals, exclaiming "*Vive la glorieuse France! Vive le glorieux Empereur Napoleon!*"

We visited the Hotel de Ville. Here they preserve the Napoleonic banner, a great white flag striped with a band of orange, and on it the three bees. When Napoleon was King of Elba it floated over the town, the guns firing a salute when the Emperor went out. A veteran of Solferino, a fine old man, reverentially unfolded the flag for me to see.[1] In the Council Chamber, on the first floor, hangs the Emperor's portrait, a copy of the picture by Gérard, representing him holding the sceptre, an ermine mantle over his shoulders, crowned with a golden laurel wreath. The portrait of Cosimo de' Medici hangs as a pendant. At the table, on the green cloth, each councillor has a little wooden bowl before him filled with red and white beans to drop into an urn at election times. On the ground floor is what remains of the imperial library. The titles of the books make an interesting study, showing the almost universal range of the Emperor's literary tastes. Side by side with the works of Vauban and Maurice Saxe, with books on mechanics, chemistry, and military science, are ancient and modern history, archæology, natural

[1] See p. 270 as to the authenticity of this relic.

history and literature, Montaigne, La Fontaine, "Don Quixote," and sixty volumes of Voltaire.

The most astonishing discovery, however, is a large number of imaginative works, principally *Le Cabinet des Fées*, in forty volumes, containing stories and legends of all countries, from "The Arabian Nights" to Fénelon and Perrault, and fables of India and China. Napoleon, the type of brute force, was also a dreamer. What else but a dream was his stupendous project of uniting the whole of Europe in one vast empire? And we are presently to see him, like Louis of Bavaria, dreaming of some fantastic palace on the summit of Volterraio, losing himself in ecstasy, on Monte Giove, at the sight of sky and clouds, at the midnight heavens teeming with stars; loving to wander in shady woods by murmuring streams on Monte Marciana. In his boyhood he had loved Ossian and his romantic poetry, and all his life he retained something of the old Corsican superstitions he had drunk in with his mother's milk. If these dreams of the past were put aside in his working hours, we may still imagine that before he slept at night he allowed himself to turn the pages of "Ali Baba," "The Fair One with the Golden Locks," or "The Blue Bird."

A marble tablet on the façade of the Hotel de Ville recalls another memory. The inscription is in Italian, and runs something like the following:—

"Here, at Porto Ferraio, in 1802, the little Victor Hugo was brought. Here he learnt his first words, those words which later were destined to spread over the world in sacred fire. Here, in the three years he spent on this island, he breathed in with the air some particles of iron and sea,[1] which, in strengthening his delicate constitution, preserved for France the pride of his birthplace, for the century the glory of his name, and for the cause of humanity an apostle and an immortal genius."

In 1802, a few months after his birth, Victor Hugo was brought to the island of Elba. He was born at Besançon, where his father, Joseph Hugo, a major in the army, was quartered. At the age of six weeks he had been taken to Marseilles, a terrible journey for so young a child, and, moreover, so delicate that the doctor despaired of his life. To add to his misfortunes, his mother had been obliged to leave him, and go to Paris to present a petition for her husband's unduly retarded promotion. The father had to take charge of the baby, who cried incessantly during his mother's absence. When she returned, she brought with her an order to proceed to Elba, which had lately been incorporated with France.

The little family set off at once for Porto Ferraio and settled down there. At first, little Victor's health did not improve; for a year after his arrival at Elba he was still unable to hold up his head, "weighted," as his admirers said, "so heavily by his great thoughts, still in embryo." The child was well made, however, with broad

[1] Allusion to the iron mines; see pp. 32, 273 note.

shoulders and chest, and with the help of the fine sea air and beautiful climate he had begun to develop, after three years' stay at Elba, the robust health he enjoyed all his life. His father was ordered to Italy with Joseph Bonaparte, and Victor went with his mother and brothers to Paris, rue de Clichy, at the end of 1805 or beginning of 1806.

It was at Elba that Victor lisped his first words, which a story has kept for us. Dumas *père* says in his Memoirs that one day in a struggle with his governess, who was threatening him for disobedience, he cried "*Cattiva!*" which means *naughty* in Italian. How had he heard the word, and why had he remembered it? There was joy all through the house when it was known the child had spoken. Thus the first word used by the poet was in a foreign language.

But Elba "recalled no memories to the child as yet." Nevertheless, later, a strange analogy was found between the journey to Elba made by the author of the "*Ode à la Colonne*" and that by Napoleon ten years afterwards. "The rugged and severe landscapes of this obscure place were the first scenes of nature reflected in little Victor's eyes. The young life was already in harmony with its future destiny—the slender thread was being silently woven into the splendid tissue of later years."

While I read and copied the marble inscription, a black arm was suddenly thrust in front of me and a black hand brandished a black purse before my eyes. I turned hastily and drew back, startled at the sight of a man in black—if you can give the name of man to a mere black bag, surmounted by a peaked hood, pierced by two holes, through which looked two burning eyes. This was one of the "Penitents," in quest of alms. He followed me with his black arm, hand, and bag deafening me with a little bell attached to his waist, which he rang furiously until I pacified him with two sous.

I was told that this was the usual custom when one of the confraternity died, the collection going to defray the funeral expenses.

That evening I sat at the door of the Ape Elbana, enjoying the delicious evening breeze, while the townspeople walked and talked, guitars and accordions made music, and children shouted ; suddenly the church bells began to toll, and from the farther end of the town came lamentable cries, growing gradually nearer, while the shop people closed their shutters and the music stopped. A strange procession next appeared on the public square. A coffin was carried by four strong men ; on each side of it walked a crowd of people of all sizes down to small children, all wearing black cloaks and each carrying large candles, chanting psalms as they went. Those who headed the procession waved lanterns mounted on long sticks, or carried crosses or banners. This was the funeral. When I remarked on the lateness of the hour, the hotel porter told me that this was the fashion for any important person ; "it was much the best style."

The procession stopped at the church door. The hooded assistants dropped their tapers on the ground, throwing handfuls of earth on them to extinguish the flames. They then entered the church, each receiving at the door five or six tiny candles, almost as small as matches. They grouped themselves round the coffin as the candles burned, making an extraordinary bleating cry, "*Bai—ai—ai!*" beginning quietly and slowly, and suddenly growing sharp and furious, intolerable to the ear. This was the old Corsican lament. When the candles were nearly burnt out, the priest finished his prayers, the coffin was raised again on the bearers' shoulders, and at the threshold the large tapers were picked up and re-lighted by the little ones. The procession moved towards the cemetery by the road near the sea, while in the town the shops reopened their shutters and the guitars and accordions resumed their music. For a long time I followed with my eyes the path the procession had taken, by the reflection of their candles on the water. A lighted lantern is left on the grave for the night, that the dead may not be quite alone. This funeral of the black cowls goes to the "Black" cemetery. The white cowls have a "White" cemetery. The two confraternities have nothing to do with each other, either in time or eternity.

Porto Ferraio is divided into Black and White, like Guelph and Ghibeline, and if the rival cowls do not come actually to blows in the street, they nevertheless always look askance. The two societies rival each other in procuring the most beautiful sites and attractive tombs for their respective dead. Except in rare cases, the dead are not buried in the earth. Under beautiful porticoes are catacombs of white marble; niches are cut in the thickness of the wall, symmetrically arranged as the cells of a honeycomb. Here the coffins are laid and hermetically sealed. The long corridors are beautified by inscriptions, flowers, and paintings, and there is nothing gloomy or sinister about this last resting-place of the departed. The white tombs with large windows, as I saw them amongst their surrounding trees, reminded me of the Trianon Palace.

* * * * *

All the roads in the island radiate from Porto Ferraio. Several mail carts leave the town every morning, each drawn by one lean horse with long legs, reminding one of a grasshopper. The shafts, instead of being harnessed to his flanks, are tied on his back, and point into the air. If he breaks into a gallop, one is tossed about in a kind of salad basket, and unless one holds on firmly to the sides, one would soon find one's self sitting in the road. The baggage is tied in its place by ropes. Otherwise it would never arrive intact.

One of the roads leads westwards, towards the great mountain on the horizon, whose summit is enveloped in clouds. This is the road to Marciana. It ascends at first through cultivated fields and aloes, with here and there a farm, and one meets a few peasants going to the town, all mounted on donkeys—the woman sitting astride on the animal's neck, the man on his back, the son on the crupper, and various small babies in paniers hanging on the animal's sides. The poor donkey can hardly be seen for the family he carries. Only his head, his tail, and his feet are visible. He goes at a very slow trot, and never seems distressed.

The seashore is curved into a deep semicircular gulf, and Monte Capanno, with its 3,000 feet of altitude, rises straight from it. Clouds always float about Monte Capanno and its neighbour Monte Giove. Below is the blue sea and the sunny shore, where a solitary fisherman, looking like an ant in size, is beaching his boat and spreading out his nets to dry, while up above a hurricane is raging, the thunder rumbles, and flashes of lightning zig-zag down the mountain side. Now and then, when the clouds are torn asunder, patches of snow are visible. A veritable Olympus, where Jupiter and the gods reign apart.

I asked my driver if our pace could not be hurried a little, as the accumulated mass of clouds over our heads might break on us before we reached Marciana. He shook his head, saying there was nothing to fear as yet; and indeed the sun shone upon us all the road, which skirted the gulf (called the Gulf of Procchio), then ascended the side of the mountain, until a last descent brought us to Marciana Marina and l'Auberge de la Paix, Ventura Braschi, *bonne cuisine.*

MARCIANA ALTA.

MARCIANA MARINA.

Neither Signor Ventura or his wife could speak a word of French, but they were full of kindly feeling and shouted very loudly to make me understand. I did my best to explain what I wanted, and while waiting for the "bonne cuisine" set forth on the sign (which resolved itself into maccaroni and eggs) I strolled to the harbour where the fishing-boats had come in empty, the sign of a stormy night.

The clouds had come down the side of the mountain, and the sky was overcast. The sun had disappeared behind a grey curtain. The rough sea broke monotonously on the shore, and a dull feeling of depression had settled on everything. Porto Ferraio seemed very far away, and the near presence of the great mountain, although invisible behind the mist, weighed down on one like lead. It had turned very cold. What a change in the aspect of things in a few hours! A fine penetrating rain began to fall; one could almost imagine oneself on some desolate shore in Norway or Spitzbergen. After dinner, as I went to my bed-room in another building, I could hardly walk for the violence of the wind, which blew the sand against my face. Showers of spray fell into the streets, and the only light to be seen was a tiny lamp burning before a shrine of the Holy Virgin in the market-place. My thoughts travelled back to just such a night as this, the last scene of the love-story of the King of Elba and the fair Countess Walewska. They met on Monte Marciana, snatching a few hasty hours together, and separated in storm and hurricane.

The next morning I was awakened by the sunlight. I intended that day to ascend Monte Giove and see Marciana Alta (Marciana on the Mountain), the twin-village, as it were, of Marciana by the Sea. On the Mediterranean coast these double villages are very common, and are found also in France, Italy, Corsica, and Spain. Their object was to protect the population against the attack of pirates, who, up to the middle of the nineteenth century, when Algiers was taken over by the French, invaded the coast, killed the inhabitants, and pillaged their property. Watch towers, the ruins of which still exist on rocks and headlands, were built round the coast, and the approach of the pirates was signalled. The people of the lower villages then collected their most valuable property, and fled to the higher ones, fortified to repel any assault. The pirates rarely ventured so high, as they might easily have been crushed in climbing the steep ascents by showers of stones and rocks. Indeed, they hardly knew where the villagers had taken refuge—it seemed somewhere up among the clouds.

I asked to be directed to Marciana Alta, and Signor Ventura came out with me and pointed to the mountain. Where we stood the sun shone, the atmosphere was warm, and the sea calm and smiling, but the mountain was still cut across by a thick veil of cloud, completely hiding the upper part. Behind the veil is Marciana

Alta. I had only to follow the path, always ascending.

I began to climb, therefore, keeping on steadily. The air felt warm and damp. Before me was that thick curtain of cloud, behind me when I turned was Marciana Marina growing smaller and smaller, and an immense panorama of coast line stretching out at my feet. Soon I reached the cloud, and everything disappeared, before, behind, and all round me. Nothing was left but mist, which gathered in drops of water on my clothes and beard just as it covered every plant and blade of grass. The aspect of the vegetation had changed. I was now in a northern climate, heather grew round me, and large chestnuts, still bare of bud or leaf, while at Porto Ferraio the myrtles were in full flower. Then I came to ferns and moss, with tiny streams falling in miniature cascades. The path became steeper, but was still clearly visible through the mist. I met a woman and a mule, looking like phantoms as they came towards me. She was going, no doubt, to the lower village to buy provisions, as food must be scarce on the mountain. She murmured "*Buona sera*" as she passed, and seemed much surprised at the strange language in which I replied. After another half hour, objects grew more distinct, the sun began to peep out, and, above my head, Marciana Alta broke through the clouds.

It was a curious spectacle. Before me shone a northern sun in a cold, clear atmosphere; behind, the thick veil of cloud hid the base of the mountain, just as from below it had concealed the summit. I felt as if I were cradled in folds of cloud, suspended over nothingness. Most wonderful of all, is the fact that people live here; at least, judging by houses and a church tower, there ought to be inhabitants, for I saw none there. Everywhere was dead silence; no sound from below, and no sound from this mysterious village, with its rugged houses closely packed together, within a stone rampart. It was like a Corsican stronghold, wild and forbidding—the nest of a bird of prey.

I climbed some steps and passed under an archway, climbed more steps, and found myself in a narrow alley, with a blackened, sticky pavement. A woman, with a profile like a vulture, was sitting at her door, dressed in black, with a black handkerchief on her head. Her eyes were bright and gentle, however, as she looked at me with a perfectly impassible expression. Presently another woman appeared, also in black, leading a black goat by a cord. Then a third, this one quite young, carrying a load of hay. But where were the men?

Close by was an inn; and partly to rest after my climb, partly to inquire for a guide, I went up to it, and heard voices through the doorway. So far, so good; here, there were some men. Some men! *All* the men in the village were here. I had been wondering what they found to do in this out-of-the-way place. The answer is simple—they do nothing.

At least, they drink, smoke, play cards, and talk,

from morning till night, every day and all the year round. It is the typical Corsican village, the amazing existence led by these people who live in complete solitude, year in, year out, seeing nothing —separated from the rest of the world by the clouds—and spending their time drinking vermouth, and discussing the destinies of Europe. The main objects of their lives are to talk politics, and to record their votes every two or three years. During the summer months a few try to cultivate the mountain side, and raise crops: a little lower down they plant vines, which do fairly well, but the work is hard, and few of them take this trouble. The more enterprising spirits emigrate to try their fortunes in America. But as soon as they accumulate a small sum—a real fortune here, they hurry back to their native soil.[1] Some keep pigs, which pick up enough to feed them, others keep goats led to pasture by the women, or they grow potatoes, or pick up chestnuts. The small sums they make in this way pay for their wine and tobacco.

As I entered the inn the cards were laid aside, and the Governments of the old and new worlds, which were having a bad time, had a few minutes' respite, as pipes were put down, and the politicans looked me all over, saying to each other "*Inglese!*" I asked if anyone spoke French. One of them

[1] The island of Elba belonged to Spain for a great part of its history (see pp. 30 and 37), and its emigrants made their way to the old Spanish colonies in South America. Most of the fortunes, large as well as small, have been acquired there.

rose and holding out his hand, answered, "What do you want, Sir?" I heard murmurs, "*Francese, Francese, come l'Imperatore*" ("a Frenchman like the Emperor!") I begged the man to tell me if he knew any one who could guide me to the summit of Monte Giove, and to the Madonna's Hermitage. He beckoned to a man who was sitting on a bench, half asleep—a man of herculean build, displaying a muscular, hairy chest through his shirt, unbuttoned at the neck. He was bare-footed, and carried a stick, or, rather, a heavy club. It would hardly be pleasant to meet him suddenly in the maquis if one were alone. And this giant of strength spent his time lolling here, in absolute idleness! When he understood what I wanted, his eyes lit up, no doubt at the prospect of money so easily earned, and he ordered something to drink at once, on the strength of it. He then took charge of my small amount of luggage, and said he was ready. With his really alarming appearance I found this man was the good giant of the children's fairy tales, ready for anything asked of him in return for bite and sup in the kitchen.

The road to the Hermitage is paved like a Roman way with blocks of rough stones. Here and there are shelters for wayfarers against the rain, wind, and snow, of which last there still remained large heaps in the hollows facing north. "In a month's time we shall be roasting," said the man in his *patois*. That day, the beginning of April, I shivered in spite of the exercise of walking.

THE GULF OF PROCCHIO, MONTE CAPANNO, AND MONTE GIOVE.

The fog, as I feared, now covered the mountain-top. When we reached the Chapel of the Madonna, we could hardly see ten paces in front of us. One might be either at the top of a mountain, or the bottom of a well for all our eyes could tell us. I could dimly make out the walls of the chapel, a few crooked chestnut trees with bare branches, and a little house with closed doors. The house was inhabited, as, in answer to my guide's knock, an old man, with a head like a goat, opened the door. This was the hermit.[1]

He could certainly not complain of the worry of neighbours, nor could gossipping be his besetting sin. Here he lived with his wife and his goat, as dead to the world as an Indian on the Pampas. Marciana Alta was to him the centre of civilisation, where he spent the winter: Marciana Marina an important expedition: and if he went twice a year to Porto Ferraio, it was the extreme limit. Here, however, he was king; and in his wretched hut he must often have been a spectator of extraordinary atmospheric conditions: and I wondered why his hut had not been torn from the ground or destroyed by lightning, in some of the violent storms peculiar to southern climates. He seemed indifferent to all

It is not unusual in Provence, and the Pyrenees, and other southern districts, to come across these lay hermits, who no longer have any religious characteristics, but are charged by the communes or churches with the care of certain famous sanctuaries, which they look after, in return for the gratuities bestowed upon them by pilgrims and visitors. Some return every night to their own village, others live in the hermitage, and spend the rest of their days in its tranquil solitude. Monserrat is another retreat of the same kind.

these trials; whether deafened by the howling wind, frozen one day, baked on the next, or smothered in fog—fogs so dense that they give one the impression of being enclosed in a shroud. He smiled on seeing visitors, for he is in charge of a register, with a pencil attached, and all those who come since Napoleon's time are asked to inscribe their names. He keeps the keys of the little chapel, which he shows, and also a print by Epinal of Napoleon. This appointment is his only source of income, and, judging by the number of visitors who come, it is unlikely he will ever make his fortune.

In one of the four rooms of this little house Napoleon stayed, and received Countess Walewska, on September 2 or 3, 1814. A wooden crucifix more than a century old, nailed to the wall was, perhaps, a witness of their meeting; and the hermit's bed, consisting of a plank on an iron frame, with a mattress of dried fern, was probably scarcely worse than the Emperor's.

Everything here appeals to the imagination, from the damp walls of the little chapel which had sheltered him, to the altar steps where knelt Madame Mère, who came up from Marciana to pray and offer a candle to the Madonna if she would protect her son from harm. At the entrance to the chapel in a stone semicircle, lichen-covered, are four fountains filling their carved basins with a continual splashing. The façade of the chapel is painted in fresco, and the Emperor's visit is commemorated by a marble plaque, placed there in

1863. It sets forth that he stayed here from August 23 to September 14, 1814. The last date is an error. The Emperor left the Hermitage on September 4 or 5.

The fog was as dense as ever, and I gave up all hope of seeing the splendid view which in clear weather is to be had from this height of 2,500 feet. The hour grew late, and if I was to sleep at Marciana Marina, I must turn back, as the descent is long and difficult. The old man tried to make me understand that I must wait a little. "*Poco, poco, Signor*," he said, waving his arms like a windmill, to indicate that the fog would soon disperse—when I should be able to see "*La Corsica.*" I felt rather doubtful of such a chance, as the fog seemed to thicken rather than disperse. But I know that the most unexpected things happen on a mountain top, and I turned back into the hut, to warm myself and wait. As for my giant, he seemed on the contrary to suffer from heat, in spite of his bare feet and open shirt front, as he found a jug of cold water under the table and drank several tumblers full. While I dried my clothes, the old man went out to report on the progress of the fog, which rolled past in great puffs like smoke. Suddenly, as we looked, the heather shivered, a wind rose, the bare branches of the trees showed more distinct, and flecks of blue appeared in the sky. "*Venite, Signor, venite,*" cried the old man. He led me to a rock, rudely carved, forming a rough throne where they said the Emperor used to sit.

As we reached the place the fog parted as if touched by a fairy's wand, rolling down the mountain side, and only shreds of it remaining here and there, looking like great tawny-coloured birds perched on the rocks. The atmosphere was bathed in radiance, and right in front of me, beyond the sea, in the golden western light, was the serrated line of the Corsican mountains, all the snowy range from end to end of the island. It was a sight I shall never forget.

The old man was delighted at his triumph. He gazed as I did at the setting sun opposite to us, now nearly touching the horizon. As it sank lower, the disc grew sharp and clear as if cut in metal. The fire was gradually extinguished, and in the luminous transparency which comes before twilight, the smallest details were clearly defined. "*Bastia!*" cried the old man, taking hold of my arm and pointing out some little white objects gathered close together. They were houses in the Corsican town: I could almost distinguish the windows.

For five minutes this lasted, a violet light spread over the sky above Corsica, like lilac blossom in the garden of Eden. The sea, smooth as the blade of a sword, reflected the marvellous colour. But now the clouds began to gather again, the fog drew together like a curtain, veiling the radiant infinity of sea and sky. Winter fell on me in the growing darkness, and the wind blew cold through the bare branches. The old man pulled his fur cap over his ears, and I made haste to descend, as I had to reach Marciana Marina that night.

I passed through Marciana Alta where the lights began to appear in the windows of the dark, rugged houses, and caught sight of Poggio, another village half hidden in the clouds. When night fell I had only accomplished half the journey. I had left the fog behind, however, on the mountain top, and when I descended the last slope to regain Signor Ventura's albergo the night was as clear as a night in the East. The good man was growing uneasy about me. I passed the Holy Virgin behind her grating, with the steady little lamp burning. No trace of last night's storm was perceptible in the warm, balmy air. I had been through every imaginable scene and aspect of nature during the last twenty-four hours, as if the island had come unfastened from her moorings and had floated across the sea from South to North, from the kingdom of light to the sad country of Cimmerian gloom.

* * * * *

Two years later, I paid another visit to the Madonna's Hermitage—this time in the month of May. The mountain, from base to summit, was bathed in sunshine, except where the forest of chestnuts, as far as Marciana Alta, gave a delicious shade. The dismal village had awakened to life. Birds sang in the trees, some of the men worked in their vineyards, and others were busy white-washing their houses, while a few strummed on guitars at their door-steps.

On my asking for an inn where I could stay the

night, I was taken to a gloomy-looking house down a flight of steps still damp from the winter's rains. The side of the house away from the street rose like a fortress, straight from the precipice. At dinner-time, however, while I ate my beefsteak my hostess placed a vase of flowers on the table, and her husband sat down at an ancient harpsichord and strummed with all his might, to amuse me as I dined. When bedtime came, the woman went out, and returned with a bunch of herbs, which she plaited into a little wreath. This she hung on the head of my bed, saying, "This is the Holy Ascension herb (it was the eve of the feast) and I gathered it on the mountain for you. It brings luck to the stranger."

After bidding good-bye to my kind hostess the next morning, I followed the familiar path and the paved road with its stone niches, now serving as shelters from the sun on this shadeless road. As I ascended the air became more rarefied, and in the blue immensity round me I could hardly distinguish where sky and sea met. Thousands of flowers carpeted the ground, mostly red and white Alpine roses with their golden hearts. At the Hermitage I found a little flickering shade came from the budding chestnuts, and here were the gurgling fountains and the little lawn studded with pale violets and purple cyclamen.

I could see Corsica, like some great Leviathan, sleeping in the water, and the island of Capraia at its side. I saw the sun set again behind its mountains, and when night came the old hermit with the goat's head, who remembered me, prepared for me one of the little rooms which had sheltered the Emperor and Walewska. I dined off a bowl of milk and a plate of broad beans. The hermit also gave me a bowl of water which he explained was for the purpose of softening the bread, which he only bought fresh every month. The mattress was as hard as the bread, but the charm of the situation brought pleasant thoughts, and from the uncurtained window I was almost dazzled by the stars.

Thus did Monte Marciana appear to me in summer, but she fastens on every cloud that floats by, and is soon veiled again from the rest of the world.

* * * * *

The other great road in the island leads to Porto Longone Rio Marina, and the iron mines—in the opposite direction to Marciana, that is to say, to the south and east. Slightly ascending, it skirts the bay of Porto Ferraio, and follows all the developments of its beautiful contours. At one point are some Roman remains: blocks of stones in regular order, crumbled steps, ruined arcades. Here an amphitheatre stood by the blue sea, for witnessing galley races, either by oar or sail, or war galleys in mimic battle.

The horse slackened his pace as the road grew steeper, then resumed his jolting trot. We passed through a pine wood, and at the highest point a custom-house. Then we began the descent on the eastern side of the island.

Capoliveri was the first village we came to, a forbidding-looking place, and with a bad reputation. The Romans in ancient times, and the Persians of the middle ages, made a sanctuary of it, recognised by law, for debtors, false coiners, bankrupts, runaway slaves, and convicts escaped from prison, who all sought its refuge from the Continent. Hence the name Capoliveri, *Caput Liberum* in Latin, Capo Liberi in Italian. A riff-raff population is the result, whose disorderly conduct is the terror of the island. It looks like a fit haunt for brigands, perched as it is at the top of a steep hill; and one expects to see the muzzles of guns gleaming up there from the walls. In Napoleon's time he was forced to send 220 soldiers and gendarmes against them: his only means of collecting their taxes. The people have somewhat improved since then, but they do not mix with the other inhabitants of the island.

The road descends to the sea-level, where the thick leaves and flowers of the aloes grow down to the water's edge. Here we came to the little harbour of Porto Longone, where food and lodging are to be had at the *Albergo della Maria*. I found the people pleasant. Above the town, on a rocky eminence, the Spaniards built a citadel in 1605—19. It includes a convict prison, and a church with Spanish tombs.[1]

[1] The prison or *ergastulum* of Porto Longone can contain 800 convicts. Another prison at Porto Ferraio holds 400.

The road from Porto Longone to Rio Marina is a triumph of engineering; now rising, now falling, and alternately revealing and hiding the sea. About a mile out from Porto Longone, on the left-hand side of the road is a footpath leading down a gorge.

Here I left the carriage, and at the end of the ravine amongst giant aloes, stone pines, and cypresses, I found the humble chapel of Monserrat, offering shelter to the pilgrim under its vine-clad trellis. It is almost overhung by sharp, needle-shaped rocks, where shepherd boys in search of their flocks call to each other. At the extremity of the valley is the sea, and through the network of pines and cactuses I could catch sight of a sail as it swept by.

It is an exquisite place, with a Virgilian simplicity and charm, and one might well remain with peace in one's soul and let life slip by. No echo of the world's revolutions can have sounded here. Pan and the Dryads surely hid from each other in these thickets, and it looks to-day just as it must have looked when the first Christian hermit built the little white-walled chapel, and as the Emperor visited it.

But I heard the driver impatiently cracking his whip down there on the road. I was obliged to tear myself away, and go: and we drove through Rio Montagna, whose regular, cube-shaped houses looked like dominoes piled on one another. At a fork of the road is a solitary chapel with a triangular pediment, and a portico like a Greek temple, where one expects to see Daphnis bringing an offering of a young goat or new-born lamb.

At the next turn of the road, alas! all poetry was at an end. We came into thick, black smoke, issuing from high factory chimneys. This was Rio Marina. Good-bye to balmy woods, to rural valleys, to pure skies, to murmuring pines, and peaceful country folk on their donkeys. We are now in the land of iron.

Rio Marina is the defilement of the island. Nowhere could be found a greater contrast between green, beautiful wholesome nature which God made for man, and the physical and moral blemish the world has imposed on nature, by human manufactures. The first impression was wholly bad. Bold-eyed women were washing linen in a corrugated iron shed, shouting jokes to each other. One of them caught sight of me, and said a word to the others, and all stared at the stranger with impertinent curiosity. I stared also, but not an eye was lowered. A beggar approached—the first I had seen on the island—a miserable, sordid, creature, bent almost double. "*Signor, la carità*," he said, catching hold of me with a claw-like hand, "*la carità! la carità!*" I understood that he was old, had worked in the mines, and that a large piece of rock had crippled him.

Further on were houses, six stories high, like those of a large town; one felt that the people were packed one upon another inside, with swarms of children, and stifling smell of cooking. Rags hung from the windows, and untidy heads peeped out. Every now and then a basket was lowered by a string into the street. Into this receptacle the postman deposits letters, the tradesman his meat, bread, and vegetables. The inhabitants thus save their legs, and as the dinner hour was near, the baskets were coming and going continually.

What I noticed specially about the town, however, was the reddish colour of every object. The rusty iron dust covers the houses, even to the leaves on the trees, the grass, the people's faces, and their hands and clothes. The wind carries it along, and I was soon thickly covered myself.

I met a drunken man, who, like the beggar, was the first I had seen on the island ; he pounced on me, taking my hand and squeezing it effusively, gabbling some words I could not understand. As it was past mid-day, and the sun burning hot, I took refuge in an inn—*Albergo Ristorante.* There I found a dirty room, a soiled table cloth, flies in the water-bottles, and greasy cooking on greasy plates. My unpleasant meal was shared by some commercial travellers, who also joined in my ineffectual complaints. When my bill was presented I was charged twice as much as my companions. I refused to pay, and the others coming to my help, the landlord, like a whipped dog, consented not to rob me more than the other guests. He received his exorbitant payment with a sulky, supercilious air, and, without any acknowledgment, returned to the bar to wash the glasses with his dirty fingers. Oh! this hideous industrialism, corrupting, and soiling everything it touches! bringing to light all the vices and baseness of life, which increase at its touch.

The mines are not specially interesting. They are worked from the surface, and one has only to stoop, as it were, to pick up the iron. It is carried in small waggons to the boats waiting at the foot of the mountain. Any iron of inferior quality is kept back to be sifted in the workshops. The yield is considerable; it is worked at small expense, and amounts to 300,000 tons per year. Many of the boats come from England.

The mines seem to be inexhaustible. Etruscan and Roman coins have been found there, proving a very early date for the first workings, and the mountain to-day looks like the mass of craters on the surface of the moon. The miners' faces can hardly be seen for the coating of dust adhering to them, and the surface of the ground sparkles in the blinding sun like a carpet of diamonds.

I was glad, as I returned, to see the solitary valley of Monserrat, and the untarnished beauty of the Bay of Porto Ferraio with its Genoese turrets. Up to the time I visited it, Rio Marina was hidden away behind its mountain barrier, and the rest of the island was untouched—but not for long. Now, alas! furnaces are appearing near Porto Ferraio; two great chimneys, 200 feet high, tower above the bay, harsh and red, like two monstrous guillotines, vomiting their smoke and flames over the splendour and purity of the island. In the place of radiant Phœbus, Vulcan now reigns with his attendant Cyclops, and the clamour of his blast furnaces.

It is, of course, perfectly natural that the mining company should wish to extend their business, but what of the inhabitants of Porto Ferraio, whose fresh air is poisoned and beautiful sky blackened by this invasion? Instead of protesting, as might be supposed, they welcomed it with joy, foreseeing future prospects of sinecure appointments, so dear to the Southerner. They were not aware that business companies, unlike Government schemes, do not employ useless individuals, and that furnaces require stokers instead of clerks. Salaries would be earned in future by shovelling coal, and not by reading the newspaper comfortably in arm-chairs. Peasants would be forced to leave their peaceful fields, their pleasant means of livelihood, and for a higher and more immediate gain become mechanics, scorching their faces and chests at the furnaces. Like the savage African tribes, who dance round their blood-stained idols, in their ignorance they jumped for joy before the Moloch who was to devour them.

* * * * *

Such was the island as it appeared to me. Besides the two great roads to Marciana and Rio, which cover fifty miles of ground in their innumerable windings, there is only the road on the south coast to Campo, the remaining town on the island. This is the town of marble quarries, where Pisa obtained material for her palaces and churches. Long after Pisa's downfall, the remains of her magnificence might be seen scattered about the quarries. Shafts and bases of columns, capitals only half hewn—ruins of a glory suddenly vanished. San Pietro in Campo is perched on the mountain above the little harbour of Campo Marina. According to the island custom, the eagle's nest is built as a refuge for the inhabitants of the lower town.

Beyond Campo the roads are only mule-paths, narrow foot-ways climbing above inaccessible headlands and deep gulfs, or traversing jagged mountain tops. A steady head and untiring feet are needed to climb to all the summits in Elba. Opposite Porto Ferraio, on a peak of 1,292 feet, is a ruined fortress—the doors and windows now only visited by clouds. This is Volterraio's ancient stronghold. The Emperor once formed the project of climbing to it, but allowed himself to be dissuaded by his attendants. How were the walls built on this precipice, which man hardly dares to climb for fear of being blown down by every gust of wind? Popular tradition says it is the work of giants—and certain it is that only supernatural beings could inhabit such a place. There are cisterns for collecting rain water in the fortress, and space for lodging five hundred men.

The highest point of the island is Monte Capanno, neighbour to Monte Giove, and, according to ancient geography, it measures over 3,000 feet.

The island is $17\frac{1}{2}$ miles long from east to west, 12 miles from north to south. Its circumference, measuring the indentation of its coast line, is 52 miles. The women are good-looking, with regular features, complexions like milk, and quantities of fine wavy black hair. Occasionally one sees reddish blondes, like the Florentine type, but they are rare.

The history of Elba is, like that of most of the Mediterranean islands, a recital of misfortunes. Any foreign people with an armed ship at command can dispute the possession of these sea territories, with fire and sword in hand. Elba, by reason of her small size, would no doubt have been overlooked by covetous neighbours, were it not for her rich and ill-omened iron mines, which as far back as memory reaches have been her curse in attracting the foreigner. The Etruscans, long before Rome existed, were the first people to conquer and colonise the island. They were succeeded by the Carthaginians and Romans, who sent swarms of slaves to work the mines. The Goths, Visigoths, and Ostrogoths next passed the straits, and took possession of the island, bathing it in blood. Then it fell into the hands of the Lombards, the Germans, Pisans, Genoese, and Spaniards. The French appeared next, and war having broken out between Francis I. and Charles V., the Sultan,

Soliman, ally of the King of France, sent the Ottoman fleet against Italy and her islands. The fleet was commanded by the famous corsair, Barbarossa, who had attained the position of admiral by his audacity and cruelty. Not content with bombarding the coast, he landed and raided the island, killing men, women, and children, and setting fire to everything in his reach. The ruin he left behind him was so terrible that fresh colonists were sent over from Italy, and the few miserable survivors, hidden in caves and woods, were quite unable to rally after so many disasters.

In 1548, Cosimo de' Medici, Duke of Florence, united the island of Elba to the dukedom of Piombino and founded Porto Ferraio. He fortified it and called it Cosmopolis, a name it retained to the beginning of the nineteenth century.[1] Its misfortunes, however, were not over. Italians, Spaniards, Turks, and Frenchmen still wrangled over this scrap of country, and besides these, there were Corsairs from Algiers, who pillaged the island in passing, and the English, anxious to secure a foothold between Italy and Corsica.

Elba, however, at last began to weary of her miserable lot, and determined to free herself once and for all. In 1799, France had landed some troops and occupied Porto Ferraio, alleging as

[1] "Cosmopolis," or city of Cosimo. Above the mouldering oak door of Forte Falcone, which dominates the town, is the inscription: *Templa, mœnia, domos, aras, portum. Comus Med. Florenti. A Fundamentis erexit.* A.D. MDXLVIII. (Cosimo de'Medici, of Florence, erected these temples, walls, houses, altars, and this harbour, from the foundations, A.D. 1548.)

pretext her rupture with Tuscany. The people of Elba secretly arranged a terrible revolt, under an apparent submission. Every French inhabitant was marked for destruction, and the massacre was simultaneous. The convicts were all liberated in these new Sicilian vespers, to help in chasing the wretched survivors, who, like wild beasts, were hunted through the woods, and into the ravines and caves of the mountains, where they had taken refuge. The inhabitants of Capoliveri were true to their infamous reputation. They offered shelter in their village to the fugitive French people, who imagined themselves secure in this sanctuary. Defenceless and helpless within the walls, they were all massacred. The dead bodies were cut in pieces, and exhibited in triumph by their butchers, following the example of Attila and Alaric.

In 1801, Porto Ferraio was again blockaded by the French fleet, bombarded in 1802, and in the same year that the Treaty of Amiens had officially given Elba to France, the island sent a deputation to Paris. The delegates were received by the First Consul, to whom they promised their fellow countrymen's loyalty, giving the assurance that they would consider themselves, henceforth, faithful Frenchmen, and begging in return for protection against invaders. Soon afterwards an attack from the English was repelled by an alliance of French and Elban troops.

Twelve years later, when the Treaty of Fontainebleau bestowed the island on Napoleon, its population had risen to 12,000. The poor inhabitants were, however, greatly lacking in the material well-being and culture of civilisation having, up till then, employed all their resources in defending their lives against repeated bombardments, fire, and pillage.

The houses were small, with low ceilings, and the families accustomed to sleep together in the same bed, without distinction of sex, and with a complete absence of clothing. The lower classes in both town and country used only common earthenware cooking utensils, and for food they had dried vegetables imported from the mainland, cheese made of goats' milk, coarse and unwholesome bread, and salt meat. They flavoured their badly-made wine with ginger, making it still more indigestible. Chestnuts were ground into a sort of polenta, and kneaded into a hard cake, which was stored from year to year. The inhabitants of the coast lived almost exclusively on fish; besides their coasting trade with Italy, they gained small sums by coral and pearl fishing. The oysters have disappeared, however, for want of proper preservation. Tunny fishing is carried on twice in the year, and like the salt marshes and vines, is monopolised and farmed out by the conquerors, and only benefits the contractors and the foreigner.

Any wealth the island possesses, exists in Porto Ferraio only, in the middle-class society of a provincial town. Porto Ferraio is the seat of government, and at times has been a flourishing port. Under the *régime* of the dukes of Florence, art and luxury were not unknown, but blockades and incessant fighting have ruined it. Between this town and Marciana Marina a hatred exists through trade rivalry. Porto Longone is purely military.

In curious contrast with their primitive manners, these people take great pleasure in public recitations of verse by Ariosto and Tasso, on Sundays and fête days, and organise competitions for improvising verse. Visitors to the island sometimes represent the people as savages, sometimes as gentle and cultivated. The women, who are mature at thirteen or fourteen, are fond of adorning themselves with large, black straw hats, trimmed with ribbon, large gold earrings, and long-waisted tight corsets, like the pictures of Spanish infantas; they are laced up in these steel cases from earliest childhood.

The island is a prey to all the diseases resulting, especially in hot countries, from a total ignorance of hygiene, and a form of diet contrary to the most elementary laws. All kinds of skin diseases flourish, *i.e.* leprosy and scurvy; and dysentery and typhus are a scourge. The undrained marshes are a constant source of fever and ague to the people who live near them, and a danger to any traveller exposing himself to the damp evening air.

* * * * *

II

THE EMPEROR'S ARRIVAL.

It was on May 3rd that the Emperor came in sight of Elba and his new kingdom.

The sky was radiant, the sea calm and smiling, between seven and eight in the morning, when the lookout on the fort signalled a frigate flying the English flag, and carrying full sail in the light wind, making directly for Porto Ferraio.

General Dalesme, the French commandant of the fort, at once took all the usual military precautions; he ordered the harbour to be closed, the guns on the ramparts to be loaded, and the garrison to be placed under arms. The townspeople meanwhile ran to the shore, full of excitement and curiosity. What vessel was this, and what was she doing here? Was she the precursor of another bombardment, the landing of a new enemy?

The islanders were entirely ignorant of events that had recently taken place, as during the five last months of the war they had been blockaded by the English, and all communication with the mainland cut off. They were in constant fear, therefore, of having to pay again for their masters' quarrels.[1] A rumour of the fall of the French Empire had reached the island, and had thrown it back to anarchy. On April 21st, the garrison at Porto Longone, including a number of old Italian deserters and thieves transported to the island, had mutinied. On the same day Napoleon had been burnt in effigy at Marciana Marina; and on April 22nd, General Dalesme, to avoid a similar mutiny at Porto Ferraio, had offered to send back every foreign soldier who desired it, to his own country.

The English, for their own part, lost no opportunity of getting possession of the island. A man-of-war was sent on the 27th, with a flag of truce, to inform General Dalesme of the fall of the Empire and the restoration of the Bourbons, calling upon him to surrender, on the ground that the Treaty of Peace signed between France and the allied Powers had ceded Elba to England. Dalesme refused to surrender the island until he had further instructions, and demanded a safe conduct to Paris for one of his aides-de-camp to obtain information. The man-of-war retired. On the 28th another English vessel, with an envoy from the Provisional Government on board, confirmed the abdication of Napoleon and called on General Dalesme to substitute the white flag for the tricolour and Imperial eagle, informing him that Elba had been chosen

[1] Pons de l'H., 7, 86; Mém. aux Puiss All., 4, 305; Peyrusse, 233; Mme. Durand, 247; Monier, 22; Waldbourg-Truchsess, 51; Fabry, 64; Gen. Vincent, 157.

as the ex-Emperor's retreat, and that he would shortly arrive there. General Dalesme was incredulous and inclined to be defiant, and while obeying orders as to the flag, kept a watchful eye open for treachery. No one believed that Napoleon was coming. Most of the inhabitants were firmly convinced that the island was taken by the English, and the most patriotic spirits talked of exterminating the foreigners, and asserting their independence.

In the meantime the frigate was sailing quietly over the calm blue waters, in the golden sunlight, and gradually approaching the island. Although she presented a friendly appearance, General Dalesme still feared being taken by surprise, and when she was within a short distance from the shore he sent a despatch-boat to warn her that if she came any nearer, he would open fire. For answer, she ran up a flag of truce, took in her sails, and cast anchor. It was then two o'clock in the afternoon. The frigate was none other than the Undaunted, with the Emperor on board, and by reason of contrary winds had taken four and a half days in crossing from Fréjus to Elba.

The Emperor was fully aware of the terrible struggles in our former occupation of the island, and he felt anxious as to the reception his future subjects might offer him. Perhaps he might find the island in the throes of a revolution, of a general massacre of the French, and even if Elba remained loyal to France, would he himself be acceptable, arriving without their invitation? Would he meet

PORTO FERRAIO—THE PORTO MARINA, WHERE NAPOLEON LANDED, MAY 4, 1814.

with the same reception as he had experienced in the south of France; the same threatening attitude? He had asked the English Commissioner at Fréjus "if he might rely on 100 sailors from the Undaunted as a protection during his first days in the island, until the arrival of the 400 men from the Guard allotted him by the Treaty of Fontainebleau (Article XVII of the Treaty)." He had even foreseen the possibility of being unable to land, and in that case, of retreating to England.[1] The statements of a fisherman who had been interrogated and summoned on board the previous evening, had increased his fears; the two Commissioners, an Austrian and an Englishman, who were with the Emperor and were responsible for his personal safety, both objected to his landing until his safety was assured.

Moreover, he had no wish to enter the island furtively, as a fugitive, or even as an ordinary individual. He was Napoleon the King, and he would be royally received.

The day dragged on, in uncertainty on both sides. The Emperor spent the time in walking up and down on deck, wearing a sailor's sou'-wester.[2] Later in the afternoon, a boat left the Undaunted and rowed to the harbour. In it were General Drouot, the Polish Colonel Jerzmanowski, Col. Campbell, the English Commissioner, and Major Clam, aide-

[1] Campbell, 40, 60; Waldbourg-Truchsess, 12. It is interesting to compare this first idea of Napoleon's, of seeking a refuge in England, with the same project put into execution the following year, after Waterloo.

[2] Peyrusse, 232; Pons de l'H., 14.

de-camp to General Koller. Making their way through the crowd on the quay, they asked to speak to General Dalesme, and presented a letter to him from the Emperor, written at Fréjus, on April 27, informing him that as he was compelled by circumstances to renounce the throne of France he was, from henceforth, the King of Elba, and he expected the island at once to be formally handed over to him, with its armouries, magazines and storehouses, and the property belonging to the Imperial estates.[1] He begged General Dalesme to inform the inhabitants of the island of his wishes, and in a few adroitly flattering words His Majesty gave them to understand that in the choice of their island he had been guided by their gentle manners and the mildness of their climate. In conclusion, Major Clam added: "The Emperor must be obeyed," and Colonel Jerzmanowski observed, with his hand on the hilt of his sword, "I hope we shall not have occasion to use force."

General Dalesme gave every assurance of his personal devotion and respectful submission. He at once summoned a council of the authorities at Porto Ferraio, presenting to them the envoys of the Emperor, whose letter he read aloud, and requested them to communicate its contents to the inhabitants. This official announcement took everyone by surprise. The arrival of the Emperor Napoleon, his wish to establish himself in the island after laying aside the government of the world, came like a thunderclap to these simple people, bewilder-

[1] Corres. Imp., xxi., 563.

ing to their pride; almost as if Tarascon should suddenly learn that the Czar of all the Russias, or the Emperor of China, had abandoned his throne and palaces to retire within its walls. The small minority of doubtful or hostile individuals were swamped in the general enthusiasm. The people became delirious with excitement.[1]

It was agreed that a deputation consisting of General Dalesme, the Sous-Préfet, the Commandant of the Elban National Guard, and M. Pons de l'Hérault, the Administrator of the Mines, should wait upon the Emperor, and assure him of the loyalty of his subjects. They embarked immmediately in the frigate's cutter, while the flag, with its fleur-de-lys, flying over the citadel, was lowered.

* * * * *

At this point it seems advisable to give a short description of one of the members of the deputation—namely of Pons de l'Hérault—whose name was connected more than once with the Emperor's fortunes, and who has left a very interesting memoir of events in the island of Elba.

He was born at Cette, his father a Spanish innkeeper, and his mother a Frenchwoman. He began life as a captain of a merchant ship, then he

[1] Helfert (p. 70) says that existing in the family archives of the Austrian Commissioner, Koller, is a Protest from the Elbans, complaining that under the pretext of ridding the earth of a scourge of the human race, he had been sent to their island, "that he had shed enough blood to submerge it, that he ought to be kept in the tiger's cage at the Jardin des Plantes, in Paris, among the animals he resembles, or perhaps that Corsica should take back the Minotaur she produced." This protest, signed "*Finanza et Buonafede*, deputies of the island," is evidently fictitious—and printed in Paris.

became a naval officer, then a captain in the artillery, and when stationed at Toulon had known Bonaparte, at that time a general. He had entertained him at his house for two days, and had initiated him into the delights of a Provençal *bouillabaisse.* He was an ardent Republican, in former times a Jacobin and disciple of Robespierre, and had disdained to accept any favours of the Empire. In 1809 he was only appointed as Commissioner of the Mines at Elba by the special favour of Lacépède.

He was a curious, uncouth product of the Revolution, with much of the old Roman and bureaucrat about him, of the type of Cato, with a large nose, and wearing spectacles; stubborn, stiff and solemn, he would rather be cut in pieces than act or speak against his principles. Under the surface he was as ingenuous as a child, and had the best heart in the world.

The personal fascination of Napoleon made a conquest of Pons de l'Hérault as soon as they met again after so many years. In his own words, "he had always admired him while hating him. He regarded him not as a tyrant, but as the greatest genius in the world," and he became one of his most faithful servants. He earned the respect of the Emperor by his stubborn honesty of principle, was in daily intercourse with him, and was thus able to keep a diary of everything that occurred in the island. These memoirs, stowed away in the library at Carcassonne, and recently published, exhibit both the qualities and defects of their author. Truthful and exact in every sense of the words, with the exception of a few mistakes of memory, they are inspired solely with the intention of relating things exactly as they occurred.

But the relation of a fact, while absolutely truthful, may at the same time be incomplete and misleading if the narrator is ignorant of its full bearings. Pons was so simple and upright, so incapable of dissimulation, that he took for granted the good faith of all the Emperor said or did: one side of that complex and subtle mind entirely escaped him. This method of writing history was evidently agreeable to the Emperor, as he encouraged Pons in his diary; and it remains the only complete history left of the ephemeral royalty on the island of Elba.

Outside this limited view of the events which he saw before him, Pons was inclined to launch out and exaggerate whenever his own private affairs were connected with the Emperor's, giving them an importance they did not possess. If the Emperor disagreed with his opinion and expressed his views, it became a dispute. The next day when the Emperor, his mind full of other things, gave him his hand, without mentioning the previous occurrence, Pons concluded that he was incapable of bearing malice, and was as gentle as a lamb. Even while actually opposing the Emperor's will, he remained his dupe.

This accounts for the false point of view which Pons took of the facts he recorded. Nevertheless his memoirs, by their extent and their sincerity, are extremely vivid and useful, although in spite of a classification made by their compiler, they are in an inextricable muddle, as Pons never finished the work he had begun. They are hardly dated at all, and to arrange them in sequence, the compiler was obliged to consult different historical authorities, such as Colonel Campbell's Journal, the Imperial Correspondence, the Registers of the Island of Elba, and Peyrusse's account books—as no Gazette with a record of each day's events is to be had.[1]

* * * * *

As the members of the deputation climbed the ladder to the deck of the English frigate they were trembling with emotion and excitement. Colonel Campbell presented them first to General Bertrand, sitting pale and sad, in the state cabin. The Emperor appeared. "By an instinct," says Pons, "we all gathered close together. He stopped and looked at us. We made a movement to approach him, but he came towards us. He was not like Themistocles, banished from Athens, or Marius at Minternæ. He was like no one else. He wore the green uniform of the Chasseurs de la Garde, with a colonel's epaulettes, and the simple Chevalier's Star of the Legion of Honour. He was quiet, his eyes

[1] Many of the Emperor's companions, who made their notes day by day, added the dates only after the event, and more or less approximately. Napoleon's letters, again, exact as they usually are, sometimes give two versions and appear contradictory. At Elba the Emperor dictated as the ideas came into his head to any of his suite who happened to be present (Pons de l'H., 199); he spoke rapidly, and the difficulty of following led the writer to put the sentences down as they came, with many repetitions and subsequent alterations. In Elba the system produced little inconvenience, as Napoleon could give his orders by word of mouth, and see to their execution in his kingdom of 17 miles by 11. There was now no question of the administration of an empire.

bright, his expression kindly. He was bareheaded, and his hands were clasped behind his back. As he half-turned we saw that he held a sailor's hat in his hand. We stammered a few words, and the Emperor seemed to understand our difficulty and answered us kindly, as if he had heard all we had to say. Then he spoke of the recent events, his own misfortunes and those of France, and expressed his intention of devoting himself to the happiness of Elbans." It was arranged that the Emperor should enter the capital the next day.[1]

On shore the excitement increased. The emotional southern natures were in a ferment. People went about Porto Ferraio with their eyes starting from their heads, telling of the wonderful things that had happened, and carrying packets of candles ready for illumination. From the deck of the frigate at nightfall the Emperor could see the town lighted up in his honour. The walls were covered with proclamations hastily printed, "People of Elba! The course of events has brought the Emperor Napoleon amongst us. Your future happiness is thereby assured. Let us give free play to the joy we feel, and rival each other in zeal for welcoming our Sovereign: thus giving pleasure to his paternal feelings."[2]

The civil, military, and religious authorities met in council during the night to arrange for the next day's ceremony, and a summons was sent to each

[1] Pons de l'H., 13, 14.
[2] Proclamations of Gen. Dalesme and the Sous-Préfet.

commune and parish in the island that their mayors and priests should attend. Only the French inhabitants did not share in this general enthusiasm. They were almost stunned by the overwhelming events, and feared any action which might compromise them. Some continued to wear the white cockade which they had only pinned on five days before, while others hid it in their pockets.

As soon as the day broke the crowd began to gather on the jetty at the harbour, climbing to the roofs of the houses to catch the first glimpse of the Emperor, and a whole flotilla of small boats and fishing-smacks, flying multitudes of flags, surrounded the majestic frigate which carried their Cæsar. Some of the boats had musicians on board, playing on guitars, tambourines, and flutes; others were crowded with men cheering and waving their caps at the ends of their oars. All the morning, officers were coming and going with instructions from the Emperor, who chose a flag for himself designed from an engraving of old armorial bearings of the time of Cosimo de' Medici—a white ground with a diagonal stripe of reddish-orange, bearing three bees. For the sake of a little exercise he landed for an hour or two, and returned to lunch on board.[1]

At the stroke of midday a gun was fired from Fort Stella,[2] answered by the guns on the ramparts.

1 Pons de l'H., 34.

2 Fort Stella is below Fort Falcone, and commands the entrance to the harbour of Porto Ferraio.

The new flag, made hastily out of sail-cloth, was run up at Porto Ferraio, and the English frigate replied with twenty-one guns. The Emperor went on board the Admiral's barge, while the English sailors, mounted on the yards, gave three cheers, and the Elbans broke into frantic applause. The boat made good way over the blue waters, the bells rang, the bands played, and the people sang—

> "*Apollon, exilé du ciel*
> *Vient habiter la Thessalie!*"[1]

As the Emperor landed, his face fell, and the reality of the situation dawned on him. This country where he was setting foot suddenly appeared in its true light—a prison. Viewed from afar, the distance had softened it, and even from the deck of the frigate, the dazzling sunlight and surrounding blue water had given it an air of unreality; but on close inspection it was only a small Levantine town, yellow and dirty, evil smelling, the houses piled together in the growth of centuries, leaking with fœtid water. And this was his capital! These strange people from their mountain villages with their rough voices and cut-throat expressions, were his subjects! Those who were nearest to him noticed the look of surprise and disgust on his face. But he regained his self-possession at once, and came forward smiling to the authorities waiting for him.

The mayor, Traditi, was the first, as with a deep

[1] Pons de l'H., 35.

bow he presented the keys of the city on a silver salver.[1] He had a speech ready, which he had even written out, but he was unable to read a word. The Vicar-General advanced with a canopy, covered with tinsel and festooned with paper roses. Under this the Emperor took his place, and they proceeded to the parish church, where a feeble little bell was ringing to its utmost capacity.[2] The Emperor was dressed as on the preceding day, in a green coat, with white breeches, and shoes with gold buckles.[3] He wore the Star of the Legion of Honour, and the decoration of the Iron Cross.[4] To everyone's delight he carried his own well-known hat under his arm, and on it, instead of the tricolour cockade, was pinned the Elban cockade with the three bees. The oddest escort followed him. Bertrand and Drouot (the two Pylades), and General Dalesme, then the two foreign Commissioners, Peyrusse and General Jerzmanowski, who walked together, with the two Comptrollers of the Palace, the doctor, chemist, and two secretaries. These formed the Emperor's household. The staff of the English frigate followed, and every public official which Porto Ferraio could muster, either

1 Signora Traditi, granddaughter of the mayor, has these keys in her possession. *Cf.* p. 271.

2 Gen. Durand, 249; Pons de l'H., 39, *et seq.*; Waldbourg-Truchsess, 52. It is still customary on fête days at Porto Ferraio to decorate the churches with these garlands of coloured paper, entwined with bits of scarlet cloth and gold spangles.

3 Peyrusse, 234; Monier, 24.

4 Napoleon was crowned at Milan with the Iron Crown of Lombardy, May 26, 1805, after the Cisalpine Republic had offered him the hereditary monarchy of Italy.

civil or military, brought up the rear. Their wives, with all the ladies of the town, had hung shawls and draperies from the windows and balconies, and stood there, gaily dressed. The streets were strewn with branches of box and myrtle.

It was barely three minutes' walk from the harbour, where the Emperor had landed, to the church, but the crowd was so great that the procession was forced to pause at every step.[1] The National Guard, trying to keep order, was jostled and pushed, so were the dignified Bertrand and correct Campbell, so was even the Emperor himself. He took this somewhat brutal enthusiasm quite resignedly, but the Vicar-General grew crimson with anger, and full of the importance of the ceremony, addressed the crowd, shaking his fist furiously.

The swaying canopy at last arrived at the church door, where a prie-Dieu was placed, covered with the least shabby piece of drapery which could be found. Two hastily appointed attendants, ignorant of their functions, and paralysed with fear, conducted the Emperor, and remained at his side, imitating all he did, and even being prompted by him as to their movements. The clergy knew their duties no better, and the Vicar-General, still excited by his struggle in the street, made more

[1] "The Porta Marina," says Pons, "opens on an oblong Piazza, communicating by two streets of shops with the Piazza d'Arme, a vast square, with the Municipio and the Cathedral on opposite sides." The place remains unchanged, save that the Piazza d'Arme has been planted with trees, flowers, etc.

than one mistake. He only recovered himself two days later, in a wonderful injunction, in which he said that the island of Elba, already so celebrated for its natural productions, was to become immortal in history by receiving the anointed of the Lord. "Fathers, tell this to your children. Let the multitude assemble from afar to gaze on the hero!"[1]

The time came for the Te Deum, and the Emperor, kneeling at his prie-Dieu, prayed, or seemed to pray. Perhaps his thoughts went back to another Te Deum, sung in Notre Dame, and the mean futility of the present ceremony was overwhelmed in the tragedy of the contrast. The wave of emotion passed from him to the congregation, and at the words: "We therefore pray Thee help Thy servants," and "In Thee, O Lord, have I put my trust," the people all knelt as at a signal, prostrating themselves to the floor.

At the conclusion of the service, the procession returned by way of the Hotel de Ville, prepared for the Emperor's temporary residence. The large reception room was hung with pictures and glass chandeliers, and an arm-chair raised on a small daïs, wreathed with paper flowers, did duty as a throne. A band of three violins and two violoncellos played national airs. Here the Emperor held an audience of the French inhabitants wishing to be presented, the magistrates, and municipal officials. After the usual formalities he began to speak to the Elbans

[1] Charge of Giuseppe Felippe Arrighi, Vicar-General of Elba under the Bishop of Ajaccio, May 6, 1814.

of their country, of the various mayors of each commune, and of the changes he proposed to make. He seemed to know the precise wants of every commune, the number of inhabitants, and the resources of each. He knew how much revenue came from the salt workings, how many boats were used for the tunny fisheries, and which was their best season ; moreover, he not only conversed with the Elbans about their habits and ancient customs, their chestnut trees and chestnut flour polenta (he spoke in Italian to those who did not understand French), not only did he tell them the dates of the foundation of their towns and villages (of which most of them were quite ignorant), and all the details of their history, but he appeared to know better than any of them the topography of their island, and informed them, almost to a foot, of the height of their mountains. The Elbans listened, their mouths open with astonishment.

The key to the mystery was simple. The Emperor, while at Fontainebleau, had sent to Paris for any papers that existed on the history of Elba, since its annexation by France. He also found in his library, books and maps containing full information about his future kingdom, amongst them the "*Voyage à l'île d'Elbe,*" by Arsène Thibaut published in 1808. In the catastrophe which shook the whole of Europe, and lost him his throne, he remembered to put this guide book in his pocket, and master its contents on the journey. No doubt the book was not absolutely correct as to archæological details, but it was worth taking the risk, and for the political history of the island he had gone to the papers of the sub-prefecture that very morning, on board the English frigate. His command of detail, and his power of deception, never left him, and the effect he made was, as usual, unerring. The Elbans were astounded.[1]

The day dragged on slowly, and seemed an eternity. All the Emperor's attendants were worn out, but so far from his being tired, he suddenly asked for a horse, to ride across the country.[2]

However, on the arrival of two strangers for presentation, he remained closeted with them, in private; and the interview remaining secret, it was supposed that they were messengers bringing news from Marie Louise, or from some of her followers. When they left the Emperor, they returned at once to sea.

Afterwards the Emperor visited the citadel, and in the evening gave more audiences, while the town was illuminated as on the previous evening, and the inhabitants danced in the streets.

And, while in the popular imagination the conqueror of Austerlitz had turned shepherd and, like a fallen Apollo, would henceforth feed his flocks, while his people, in this Mediterranean island under the warm Italian sun offered him their poor and humble welcome, Louis Stanislas-Xavier of France, called Louis XVIII, collected his followers and

[1] Peyrusse, 223; Beausset, *Mémoires*, Paris, 1827, II., 243; Pons de l'H., 42, 61. *Cf.* Campbell, 207.

[2] Pons de l'H., 44.

made his entry into Paris. On this 3rd of May, as the Emperor landed in Elba, he received at the gate of St. Denis the keys of the capital. In a carriage emblazoned with fleur-de-lys, drawn by eight white horses with nodding ostrich plumes, he drove through Paris, and after hearing at Notre Dame the "*Domine salvum fac regem*" before the very altar where, ten years before, the Pope had anointed the usurper, he returned to the Tuileries.

* * * * *

The slow journey from Fréjus to Elba had quite rested the Emperor after his hard travelling across France, and he now felt a great desire for activity. His household were all preparing to go to bed (no one had slept on the previous night) when, at midnight, while all the inhabitants of the town had retired indoors and the mountain villagers gone home by torchlight, the Emperor sent for Marshal Bertrand, General Dalesme, and M. Pons: expressing to the last-named his desire to breakfast with him the next morning at nine o'clock at Rio, and pay a visit to the mines. Bertrand, foreseeing that he would be of the party, exclaimed that it was impossible; but General Dalesme placed himself at the Emperor's service, and the Commissioner of the Mines replied that breakfast would be ready with an official reception, at the prescribed hour.[1]

Pons, therefore, saddled his horse, lighted a lantern, and rode post-haste across the island to arrange for a meal and a reception worthy of his

[1] Pons de l'H., 45.

guest. Before daylight broke he ordered nets to be cast into the sea. The nets caught a fish weighing more than 25lb., besides a number of smaller ones. It was a second Miraculous Draught of Fishes. The fishermen were overcome by the miracle—surely God's hand was in it! Pons also sent for a gardener, and ordered his garden to be filled with flowers.

At five o'clock in the morning the Emperor with his suite left Porto Ferraio. When he arrived at Rio, the ships in the harbour ran up their flags, the merchant-men held fuses ready to the breaches of their guns, old carbines were fired off, for want of better, and the miners, pick in hand, lined the roads, shouting a welcome. A bevy of young girls advanced to meet his Majesty and kiss his hand, and the Mayor of Rio Montagna, once a great slayer of Frenchmen, knelt on one knee, saying, "*In Te Domine, Speravi.*"

It was quite impossible, however, to foresee everything, and the garden was found to blossom almost entirely with fleur-de-lys! The gardener had without reflection simply planted what flowers he could find and the Commissioner had not noticed them. The flower sacred to the Bourbons, the cursed lily, reinstated on the throne of France by foreign artillery, was now thrown at the Emperor's head! "*Me voici logé à bonne enseigne!*" he said with a rather sour smile. Pons felt much distressed, and the miners made matters worse by addressing the Emperor as "M. le Duc," "M. le Comte," and even simply "Monsieur." The good Pons wished he could sink under the earth. Drouot reassured him the next day by telling him his appointment was confirmed. The Emperor no doubt understood that the revenues from the mines, which formed such a considerable part of his budget, required the honest direction of Pons.

The Emperor paid visits to all the communes of the island. General Bertrand wishing him to feel that he ruled over a great people, gathered all the available material together to welcome him wherever he went. The Emperor easily recognised the same faces appearing again and again, and was not in the least deceived, but not wishing to vex the Grand Marshal, he made no remark. He was escorted on these small journeys by the following: Two chamberlains, two orderlies, a captain of police, sous-préfet Balbiani (who now ranked as Commissary-General of the Island), the Mayor and President of the Court of Porto Ferraio, Bertrand, an English naval lieutenant, the English Commissioner, Campbell, and the aide-de-camp of the Austrian Commissioner. Triumphal arches of chestnut and oak boughs were erected for him and his suite, children and young girls strewed flowers before him, and everywhere guns were fired, municipal deputations presented addresses, and the clergy from the different parishes formed processions. At dinner he invited six chosen guests, who were puffed up with pride. Marciana Marina, where he was once burned in effigy, became loyal, and on the day of his visit, sang a Te Deum, following the example of the capital.[1]

He visited the forts, examining their turrets, their cellars, bastions, and stores. He criticised the various strategic points on foot, or on horseback, often walking for ten hours under heat that would have felled an ox. At the end of a fortnight everyone was completely knocked up. "He alone was perfectly fresh and well. He gave orders which had to be executed on the spot—everyone working the flesh off his bones."[2]

* * * * *

It was now necessary to choose a lodging for the Emperor.

Porto Ferraio could not boast of many palaces, nor indeed of many houses suitable for the purpose. The Emperor had at first been received in the Hotel de Ville, in a few rooms hastily adorned with furniture borrowed from loyal citizens. This state of things was most inconvenient to him, as he was liable to constant interruptions and expressions of loyalty, springing, no doubt, from praiseworthy sentiment, but very tiring to the Royal visitor. The rooms were, moreover, exposed to the unpleasant odours from the gutters in the streets, where every house threw its refuse, and although the inhabitants were accustomed to this incon-

[1] Pons de l'H., 28, 82; Campbell, 84; Peyrusse (Appendix), 25: "Note of expenses, to the Mayor of Longone on the occasion of His Majesty's visit, 70 francs."

[2] Pons de l'H., 67, 300; Campbell, 98; Fabry, 76.

venience, and scarcely noticed it, the Emperor felt as if he were living in the Augean stables.

He thought at first of taking one of the barracks of the citadel and changing it into rooms for his own use. It was large enough to contain all his household. But General Bertrand objected to this arrangement, thinking that each officer would be better in his own house.[1] The Emperor finally decided to pull down a number of small sheds and windmills on the slope of the hill, and to alter two houses occupied by the engineers and artillery, joining them by a central building. This became the Mulini Palace, as the Elbans called it, naming it after the windmills previously standing there.

The Emperor was his own architect, drew the plans for the masons and carpenters himself, and moved into the building while the plaster and paint were still wet.[2]

In the design the ornamental and useful were closely allied. On the ground floor was a large room, looking on to the garden, intended for various purposes, prescribed by the Emperor, "This room will be used as a theatre, a bath-room, and a dining-room for myself and my household. For these purposes you will arrange" (these instructions were addressed to Bertrand, the Grand Maréchal of the Palace) "that a flat ceiling is constructed, six windows with Venetian blinds, and a stage on trestles three feet high. Here I should

[1] Pons de l'H., 58. [2] Pons de l'H., 147.

like a billiard table, and, at the end of the room, a small addition with a bath. A folding partition must be arranged in the room, dividing it, if necessary, into two. The room can also be used for receptions—and for this purpose there must be chandeliers, and marble tables, to be used as buffets. The room will thus answer all my purposes." When the building lingered on into June he said, "Give orders to the builder that everything be ready at the end of next week."[1]

On the ground floor was also the Emperor's bedroom, which communicated with the large room by a glass door. On the first floor was "a lofty room extending over all the centre of the building."[2] This was a room with four windows to the town and four to the sea, which has been described, and appears in the illustration.

Furniture was necessary, and the Emperor possessed none, but the palace of Piombino, belonging formerly to his sister Elisa, was full of it. The Emperor had no scruples, and although the palace was now annexed by Austria, he sent over a ship to take possession of its contents. This was accomplished successfully, and the quarter-master in charge of the expedition gave the Austrian Commissioner (who protested in vain) by way of payment "a precise inventory of all he had taken for the use

[1] Corres. Imp., xxi. 578. The folding partition was only arranged in November: "Nov. 24. Design for sliding partition, 438fr. 64c. On the margin the Emperor wrote, 'Approved at 400 francs. Signed Napoleon'" (Peyrusse, Appendix, 47, note 81).

[2] Peyrusse, 250.

THE GARDEN AND TERRACE OF THE MULINI.

THE GRAND SALON OF THE MULINI.

of the Emperor." Everything was carried off, even to the venetian blinds and parquet flooring.[1]

A propitious storm provided what was lacking. Prince Borghese, Pauline's husband, who was obliged, for political reasons, to leave Turin, had sent some of his furniture to Rome by a Ligurian boat. This boat, owing to stress of weather, had to take shelter off the island of Elba. The Emperor thereupon seized all the furniture, saying: "It must not go out of the family." An inventory was made, however, of all he took, and Prince Borghese had the satisfaction of receiving a complete list in lieu of his possessions. The Emperor bought the furniture belonging to the old garrison, who were leaving Elba, for his suite.[2]

Linen and wardrobes for the household were still needed, as, on the 10th of April, at Orléans, the Provisional Government had seized the waggons containing all the Emperor's official clothes in velvet and silk, the greater part of his linen, and his pocket handkerchiefs. Six dozens of shirts were all that was left him.[3] Hearing that the cargo of an English prize ship was being sold in the island, the Emperor commissioned his people to

[1] Gen. Vincent, 193, 194; Pons de l'H., 140; Campbell, 65, 85; Peyrusse, 236, Appendix 16, Note 10 and 34, Note 44. The expedition cost 3,282 francs. Elisa Bacciochi had received the Principalities of Lucca and Piombino from the Emperor, in 1805–1806.

[2] Peyrusse, Appendix, 34.

[3] Meneval II., 184; Gen. Durand, 244. For the seizure at Orléans, see p. 83. The linen belonging to the Emperor at Fontainebleau had been packed before he left in the baggage-waggons of the guard, and only reached Porto Ferraio on May 26. It had not been unpacked by the end of July (Reg. de l'I. d'E., No. 31).

buy what was necessary for him, at a fair price, *i.e.*, "cotton cloth for underclothing, cambric for window curtains, muslin for mosquito curtains, green cloth for table coverings, and for the footmen's livery."[1]

When the Emperor was settled at the Mulini Palace he gave a house-warming party, to which the principal Elban ladies were invited. When each was presented to him in turn, he asked her name, whether she were married, and how many children she had.[2] This duty accomplished, strict etiquette was re-established at the little court, and the King, who was still called "Emperor," only received his subjects in formal audience, after previous request, giving all his time to the organisation of his government.

* * * * *

The Society surrounding the Emperor, and the persons attached to him, were composed of various elements.

Bertrand and Drouot represented the remains of his former glory, Bertrand, who had been with him since his Egyptian days, was Grand Maréchal of the Palace in the place of Duroc, killed by a spent bullet at Wurtzen. He had followed him to Elba, as he was to follow him one day to St. Helena.

1 Corres. Imp., xxi. 580. This "English prize" was apparently some merchant vessel which the English had captured during the late war.

2 Pons de l'H., 147; Campbell, 81; Fabry, 79. The Emperor had given a first fête at the Hotel de Ville on May 16 in honour of his arrival in the city.

He was the Emperor's shadow, the perfect type of heroic and passive fidelity, a born grumbler, perpetually crying for rest and peace, and never attaining them. The most tedious duties were always assigned to him, but by constantly complaining he always obtained his own way. Drouot was "l'homme de Plutarque." Wise in council, brave in danger, unimpeachable in conduct, kind-hearted to all, he was the embodiment of happy, active service. Any business of great delicacy was always entrusted to him. He had refused, on leaving Fontainebleau, 100,000 francs offered him by the Emperor, as he would not have it appear that in his exile to Elba he was acting in self-interest.

Bertrand, beside the office of Grand Maréchal, held the control of *Affaires Civiles*, for which he received 20,000 francs annually. Drouot was Military Governor, with 12,000 francs.[1]

Peyrusse (called also "Peyruche," and by the Emperor "Peyrousse") was Financial Secretary. He received a salary of 12,000 francs, and the title of Pay-Master and Receiver for War and the Interior.[2]

He was a native of Carcassonne, a good-hearted officer, thin and curly-headed like all southerners, full of the joy of life, whatever happened. At Linz, in Austria, after marching all through a day "in an atmosphere reeking with perspiring soldiers," he only regretted not having seen "any of the fair sex

[1] Gen. Durand, 246; Pons de l'H., 95; Peyrusse, 242; Reg. de l'I. d'E., No. 117; Corres. Imp. xxi. 657.

[2] Corres. Imp., xxi., 568; Pons de l'H., 75; Peyrusse, 242.

who are so renowned here for their beauty."[1] He had witnessed the burning of Moscow, and the day after the fire expressed surprise at not finding a laundress for his linen.[2] He had been through the horrors of the retreat and the fearful butchery at the crossing of the Berezina: horrors so appalling that years afterwards the officers present felt their hair rise at the mere remembrance. He had seen the soldiers of the Grande Armée reduced to feeding on human flesh, dragging their dead comrades from the flames in order to eat them.[3] But nothing seemed to trouble his serenity, until he experienced the crossing from Fréjus to Elba (he had never before been at sea). As the frigate rolled on the night of April 30—May 1, he said "I thought my last hour had come."[4] When he was once more on solid ground, in his own warm southern climate, he thought the island of Elba a most desirable place, and laughingly answered those who praised him for not leaving the Emperor "I am not following him —I am going after the cash-box." As a matter of fact, he did much more than follow it. He saved it; and in the general disorder of the abdication, he managed to retrieve the greater part of the funds taken to the island of Elba.[5]

The navy was allotted, for want of a better officer, to Lieutenant Taillade, "who was anything but a

[1] Letter from Peyrusse to his brother, June 12, 1809.

[2] Letter from Peyrusse to his brother, September 21, 1812.

[3] Ségur, *Hist. de la Grande Armée*, II., 375, 407, for account of anthropophagy practised during the retreat from Russia.

[4] Peyrusse, 229.

[5] See p. 83.

mariner. He talked scientifically about the sea in calm weather, or when he was safe on dry land. But when the winds arose, the commander was prostrated. He left his subordinates to do as they thought best, and shutting himself up in his cabin, he lay in his bunk until the fine weather returned."[1] He was vain and conceited, detested by the French inhabitants of the island, and everyone enjoyed making fun of his incapacity. The Emperor had not much choice in the matter—Taillade had been living for some years on the island, he had married an Elban lady of good family, and his appointment was flattering to the local aristocracy. The Vicar-General, Arrighi, a drunkard, who had sung the Te Deum on the Emperor's arrival, became Court Chaplain.[2] This impudent Corsican went about calling the Emperor his "*cugino carnale*,"[3] which he considered gave him the right to domineer over everyone else. The Emperor merely begged him to mind his own business in his church.

Four officers of the household were chosen from the principal inhabitants. These were Doctor Lapi, who commanded the Elban National Guard, and who held, besides his title of Chamberlain, that of Director of Woods and Forests in the island; Signor Traditi, Mayor of Porto Ferraio; Signor Vantini, an aristocrat, worn out with excesses in his youth, who gave a certain tone of wit and fashion to society in the town, and who had always favoured the French

[1] Pons de l'H., 133, 349, 353. [2] Pons de l'H., 34, 73, 181.

[3] Literally, his "cousin in the flesh."

influence; and (also for political reasons) the Mayor of Rio Montagna, a ruffian who "was now like a tame cat," and was blind of one eye. Each of these officers received 1,200 francs per annum.[1]

Of the two secretaries, Rathery and Savournin, the Emperor appropriated the services of the first for himself, and gave the second to Marshal Bertrand, with salaries of 4,000 and 2,000 francs respectively.[2]

Two quartermasters from the Tuileries were raised to the rank of Prefects of the Palace. One was a gendarme dressed like an officer, rough and bad mannered, but quite harmless, the other a good soldier, who in remote Elba might manage to present an appearance in a drawing room. They each received 6,000 francs. The orderly officer, Perez, by birth a Neapolitan, was chiefly remarkable for his great stupidity, and the Corsican Paoli, specially attached to the Emperor's person, for his silliness. If the Emperor asked him the time, he answered, "The hour which pleases your Majesty," and was quite proud of his brilliant answer.[3] The ex-physician of the imperial stables in Paris was raised to the rank of chief physician to the Emperor, and received 15,000 francs.[4]

This man took his appointment in deadly earnest.

1 Labadie, 379; Pons de l'H., 77, 166; Corres. Imp., xxi. 567; Peyrusse, 242; Fabry, 78.

2 Peyrusse, 224, 242; Gen. Durand, 245; Fabry, 59.

3 Pons de l'H., 79, 80; Mém. aux Puiss All., 147.

4 Pons de l'H., 76; Peyrusse, 242. Dr. Foureau de Beauregard had served in the ambulances during the French Campaign (Peyrusse, Appendix, 113–114).

One day when the Emperor was in his bath he brought him a basin of soup. "The soup was too hot, and the Emperor sipped it to avoid burning himself. The head physician objected, as according to Aristotle, in sipping the soup, His Majesty would suck in large quantities of air, and this weight of air might bring on colic." The Emperor was annoyed, and moved impatiently in his bath, where he was kept a prisoner, but the doctor continued to develop his argument, until beside himself at last, the Emperor sent him and his Aristotle to the devil, exclaiming, "that he was old enough to know how to drink."[1]

The chemist Gatti, of not much greater ability but of a modest nature, was appointed to mix the drugs, with a salary of 7,800 francs. He and the physician had continual disputes, to which the Emperor, who believed as little in the precepts of the one as in the drugs of the other, was obliged at last to put a stop.[2] It was a veritable Sancho Panza's court.

The service of the household included a maître d'hôtel, a carver, a chef, a head cook, an assistant cook, a man to attend to the fire, a kitchen boy, two pantry assistants, a butler, two men for the silver, and a baker for the Emperor's own special service; there were two valets, three chasseurs, one of them called the Mameluke Ali (in reality a

[1] Theoretically, of course, the head physician to His Majesty was right. It is better to drink liquids than to sip them. Excess of zeal should, however, be avoided in all things.

[2] Reg. de l'I. d'E., No. 177.

native of Versailles, by name Saint Denis, who took the place of Roustan), a keeper of the wardrobe, two ushers, eight footmen, an upholsterer, two sweepers, three labourers, a lamplighter, and a porter. Of these servants some were natives of the country, others old attendants who came over with the Emperor. They were under the two prefects of the palace.[1]

The lackeys were, as always, much more arrogant and pretentious than their master, and the lowest kitchen boy gave himself the airs of a small Napoleon.[2]

An Elban woman, Signora Squarci, was head of the linen department, with an assistant, and a Frenchwoman, Madame Petronille, as laundress. A Monsieur Holard had a gardener under his direction, and a musician employed a pianist and two lady vocalists.[3]

The salaries varied between 600 and 4,000 francs. The maître d'hôtel had the 4,000 francs, the head cook 3,000, the lamplighter 1,500, the sweepers 860, the porter 800, and the 600 francs were for the musical director, the pianist, and vocalists; the care of the table, of the lighting, the floor, and the entrance

[1] Peyrusse, 242, 243; Gen. Durand, 220, 221; Sellier Vincent, Marchand, and St. Denis, *Nouvelle Revue Rétrospective*, I., 233, *et seq.*; Reg. de l'I. d'E., Nos. 5, 30, 111. The Emperor had brought two valets, Hubert and Pelard, from Fontainebleau, who returned to France with the Comptroller Colin, and were replaced by Marchand and Jillis. The Emperor's firearms were kept in a small cupboard, close to his bedroom; the mameluke slept in front of his door.

[2] Pons de l'H., 47 and 74.

[3] Peyrusse, 244; Appendix, 24, note, 23 and 128.

being considered necessaries, and the music superfluous.

* * * * *

A flock of Corsicans soon descended on the island and fastened on the Emperor in the hope of appointments. They were all his near "cousins," and aspired to a variety of places.[1]

Relying on the promises contained in the Vicar-General's charge, that "the arrival of His Imperial and Royal Highness would flood the Island with wealth," a crowd of petitioners would fling themselves in his way whenever he set foot out of doors, pressing their claims. "Sire," said one of them, an army chemist from Porto Longone, "we have had the same ill-fortune. I have been unjustly deprived of my post." "Well, then," said the Emperor, "as there is another in the same boat with me, he must not starve." Beggars offered him flowers, and asked for alms. Fraudulent nuns knelt in his way, in the middle of the road, shaking crosses and rosaries, and if he tried to avoid them they would roll in the dust almost under the horse's hoofs in imminent peril of being trampled on.[2] Serenades were continual.

Street musicians from the mainland gave uninvited concerts under his window. He refused to hear them, sending out to say he "did not like music." But the bands would obstinately continue their playing, until the Emperor was forced to send

[1] Pons de l'H., 340.

[2] Pons de l'H., 126, 268; Mém. aux Puiss. All., 71; Campbell, 66. The Emperor set down a monthly sum of 500 francs in his accounts for charity (Reg. de l'I. d'E., No. 93).

the police to them. Sculptors from Carrara brought marble busts of himself and the Empress Marie Louise, which they hoped would fetch their weight in gold, and which finally they left behind at 300 francs the pair, including pedestals. Some of these the Emperor bought, but the greater part were left on their sculptors' hands, with the additional cost of carriage.[1]

The beggars and their demands becoming unbearable, the Emperor made a new road from the Mulini, under the Porta Terra, and ordered the slippery pavements of the street to be roughened, so that he could get into his carriage and escape as quickly as possible into the country.[2]

To complete the rabble crew, adventurers came in the hope of fishing these troubled waters, either in the Emperor's service, or in his enemies'; sham military men, boasting of some imaginary act of devotion to obtain a reward; gay "ladies" who came to make conquests under Italian skies with their false smiles, and women with titles more or less authentic, who after being received at the Mulini would betray their origin by their condition after wine at dinner.[3]

* * * * *

[1] Gen. Vincent, 191, 202; Peyrusse, Appendix, 34: "To Signor Francesoni for purchase of four statues, 1,200 francs." Carrara is on the coast of Italy, north of Leghorn, 70 miles from Elba.

[2] Labadie, 49; Monier, 64; Gen. Vincent, 197. The Porta Terra which tunnels the entire width of the ramparts (named Porta Terra in opposition to the Porta Marina, opening on the port) is still existing, as well as the carriage road, made by the Emperor's orders, which joins it to the Mulini.

[3] Letter from Madame Mère to Lucien Bonaparte, cited by Larrey, II., 35; Pons de l'H., 195, 218.

THE MULINI PALACE.

A STREET IN PORTO FERRAIO.

The presence of a military governor takes an army for granted.

The Emperor, when he arrived, found a French detachment of the 35th of the line in garrison on the island. The Italian detachment had mutinied, as we have seen, and most of their number had gone back to the mainland. The French troops received orders to leave the island after the Emperor's arrival, as soon as the 400 men of the Guards had joined them. The Emperor tried to keep back as many officers and men as possible, but they were all desperately anxious to return to France and their homes. They had had enough of exile, blockades, mouldy flour, and famine.[1]

A few, however, were persuaded to stay, and were incorporated by the Emperor in a battalion, which also contained a number of Corsicans, and was kept up more or less to the number of 400 by recruits from Tuscany and Piedmont, as occasion required. This battalion, called the Corsican Battalion, or Chasseurs of Napoleon, had a captain for every forty men, a lieutenant for every thirty, a sub-lieutenant for twenty, and a sergeant-major for ten, the result being that everyone wanted to command and no one to obey, and that these 400 men were entirely undisciplined. A Corsican, called Tavelle, an old Papal officer, was addressed as "Colonel" one day by the Emperor, in a fit of absence of mind.

[1] Letter from Gen. Count Dupont to the Commandant-General of the Isle of Elba (Campbell, 18, note); Letter from Count de Chauvigny, *Miscellanea Napoleonica*, II., 154; Letter from Gen. Duval, *Archives Etrangères*, 675.

He therefore hurriedly bought himself some colonel's epaulettes, and fastened them to his shoulders. The Emperor in his kindness allowed him to use the title with the pay of eighty francs per month.[1]

A second battalion, called the Free Battalion, officially composed also of 400 men, consisted of Elban militiamen, a most unwarlike body, who only joined for the sake of the uniform, and counted many fathers of families in their ranks.

The Guards had left Fontainebleau six days before the Emperor's departure, on April 14th, at eleven o'clock in the morning, and with Cambronne at their head, started for Elba under the tricolour flag, making their way through the fleurs-de-lys, and foreign colours. They took with them four guns, the chargers, the Emperor's carriages, and the remainder of his baggage in the commissariat waggons. On the 16th they reached Briare, where they waited for the Emperor, and, allowing him to pass them, they took the road to Vermenton, Avallon, Saulieu, Mâcon, and Lyons, where they branched off towards Savoy and the Alps. In the towns where they spent the night, the inhabitants turned out the allied soldiers lodging with them, sending them to sleep out-of-doors, to make room for the veterans. At Lyons 20,000 Austrians were ordered to be ready with muskets loaded, and artillery horses harnessed, as on the eve

[1] Corres. Imp., xxi., 566. 568; Peyrusse, 246; Pons de l'H., 154, 340, 341.

of a battle, and prevented the Guards from passing through the town. They therefore skirted the suburbs where, in spite of the authorities, the inhabitants followed them, shouting "*Vive la Garde! Vive l'Empereur!*" On May 4th, the day the Emperor entered Porto Ferraio, they reached Chambéry, and on the 9th, by way of St. Jean de Maurienne and Lanslebourg, they ascended the pass of Mont Cenis, being obliged to leave their guns behind them, as these delayed their march. They arrived at Savona, near Genoa, on the 18th.[1]

The next day they embarked in five English transports, and cast anchor at Porto Ferraio in the night of May 25-26th. They landed on the 26th at eight in the morning, forming up on the Quay, and entered the town by the Porto Marina. At the Piazza d'Arme they halted and presented arms.[2]

This phalanx of scarred and weather-beaten men of all countries, including Mamelukes from Egypt with their flowing garments, and their blue or white turbans, surmounted with a gleaming crescent, was received by the Elbans with shouts of admiration. The Emperor embraced them, or shook them warmly by the hand, and made a stirring speech before all the people. The veterans wept for joy.

At their head was Cambronne. He was chiefly

[1] Sellier Vincent, 227 ; Monier, 49 ; Pons de l'H., 320, 347.

[2] Sellier Vincent, 229 ; Gen. Durand, 254 ; Monier, 48 ; Gen. Vincent, 197 ; Campbell, 41, 95 ; Fabry, 80 ; Pons de l'H., 323.

known by one celebrated speech, which followed him to the day of his death, and did his reputation no good. He was born at Nantes, on December 26th, 1770. At Jemmapes, in 1792, he received his baptism of fire.[1] He was a heroic warrior, of absolutely reckless courage in battle, most humane at other times, a protector of widows and orphans, terrible in his anger, and inflammable as powder. He returned to Nantes in June, 1793, as sergeant in the Second Legion, and took part in the war of La Vendée, amongst the Blues, inaugurating his exploits by returning alone during a retreat to retake an artillery waggon by sheer force of blows. He was promoted in September as lieutenant, but only just escaped being guillotined at Croisic, in January, 1794, for the treasonable crime of sleeping in a room hung with fleurs-de-lys and portraits of Louis XVI.[2] He fought at Quiberon under Hoche, and went, under Massena, to join the Swiss army, where at Zurich he, with his grenadiers, took two Russian guns under heavy fire. He was invested with the Legion of Honour in 1804, and was major in 1805. At Austerlitz he had his horse killed under him, and was wounded in the thigh by a spent ball.[3] On April 11th, 1809, Napoleon appointed him to the Chasseurs of the Guards, and gave him the titles of Baron of the Empire in 1810, and Commander of the Legion of

[1] Brunschwigg, 24 *et seq.*

[2] Cambronne's Biography.

[3] Letter from Cambronne to his cousin, Lefébure-Cambronne, quoted by Brunschwigg, 58.

Honour and Brigadier-General in 1813. Cambronne retained all his plebeian simplicity and his rare modesty in spite of his new distinctions. At each new investiture he exclaimed that he was unworthy, and that many others were more deserving than he. He was wounded in the leg at Bar-sur-Aube, and at Craonne and the battle of Paris he received six wounds.

At the time of the Emperor's abdication he was laid up with his wounds at Fontainebleau. He rose from his bed to escort the Empress Marie Louise, under the protection of two battalions of guards, and bring her to Orléans ; he was, however, unable to find her.[1] When he learnt, by an article of the Treaty, that the Emperor was allowed 400 men, officers, and non-commissioned officers, he wrote to Drouot "that as he had always been chosen to march against the enemy, he considered himself grossly insulted by the refusal to allow him to follow his Sovereign. His uniform, his very lining ordered him to go."[2] His request was allowed, and he had brought the Guards in triumph, threatening to put to the sword whoever stopped his way. At Vermanton, an Austrian major had refused to give up his quarters. "Very well," exclaimed Cambronne, "your men shall stand on one side, and mine on the other, and we shall see who the quarters will belong to." The Austrian major gave way.[3] When he

[1] Meneval, II., p. 182.

[2] Cambronne's evidence at his trial.

[3] Monier, 49 ; Sellier Vincent, 228. Pons says the dispute occurred at Saulieu (Pons de l'H., 320).

arrived at Porto Ferraio the Emperor held out his hand, saying, "Cambronne, I have had an anxious time waiting for you. But now you have come, all is well." Cambronne was in the seventh heaven.[1]

He was appointed Military Governor of Porto Ferraio;[2] and was, in fact, the watch-dog. He was accompanied by other officers, Major Mallet, and Captains Laborde, Combes, Lamouret, and Cornuel. Lieutenant Larabit travelled separately, and having been allowed 900 francs for the expenses of his journey he returned 300 to the Imperial exchequer on his arrival. These officers, with the Polish Colonel Jerzmanowski, formed a very devoted staff, who undertook all the military functions of the island, the care of the forts, and the command of the army, which attained the number of about 1,600 men.

As a matter of fact the Guards numbered nearly 700, instead of 400, and also 54 men of the Polish Light Cavalry. While still at Fontainebleau the Emperor had been more concerned with the terms of the agreement than the exact number of men, thinking that there would not be time to discover a slight infraction of the Treaty. The Provisional Government sanctioned the arrangement, whether with or without knowledge. What did 200 soldiers more or less matter to the man who had commanded armies numbering 400,000? The captains

1 Pons de l'H., 322.
2 Reg. de l'I. d'E., No. 2; Peyrusse, Appendix, 21; Note 20.

of the English transports at Savona had also allowed the men to pass.[1] The Guards now wore the Elban cockade with the three bees on their shakos and bearskins, and to make them cooler and more comfortable, and also to save their uniforms, the Emperor ordered waistcoats and trousers of nankin to be made for them.[2]

Five vessels comprised the fleet. On May 25th the French frigate Dryade, Captain Montcabrié, arrived at the island, bringing the brig Inconstant, which the Emperor had refused at Fréjus. The French Government would evidently not allow of a sloop. The Emperor, therefore, asked if he might have instead, besides the brig, the goletta Bacchante, which was stationed at Porto Ferraio when he landed, and had been assigned to him until the sloop arrived.[3] But Captain Montcabrié's

[1] This army represents: Corsican Battalion, 400 men; Elban Battalion, 400; Grenadiers and Chasseurs of the Guard, 2,472; Marines of the Guard, 20; Gunners of the Guard, 28; Polish Lancers, 84; officers and subalterns of the Guard, 122; Poles, 24; Mamelukes, 8; Guards' Band, 10; Drums, 14; total, 1,592, exclusive of the General Staff, Bertrand, Drouot, Cambronne, Jerzmanowski, and Lieutenant Taillade. (*Compte nominatif de la Garde*, Fieffé, 117, *et seq.*) Besides these, 50 gendarmes, chiefly Italians and Corsicans.

Of the 108 Poles, officers and troopers, 54, who were detached at Savona, near Parma, as escort for Marie Louise, only arrived at Elba on October 4 (Reg. de l'I. d'E., No. 91). The Corsican Battalion and the Elban Battalion were never complete.

The Emperor knew that at least 600 Guards were on the Roll, and gave this figure, April 27, at Fréjus, on the memorandum sent by Bertrand to Campbell (Campbell, 41), asking the English transports to convey his troops from Savona to Elba.

[2] Corres. Imp., xxi. 580; Reg. de l'I. d'E., No. 3.

[3] Fabry, 79; Peyrusse, 237; Corres. Imp., xxi. 570, 571. The *goletta* is a light boat with two masts and huge sails that give it the appearance of a seagull skimming rapidly over the waters, but make it very liable to capsize in a squall. These schooners, despite their fragility, are sometimes armed with six or eight carronades.

orders were strict. The Dryade left on the 4th of June, taking with her the Bacchante, and the old garrison of the island.[1] The Emperor was only able to keep the esperonade Caroline, with one gun, which performed the postal service between Elba and the mainland.[2]

Two feluccas, employed by the iron mines, were taken for the Imperial fleet and christened Mouche and Abeille. The xebec Étoile, of Leghorn, of 83 tons, was bought on the 5th of August for 8,822 francs. She was mounted with six guns.[3]

The brig Inconstant, of 16 guns, became the flagship, and was commanded by Lieutenant Taillade. She was used for important missions, for any small sea voyage the Emperor wished to make, or for communications with foreign countries. She was destined finally to take the Emperor back to France. The ships' crews were, severally—for the brig 60 men, including officers, for the Caroline 16 men, for Mouche and Abeille each 8 men, for the Étoile 15 men. All the vessels were miserably manned, and rarely even complete. The Elban sailors were not willing to leave their coasting trade to enter the Emperor's navy, and recruits had to be obtained at Capraia or Genoa, or wherever possible. The 20 marines belonging to the guards, distributed

1 Pons de l'H., 135.

2 Pons de l'H., 350; Reg. de l'I. d'E., No. 4. *Esperonade*, a Maltese boat, fast, flat-bottomed to allow her to be beached, one mast, no deck.

3 Reg. de l'I. d'E., Nos. 1, 43, 44, 45; Corres. Imp., xxi. 601. *Felucca*: long, narrow boat, navigated by sails and oars, ten to twelve rowers each side, two lateen sails, two masts leaning forward, a beak-shaped prow, fast goer. *Xebec*: three masts, sails and oars, pointed fore and aft, spur prow, elegant shape, fast.

amongst the vessels, served, however, to give a little stability.[1]

The Emperor had three cutters for his trips along the coast, two of them the Hochard and the Usher, were for his sole use. The last named was a present from the captain of the English frigate, and the Emperor had christened her after him.

The Civil Administration, of which Bertrand was the chief minister, included the Intendant of the island, the Administration of Estates, a Chamber of Commerce, Magistrates, a County Court, with a Genoese as president, a Court of Appeal, and a Council of State.[2] Almost everyone at Porto Ferraio enjoyed an official position, and was able to display his buttons and gold braid in the streets. To Bertrand was assigned the duty of conveying the Emperor's orders, and of checking and paying through Peyrusse the tradespeople's bills, after his Majesty's approval, who would not allow a centime to be paid away without his permission.

* * * * *

But to play at being a King, and to live, money is a necessary factor.

On April 10, at Fontainebleau, Peyrusse, after seeing that his exchequer only contained the sum of 488,913 francs 16 centimes, asked the Emperor for the necessary permission to fetch from Orléans, before it was too late, the balance of the Treasury from the Tuileries. On the next day the Emperor

[1] Corres. Imp., xxi. 571, 605; Pons de l'H., 348.

[2] Pons de l'H., 72, 81; Reg. de l'I. d'E., No. 35; Peyrusse, Appendix, 147.

roused himself from the torpor which had fallen on him since the abdication, and in sudden alarm at finding himself without money, gave Peyrusse a letter for Marie Louise, and sent him off.[1]

On the 12th he arrived at Orléans, which was gradually being surrounded by Cossacks, and there learnt from the Empress that the Provisional Government had sent the preceding day for the treasury and that the police officer in charge of the baggage waggons had delivered it over. These waggons contained 10,000,000 francs, the personal property of the Emperor, jewels to the value of 400,000 francs, 3,000,000 francs worth of silver and silver gilt plate, and the Imperial wardrobe, with the Court dresses and robes. The Government Agent had consented to leave 6,000,000 francs for the Empress, which she was willing, she said, to share with the Emperor. She therefore gave Peyrusse 2,580,002 francs, and took the rest with her to Rambouillet, where she hurriedly retired the next day.

The transport of these millions was not accomplished without difficulty across a country full of the enemy. Peyrusse covered the cases with straw and manure, and waited at Orléans for the two battalions of Guards which, led by Cambronne, was on its way to fetch the Empress. By continual pressure, he induced Marie Louise, who had no other source of income herself, to give him 911,000 francs besides, which she paid in small instalments.

Thus the Emperor departed for Elba, with the sum of 3,979,915 francs.

[1] Peyrusse, 217, *et seq.*, Appendix, 145 ; Meneval, II., 183–186.

From this must be deducted 30,000 francs Government expenses on account of the Treaty of Fontainebleau, 58,299 francs 63 centimes for the expenses of the journey, and 60,000 francs stolen at Fréjus during the night of April 26 to 27.[1] While the cases were being landed at Porto Ferraio, 20,000 francs more were stolen by a shoemaker belonging to the National Guard of Elba. The thief betrayed himself five months afterwards by the number of masses he paid for in the churches, and by the extravagant sums he gave for leather and other materials of his trade. Peyrusse, who heard of this, had him arrested, and ordered a mild form of torture for him. Under this treatment the shoemaker confessed that being on sentry duty near the coffers he had stumbled against a package containing twenty rouleaux, each of fifty napoleons, which had been forgotten amongst the straw. He had picked them up and hidden them in his shako until he was relieved, "believing that the Holy Virgin had sent him this piece of luck"; 16,960 francs were found under his mattress.[2]

The sum of 3,811,615 francs 53 centimes was treated as a reserve fund,[3] only to be used for

[1] Peyrusse, 248; Appendix, 16, 133; Gen. Durand, 243. Among the expenses of the journey we find 4,200 francs for the English sailors of the Undaunted, and 1,200 francs to the transports that brought the Guard, May 26. The robbery at Fréjus occurred during the night of April 26–27. While the Emperor was sleeping at Bouillidou his carriages went on in the direction of Fréjus, and 60,000 francs disappeared from the safes of the Controller. The thief was never discovered.

[2] Peyrusse, p. 236 and 260, and Appendix, p. 143.

[3] 3,828,575 francs 53 cent., including the 16,960 francs restored of the second theft in September.

unforeseen emergencies, and in case of absolute necessity, as the annual allowance of 2,000,000 francs paid by the French Government to the ex-Emperor, added to the revenues of the island, was sufficient for his daily expenses.

The expenses of the administration of this little kingdom (civil officials, clergy, courts of justice, bridges and roads, tax collecting) and the various receipts (including taxes on property, customs, stamps and registration, &c.) when balanced came to a sum of between 110,000 and 120,000 francs. The revenues of the island, viz., the iron mines 300,000 francs, the salt marshes 20,000, the tunny fisheries 30,000, making a total of 350,000 (with a probable increase by better management) came into the Imperial coffers. These revenues were added to his 2,000,000 of income, towards the Emperor's current expenses and the maintenance of his army. Half a million of arrears from the mines in addition gave him a bonus for initial expenses.[1] Thus the financial situation was most satisfactory.

The budget for the war department absorbed the greater part, and for the last seven months of the year attained the sum of 689,317 francs.[2] The new King of Elba with his army of 1,592 men could

[1] Reg. de l'I. d'E., Nos. 20, 32, 76, 100, 104; Pons de l'H., p. 86 and 144. Peyrusse, p. 239 and 241, and (Appendix) p. 53. 229,000 francs besides were in the hands of Pons, from the products of the mines previous to the Emperor's arrival. There were arrears of 9,166 francs 35 cent. owing to the contributions of 1813, and the treasurer had in hand a balance of 3,401 francs 91 cent. As a matter of fact, the Emperor was supposed to pay this money over to the French Government, but he kept it as a balance against the spoliation of the Treasury of the Tuileries, and the 2,000,000 promised him.

[2] Corres. Imp. 21,673.

hardly be in a position to declare war on anyone, but he felt it necessary to be ready should a blow be struck on him first. Having been till now the object of so much hatred and so much fear, it would be unwise in the extreme to feel quite secure.

The coasts of the island were bristling with forts built by its various conquerors. The garrisons of these forts were now strengthened; their weak places repaired, and guns and engineers were stationed in them, from the Guards and the Polish regiments. The old guns, balls, and powder were cleared away and sold by auction, as also the mouldy flour serving as provisions of siege.[1] The citadels of Porto Ferraio and Porto Longone were condemned to be pulled down in the near future, and to be replaced by more modern buildings.

This military play-game was the Emperor's last achievement in the great passion of his life. At Porto Ferraio he founded a school in imitation of the Polytechnic School in Paris. The parents of the pupils paid 300 francs each per year, and the Cadets, ten in number, each received a pay of 180 francs. The uniform was a black hat with red piping, blue trousers, riding boots, a sword with a white sash, and sub-lieutenant's epaulettes.[2] This was another toy for the Elbans.

In civil matters fresh orders and arrangements did not lag behind. The island was to be endowed

[1] Peyrusse, p. 241, and (Appendix) p. 54. Pons de l'H., p. 94. Reg. de l'I. d'E., 37, 50, 69 and 136. The Emperor sold this rubbish in 1814 for 77,802 francs.

[2] Pons de l'H., 73; Reg. de l'I. d'E., No. 96. The order was dated Oct. 13, as cited by Campbell (167); the first mention of it was on May 22 (Corres. Imp., xxi. 570).

with roads, with a quarantine hospital to receive doubful ships and their merchandise, with wells, fountains, with new cultivation, especially corn, which had hitherto all been imported, making the price of bread very high.[1] Porto Ferraio was to have a fire-brigade, and an avenue planted with new trees "like the Champs Elysées," where the citizens could walk on Sundays.[2] An activity totally unknown to the Elbans spread through the island: the grenadiers of the Guards took part in these new works, and mingled with the workmen like Cæsar's soldiers of old, who left the sword to take up the pickaxe, rule, and chisel.[3] The work of demolition and rebuilding went on apace, sculptors from the mainland carved chimney-pieces for houses and balustrades and urns for gardens. Every willing pair of hands found work: the island was like a beehive, and Pons, who knew his classics, could express the public feeling after this fashion: "Porto Ferraio is like Fénélon's Salentum. The illusion is perfect. Everything seems to grow. Industry lifts her radiant head, the anvil rings under the hammer, the axe and the trowel are at work unceasingly."[4]

The Emperor also undertook to cleanse his subjects. The barracks, whose noisome odours had penetrated as far as the Mulini, were cleaned and whitewashed, and the drainage improved. The

[1] Gen. Vincent, 197, 205; Pons de l'H., 279; Reg. de l'I. d'E., Nos. 8, 9, 18, 26, 57, 66, 83, 86, 123, 156, 175.

[2] Reg. de l'I. d'E., No. 77.

[3] Monier, 52; Peyrusse, 249. The commencement of the phrase is identical in Monier as in Peyrusse. As Monier's book appeared first, Peyrusse must be the plagiarist. Campbell, 208.

[4] Pons de l'H., 59.

municipal authorities were advised to keep the streets swept, and the inhabitants to provide their houses with proper sanitary appliances. Those persons who continued to throw their refuse out of the windows would in future be fined.[1]

* * * * *

The Emperor's horses had come over with the Guards to find their old master in his exile. Each one bore the memory of a battle; the glory of past achievement.[2]

Wagram, a grey Arab, had carried the Emperor at the battle whose name he bore. When he saw his master enter the stable, he began to whinny and paw the ground. The Emperor went up to him with a piece of sugar, and kissing him, said, "*Te voila, mon cousin!*"

Montevideo, a large and beautiful bay, was from South America, and had been through the Spanish campaign, as had Emin, a Turkish horse, chestnut, with a black stripe down his back, like a mule, with mane and tail black also, and four black feet. The Emperor had ridden him into Madrid during the Russian Campaign.

Gonsalvo, also a large bay, had seen the same service in Spain, Russia, and France. He bore the Emperor at Brienne, and during the battle had had the left bridle cut in two by a ball.

Roitelet, was a cross between an English horse and a Limousine mare. At Schoenbrunn in 1809 during a review, he had bolted with the Emperor

[1] Corres. Imp., xxi. 567; Reg. de l'I. d'E., Nos. 11, 48, 77, 146.
[2] Sellier Vincent, 217, *et seq.*

amongst the ranks of the grenadiers, nearly throwing his rider, and hurting many of the men. He had been across Russia, where the Emperor at first bore a grudge against him after his behaviour at Schoenbrunn, but made friends with him again, glad to find his sure feet on that icy ground where other horses slipped and fell. Roitelet, newly shod, carried him all day without a stumble. He rode him at Lützen, in the thickest of the fighting, when a ball, nearly carrying off both horse and rider, grazed the former so close that it carried off a piece of hair and skin from his hock. He rode him also at Arcis-sur-Aube, where a shell burst in front of them. Roitelet bounded to one side, throwing the Emperor, who said on mounting him again, "*Allons, nous sommes quittes pour la peur!*" After that day, when he visited him in the stable, he never missed stroking his hock, where the hair had never grown again.

The two most popular horses, however, were two white ones, who were collectively called "the white charger" of the Emperor, and who were as famous in their way as his little hat.

One of them, Tauris, was a Persian, of wonderfully graceful build, a silvery grey, slightly dappled, with a white mane and a long fine tail, was a gift from Alexander at the Congress of Erfurth. The Emperor had ridden her in the Russian battles of Vitepsk, Smolensk, Moskva, and also at Moscow. This beautiful animal, full of mettle, in spite of her slight build, had carried her master through almost all the terrible retreat. On the morning when he had nearly been taken prisoner by the Cossacks, *i.e.* October 25, on the Kolouga Road, and which the Emperor's staff charged sword in hand to clear a way for him, the yells of the Cossacks excited her so much, that Berthier (or Rapp according to some authorities) had to seize her by the bridle and prevent her from joining in the charge, and carrying the Emperor into the midst of the enemy. She bore him to the Berezina bridge, which they crossed at eleven o'clock in the evening. She was also in Saxony, Dresden, and Leipzig.

The other horse, a pure white, of Norman race, was ridden on parades, or State processions. On this account he was called Intendant, but the veterans called him Coco. Whenever they caught sight of him with the Emperor on his back, they used to shout all together "*Voila Coco!*"

Euphrate, a horse of northern breed, and Heliopolis, an Arab, both formerly ridden by the Emperor, now belonged to Bertrand and Drouot, and Cordone, an Andalusian of a chestnut colour, brought back from the Spanish campaign, a quiet, gentle animal, was intended for Marie Louise.

These horses had each a crimson velvet saddle, with stirrups and ornaments of plated silver, and at the holster a beautiful pistol with the carved head of Medusa at the butt end. The Emperor added to his stable two small horses, a Corsican and an Elban, for use on the rough roads and mountains.[1]

[1] Sellier Vincent, 230; Reg. de l'I. d'E., No. 5.

The store-houses belonging to the tunny fisheries were turned into stables, and their tenant evicted, with a compensation. The stables were "well paved, with stalls, mangers, racks for hay to right and left, and a passage down the middle." They were lighted by high windows, looking to the sea.[1]

All this care of horses was quite new to the Elbans, who used to gather in crowds to see the stables, and get a peep at these wonderful animals.

There were besides forty-eight horses of less importance, to draw the various carriages, *i.e.*, six "berlines," and a large sleeping carriage, in which the Emperor had travelled from Fontainebleau to Fréjus, two open carriages, yellow and red, and yellow respectively; a light brown and gold landau, two post-chaises, two open carts for hunting or shooting (these all came either with the Emperor, or were brought by the guards); also a cabriolet, painted yellow. There were besides, five mules with pack-saddles, four *barocci*,[2] eight artillery waggons, which served as rubbish carts in the building work organised by the Emperor, and twenty-four cart horses.[3] These, with thirteen horses for grooms, made up a total of 102 horses and mules, and 27 carriages, which were kept at the arsenal, together with the gun carriage and ammunition waggons.

The men employed in the stables, whose

1 Monier, p. 13; Pons de l'H., quoted in Reg. de l'I. d'E., 116; Gen. Vincent, 204; Sellier Vincent, 362.

2 The *baroccio* is a common form of vehicle in Italy; it is shaped like a waggon, with a canopy of netting.

3 Sellier Vincent, 229, 232; Reg. de l'I. d'E., No. 101. The cabriolet came from Rome with Madame Mère.

functions were all controlled by the Emperor with as much formality as in Paris, consisted of the chief saddler Vincent, with three men under him, one harness-maker, a veterinary surgeon (originally picked up at Saulieu to look after Tauris, who went lame), one farrier, a head groom, who had the sole right of mounting the Emperor's horses, a stud-groom, with one man under him, a coachman and eight postillions, ten stablemen, one of them a Russian, two troopers, two locksmiths, two carpenters, and a tailor to make the liveries ; 35 persons in all under the direction of a Préfect of the Palace.[1]

The two open carriages were always kept ready for immediate use, and the cart for provisions ready stocked with lemons, oranges, and bottles of wine and brandy.

The harness bore the Imperial eagle, the postillions and coachmen wore hats with gold lace, green coats with gilt buttons, red waistcoats with gold braid, and capes. The purpose of this display was to show to the people of Elba and to strangers coming to the country that Napoleon, the King of Elba, was still a sovereign, and not a mere exile.

The symbols of state were necessary to exact the

[1] Reg. de l'I. d'E., No. 5 ; Sellier Vincent, 225, 226 ; Peyrusse, 243. To this establishment must be added two grooms and three coachmen for Madame Mère, Princess Pauline, and Countess Bertrand, when these ladies arrived in Elba. There were also the barouche in which Madame Mère travelled from Rome to Leghorn, and a little chaise with two ponies which Pauline brought from Naples. The Emperor's establishment, including stables, saddlery, and household at the Mulini, accordingly numbered 75 to 80.

respect of his subjects. And something of the great Emperor seemed to remain, when, with Bertrand and Drouot galloping at his side, he drove out in his gilded carriage, with his mounted grooms, and postillions cracking their whips, disappearing amidst a cloud of dust.

* * * * *

On the 2nd of August the majestic and venerable Madame Lætitia Bonaparte, the Emperor's mother, usually called Madame Mère, landed at Elba.

She had left Orléans for Rome on the 11th of April, accompanied by her brother, Cardinal Fesch; the journey, which occupied a month, was a severe one for a woman of her age.[1] Apparently unmoved by either the splendour or the fall of her son, equally ready to reign in state at the Tuileries, or to resume the black dress and hood of her native country, she seemed like a second Cornelia, proudly indifferent to misfortune and unaltered by time.

On June 2nd, after hearing that the Emperor was in possession of the island, she wrote to him (he only received her letter on the 14th) saying that she was ready to join him. After some correspondence as to the manner of her journey, she left Rome, on July 26th. Perils threatened both by sea and land. Barbary pirates swarmed on the sea, and brigands on the roads. Madame Mère, who had a superstitious fear of the water, chose the

[1] Larrey, II., 56, 57, 62, *et seq.* Madame Mère met her brother, the Cardinal, at the Convent of Pradines, near Roannes, reaching Rome the night of May 12. She was at that time 64 or 65 years old. The exact date of her birth is unknown.

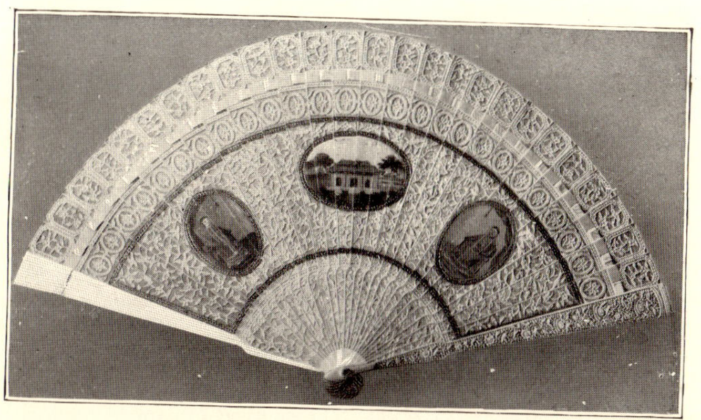

FAN BELONGING TO PAULINE BORGHESE.

BED BELONGING TO MADAME MÈRE.

brigands and dry land. She was armed by a passport, which Cardinal Pecca gave her from the Pope, describing her under the name of Madame de Pont.[1]

She reached Leghorn in safety on the 29th, with her chamberlain, Colonna, and a small suite, in two carriages drawn by six horses, an open light carriage and a cabriolet, escorted by four guards sent by her son Lucian, and from Pisa by four Austrian hussars. She embarked, on August 2nd, on the English brig Grasshopper, amidst the jeers and hisses of the mob.[2]

She was ceremoniously received by the captain of the brig (Captain Battersby) and accomplished the short voyage lying on a sofa arranged for her use on deck, a snuff-box in her hand ornamented with a portrait of her son Louis, gazing at the island of Elba on the horizon. When she was informed that the Mulini Palace could be distinguished on the top of its rock, she left her sofa, and, to get a better view, climbed with considerable agility on a gun-carriage. The Grasshopper cast anchor at Porto Ferraio that same evening. Madame Mère seemed much offended that the Emperor was not at the harbour to meet her. He had not been informed of the exact date of the arrival, and had driven out in the island. As soon as the news reached him he hastened to the spot and greeted

[1] This passport is at Porto Ferraio in the keeping of the Sindaco, Signor Bigeschi. It bears the date of June 27, when it was issued to Madame Mère ; and was stamped twice *en route*, on July 27 and 28, at Siena.

[2] Campbell, 124, 131.

his mother with much feeling, even with tears. This display of emotion greatly pleased everyone, and proved that instead of being the heartless monster represented by his enemies he was indeed tenderly sensitive.[1]

Madame Mère was received in a house close to the Mulini, rented from the minister chamberlain, Vantini, for 200 francs per month.[2] Her diamonds had been left behind at Rome to be sent later by safe hands, and she wrote to Paris and Rome for her furniture, amongst other things a large fourpost mahogany bedstead, inlaid with gold, and thirteen red chairs.[3] She extended her gracious protection to all the Corsicans on the island, who grew, in consequence, more rapacious and unbearable than ever.[4]

The Vantini Palace had been originally intended for Pauline Borghese, or as she was intimately called, Princess Paula. When the Emperor was travelling to Fréjus she met him, intending to embark with him for Elba. She was always fragile, and at that time especially very ill, her nerves shaken by the late tragic occurrences. She grew so much worse that she was unable to reach Fréjus, and was obliged to stop at Muy, some miles off.[5] She arrived at Elba, still very ill, on

1 Pons de l'H., 205, 306.

2 Peyrusse, Appendix, 142. This house exists still; it is now inhabited by the Sous-Préfet of the Island, and has a commemorative inscription inside. In the engraving it is the third on the right-hand side of the street, going up to the Mulini.

3 Larrey, 79, 84, 85, 86, 105. This is, in all probability, the bed now in the Museo di San Martino (see p. 270). 4 Pons de l'H., 208.

5 Waldbourg-Truchsess, 40; Helfert, 70; Campbell, 89, 99; Monier, 53; Gen. Vincent, 202, 203; Fabry, 55, 81.

the 31st May, and was carried to the Mulini, where the Emperor gave up his room for her, the only habitable one in the Palace, full as it was of plasterers and carpenters' hammers. After two days of this racket, her nerves tried beyond endurance, she left for Naples, promising to return when her health improved, and her brother was able to find her a residence. The Emperor took the Vantini house for her, but as Pauline did not return, he placed his mother there.

As to the Empress Marie Louise, who had been separated from her husband so sorely against her will, the Emperor continually declared she was on her way. To convince his hearers, a suite of rooms was prepared for her and the little King of Rome, at the Mulini. Her horse was waiting for her in the stable, with his English saddle and bridle, ready for her excursions across the island. Cargoes of coloured glass lamps and fireworks were ordered from Leghorn.[1] The Elbans' curiosity was stimulated by these promises, seeing in them a vista of future fêtes, and a proof that their beloved sovereign would remain indefinitely on the island.

* * * * *

There was only one blot on the canvas.

One form moved in this miniature court, with a piercing eye, an artificial smile, a watchful ear, a scarred brow, artistically concealed by a silk handkerchief. This was the official spy, Colonel Campbell, who with his faultless uniform, and his

[1] Sellier Vincent, 231, 306, 368 ; Reg. de l'I. d'E., No. 38.

elegantly correct British manners, followed the Emperor's footsteps, and as if by accident was present everywhere.[1] The Austrian Commissioner, Koller, had left on the 9th May.[2] Only Colonel Campbell remained to see what the formidable captive might have in his mind to do. It seemed wise to be a little afraid of him.

Campbell was of Scottish extraction, and had fought under Wellington in Spain and Portugal, had known the exile Madame de Stael in Sweden, and had been at the battle of Bautzen, where, through a field-glass, he had for the first time seen the Emperor moving to and fro in front of his army's lines. During the French campaign, at la Fère-Champenoise, he was accidentally caught in a struggle between French and Russians, and had been felled by a Cossack's lance. Another struck him on the head with his sword, in spite of his crying "*Anglisky polkownick* (*Colonel Anglais*)." A third nearly finished him off, when he was saved by a Russian officer.

After the treaty of Fontainebleau, he was nominated as English Commissioner, and presented himself to the Emperor, whom he found "walking up and down in his room, his hair and clothes in disorder, like a wild animal in a cage. Campbell informed him that according to instructions received from Lord Castlereagh, he must not only conduct the Emperor on his journey, but also "reside at the

[1] Pons de l'H., 10, 83, 236.

[2] Bertrand to Meneval. Meneval, 245.

island of Elba for as long as the Emperor considered the presence of an English officer would be useful to him." His personal instructions were as follows: "To correspond with the Government in the execution of his mission, and if occasion required, to call for assistance from any of the civil or military authorities of the Mediterranean." The manner and conditions of this correspondence were left to "his own discretion." This last phrase clearly signified that nothing in the nature of an open correspondence was expected of him.[1]

This mission was a distasteful one to a soldier. He was at once gaoler and spy, without being openly either one or the other, and with the necessary bearing of a gentleman. He performed his mission conscientiously, though frequently disgusted by the rebuffs he forcedly experienced. To make his position easier he had offered to retire, after the definite possession of the island by the Emperor, and had obtained an official letter from Bertrand on the 27th May, begging him to stay: "The presence of Col. Campbell at Porto Ferraio appears indispensable. I can only reiterate to Col. Campbell how much his person and his presence are agreeable to the Emperor Napoleon."[2]

Indispensable he certainly was, as failing his presence the Emperor was unattached by any tie to European Governments. He was an exile on his

[1] Campbell, 9–12.
[2] Campbell. *Napoleon at Fontainebleau and Elba*, 242.

island, cut off from any other community, and counted as a cipher: a prey to any future destiny, he might be insulted, carried away prisoner, his island pillaged and bombarded, in spite of his poor army and his brig of sixteen guns, without a single protector to utter a protest. The presence of Campbell, however, was a defence, a guarantee from the Powers, almost an embassy, giving an air of reality to this poor apology for a kingdom. It was Campbell who carried out the Emperor's desire to have the flag of Elba recognised at Algiers, and through the person of His Britannic Majesty's Consul to inform the Dey, whose corsairs he dreaded, "that the Allied Powers have engaged among themselves to have that flag respected, and that it must be treated upon an equality with that of France."[1]

It was Campbell whom the Emperor sent to Leghorn, a hostile and quarrelsome town, to arrange about quarantine and navigation.[2] It was Campbell who had asked and obtained for Madame Mère a passage on the English brig, and if any difficulty should arise with the French Government, it was Campbell's duty to try to arrange matters.

Colonel Campbell performed all these duties admirably, and the other part of his mission no less, taking daily notes of every event that took place, and making flying visits to the mainland on the man of war always kept in readiness for him in the roadstead of Porto Ferraio. These journeys were

[1] Campbell. *Napoleon at Fontainebleau and Elba*, 242. [2] *Ibid.*, 245–7.

for the object of first recruiting, and then keeping in touch with agents established on the Italian coast from Sicily as far as Rome; to compare their information with his own, and with the Austrian General Stahremberg, the military governor of Tuscany, and to keep himself in constant communication with the English officers of the Mediterranean squadron.[1] On the island of Elba he did not hesitate to make the most audacious proposals to anyone who would listen to him. If he succeeded, it was so much to the good: if not, he did not trouble himself about the risk of betrayal, as his true position was a secret to no one.

The Emperor, fully aware of these intrigues, was equally diplomatic, and could not show Campbell enough attention. In any case he had nothing to conceal. He was outwardly absolutely harmless, and a reliable witness was all to the good.

[1] "July 11. Arrived at Rome. Pursuing my intentions of seeing the different persons employed by His Majesty's Government in the vicinity of Elba for the purpose of establishing secure and confidential communication with them. . . ." (Campbell. *Napoleon at Fontainebleau and Elba*, 266). "Every possible means must be employed in order to be constantly well-informed of all that goes on in the island of Elba, and you will exceedingly oblige me by communicating whatever you know" (Stahremberg to Campbell, *ib.*, 275). "Lord Exmouth, the Admiral commanding in the Mediterranean, has for the purposes of my mission been pleased to attach to the Elba station His Majesty's brig Swallow, which enables me to communicate with all parts, and I propose to proceed to Sicily for a few days to give Lord William Bentinck all the information in my power, and to benefit by his counsel as to my future proceedings" (*ib.*, 266). "I keep a strict look-out upon all vessels belonging to this island, a list of which I do myself the honour of enclosing for your Lordship's information. I have also given the same to Admiral Penrose, commanding His Majesty's fleet in the Mediterranean, and to the naval officer on this station" (*ib.*, 343) in a despatch to Lord Castlereagh, of November 6.

The Emperor, on his side, had his secret agents, and Campbell could never feel certain that his own servant was not a spy. The information obtained was reported to the Emperor only. Poggi, the judge, was commissioned to *explorer les familles*, and to report any gossip he might hear in the social life of the town.[1] He had the gift of making people talk, and by his pleasant manners, with occasional carefully studied lapses of ill-humour, of giving precisely the opposite impression to what he really intended. He collected information while carrying on a constant deception.

* * * * *

[1] Campbell, 143, 208; Pons de l'H., 72, 81.

III

THE LAST IDYLL

THUS passed the first few months of the Imperial occupation of the island, as peaceful and quiet as life in the provinces, and untroubled by any serious event. The Emperor usually rose before dawn, sometimes as early as three o'clock, to enjoy the freshness of the air and to work and read in his study.[1]

He occupied himself by collecting a library. In passing through Fréjus he bought 240 francs worth of books and a Bible compiled by Silvestre de Sacy in thirty-two volumes. At Lyons he bought a herbarium. Several cases of books from his library at Fontainebleau had arrived by the Guards' commissariat waggons, and others had been ordered from Venice, Genoa, Paris or Leghorn; those he kept were all rebound and stamped with an N or an eagle. The books sent for his approbation were often the fag-ends of libraries, odd volumes or

[1] Monier, 56. Peyrusse has the following note in his accounts, Appendix 51: "His Majesty's study. Couch: wood painted grey with gold lions, to match the library. Yellow silk."

works without any interest, which he returned.[1] Amongst these literary remains were some books which had been forbidden by the censor during his reign. These he read, and for the greater number could not discover the reason of the censure.[2] However, during his palmy days it had been no easy matter to foresee what might displease him.

After walking for a little while in his garden he retired to rest again at about seven or eight o'clock. He rose an hour or two before luncheon, and went for a ride or drive without an escort.

The luncheon was slight and taken quickly (sometimes out in the country),[3] and after it he would resume his exploration of the island, visiting the most picturesque places, climbing rocks and headlands, a shepherd's staff in his hand. He thus ascended the summit of Giove by narrow goat-tracks. This peak, which rises near Volterraio, on the northern extremity of the island, must not be confused with Monte Giove with its village of Marciana. The peaks were both dedicated in ancient times to the father of the gods, and their name still survives. When the Emperor reached the summit he sat down to rest, like Marius on the ruins of Carthage, and "giving rein to his lively imagination, he traced the design of a solitary dwelling place on the top of this rocky hill which should be of ideal beauty, marvellous, unique.

[1] Pons de l'H., 199; Campbell, 76; Corres. Imp., xxi. 591, 655; Reg. de l'I. d'E., Nos. 38, 78, 90; Peyrusse, Appendix, 33; Fabry, 30; Hérisson, *Le Cabinet Noir*, Paris, 1887, 143.

[2] St. Helena Mem., Dec. 19, 1815.

[3] Gen. Vincent, 178.

Here should stand the principal building, there the offices, further on a garden and a well." But his dream was soon over, and, letting his arms fall, he shook his head, for money, counted by the millions which were no longer his, would be needed for such an undertaking.[1]

On another day, radiantly fine, he made an excursion to the Gorge of Monserrat. He was accompanied by Bertrand and Pons. The latter has described the occasion in his amusing style. The detail is so full that we can follow them almost every step of the way.[2]

"On leaving the Porto Longone road," says Pons, "we followed a narrow path bordered with high cypresses. The pathway leads down a ravine thick with aloes and Barbary fig trees. Through the ravine flows a stream losing itself in the sea." The whole description is a complete picture.

Pons rode one of the little Corsican horses, not beautiful, but sure-footed, and Bertrand was mounted on Euphrate, the great charger from the North which the Emperor had given him. The Emperor, who was in a teasing mood, asked his companions to race in front of him. Pons agreed readily, but Bertrand declared that it would be ridiculous, as one stride of his horse was worth four of Pons' mount, and he would be on the way back before Pons arrived. Things turned out otherwise, however. The charger stumbled over the stones of

[1] Pons de l'H., 254; Gen. Vincent, 203.
[2] Pons de l'H., 267, *et seq.*

the ravine, while the other jumped from rock to rock like a chamois. After a few minutes Bertrand announced that he would give it up. The Emperor shouted with laughter; nothing amused him so much as to tease the General, who took all his jokes in tragic earnest.

The trio next met a vine-dresser, and as the Emperor had previously noticed that the earth cast up by the spade contained white stones, he picked one up, and, showing it to the man, asked him if this kind of soil was favourable to the vine. The vine-dresser answered carelessly that this soil was not bad for white wine, but that the red wine required a richer soil. The Emperor put twenty francs into his cap.

They arrived soon at the Hermitage, and Pons continues, "The hermits have cultivated a piece of ground, planted some trees, and a few vines. The church is simple and poor, but well cared for. The hermit's cell, a comfortable little house, is built on a small terrace covered with trellised vines." The hermit came out to speak to the Emperor, and complained in a whining tone that times were bad. "The sailors of these parts used to have faith in the Holy Virgin of Monserrat," he said, "and have masses said in her honour. To-day, things are different. Their faith now has to be rewarded by a good miracle."

As the Emperor entered the chapel, he turned to get a view of the enchanting scene, grand, and yet charming "far from the bitterness of life." He

THE CHAPEL AND HERMITAGE OF MONSERRAT.

remained silent, enchanted by the beauty before him: but as if the peaceful aspect of the scene could not impress him long, he said "Yes, it is beautiful; but how much grander it must be during the equinoctial gales of this country, with lightning and storms of rain." He asked the hermit if destructive thunderstorms often visited Monte Serrato. The hermit answered that they frequently had them; but through the Holy Virgin's protection, the Hermitage had never been struck. The Emperor laughed, and pointing to the surrounding peaks, said, "These are also a help; they make splendid lightning conductors." "You are right," said the hermit; "but it is better to let the people believe in heavenly protection." The Emperor shrugged his shoulders, and to change the subject, the hermit asked him to go into the church, which was lighted by candles. The Emperor knelt for a moment, and left some money as alms. Then he ordered a basket of provisions, sent from Porto Longone, to be unpacked, and invited his two companions to share it with him.

After his lunch the Emperor, overcome by the heat, slept in his chair. When he awoke, after a quarter of an hour, he left the valley with Pons and Bertrand. "He was in excellent spirits, and these hours were the happiest he spent."

He was also shown all the natural curiosities of the island; for example, the magnetic mountain of Cape Calamita and all the vegetable phenomena, a fig-tree like that at Roscoff in Brittany, "with branches which grew down to the ground, taking root again there, and surrounding the trunk with a fresh generation of fig-trees, besides forming a beautiful tent of foliage"; an apricot-tree which the year before had produced 400 kilogrammes of apricots; a peach-tree which yielded fruit weighing each $\frac{3}{4}$ of a pound, of so surprising a size that strangers could not believe in their reality: also two carob-trees, one male, the other female, belonging to a baker, at Porto Longone, under whose shade "a table for sixty wedding guests had been laid."[1] The Emperor saw all these wonders, and was duly impressed.

But when on climbing a summit he caught sight of the sea bounding the horizon, he said, sighing, "my island is very small."[2]

* * * * *

On the southern side of the island, on clear days, a little islet, flat as a raft and barely emerging from the water, could be seen. This is Pianosa.

Of the same geological formation as Elba, Pianosa lies eight miles off, measures twelve and a half miles in circumference, and is covered with fertile soil, except where the rock breaks through. The inhabitants of Rio, Porto Longone, and Campo go there for their stock of hay, as the islet is full of springs and the grass is excellent. But it is uninhabited, as long ago it served as a kind of fort to Moorish pirates, who massacred every one living there. In 1806, colonists went over from Elba

[1] Pons de l'H., 265, 266, 270. [2] Campbell, 74.

protected by a small fort and two guns, but the English destroyed the defences, and the colonists left the island to wild goats.[1]

When the Emperor heard of the existence of this island, he declared that as it seemed to belong to no one else it was his, and after sailing over to it on board the Inconstant, announced his military occupation and colonisation.

This expedition was carried out with immense difficulty. The troops consisted of forty men, viz., twenty gunners and sappers of the Guards, and as many from the Corsican battalion, under Major Gottmann, removed from Porto Longone, and Lieutenant of Engineers, Larabit.

The troops landed, having with them a priest from Campo, a few provisions, and cases of biscuits, some workmen, a mortar, ammunition, and cartridges. The Emperor gave instructions that the guns were to be mounted in a battery within forty-eight hours, to clear the sea in case of attack.[2] Major Gottmann was next ordered to construct a bomb-proof battery under cover, to build barracks, a church, and a village for future colonists; also to kill all the goats, for the sake of the crops on the island. A tax of three francs quarterly was to be levied on Neapolitan coral fishermen, to be "paid into the office of public works on the island."

[1] Larabit, 64, *et seq.*; Corres. Imp., xxi. 567, 570, 574, 577, 579, 585, 616; Reg. de l'I. d'E., Nos. 36, 51, 81, 82, 94, 121, 137, 167; Campbell, 84; Pons de l'H., 302, 337. The nearest point on the mainland is eight miles from Elba. Pianosa is about twenty miles from Porto Longone.

[2] From the Algerine pirates, since Napoleon was at peace with England.

In the meantime some caves on the sea-shore, which had formerly been used as tombs were all the shelter available for the army of occupation. The excavations made to receive the coffins were still to be seen. "The caves can be used by the garrison," said the Emperor. "The Major will have them cleaned out, first lighting some fires to burn the insects. The priest from Campo will be curé of the parish, he will take his vestments and holy vessels and say mass in the open air, until the church is ready. The village will be built according to designs submitted to my approval."

Major Gottmann, however, in his character as temporary Governor of the island, had taken his wife and daughter with him, and refusing to inhabit a cave, ordered Lieutenant Larabit to set his sappers to work in building him a house. Larabit replied that he was busy with his battery, and would see about the house afterwards. The discussion led to a quarrel, and the two officers nearly came to blows. Continued bad weather had delayed the passage to and fro of the boats, and Pianosa was badly off for food. The garrison was reduced first to eating the goats, and afterwards to any fish they could catch, or shell-fish they picked up on the rocks. Instead of wine they had to drink brandy diluted with water, or even vinegar. Discontent, grumbling, and active insubordination followed.

As soon as the weather permitted, the Emperor despatched a flock of sheep to the famished islanders, with two milch cows, thirty hens with cocks, and some pigs. By the same boat he sent also some doors and locks left from the demolitions at Porto Ferraio, and failing clocks, "some hour-glasses for marking the time." He came soon afterwards with Drouot, on the Inconstant, to see the condition of things for himself, and smooth things down.

When his inspection was over, as he was on the point of departure, a gale suddenly got up, the brig was unable to approach the shore, and the Emperor was forced to spend the night on the island, in torrents of rain. He left the next day, taking advantage of calmer weather, loudly abusing the sea and everything connected with it.

The inhospitable rock of Palmaiola, was, like Pianosa, also occupied, and provided with a battery.[1]

Colonel Campbell at first paid no attention to what he laughingly described as the Emperor's "conquests." He had accompanied him as if for a day's amusement on his taking possession of Pianosa. "The Emperor is doing all this for the English," he said, "one day we shall take his place here." When Pianosa was fortified as a strategic position, however, he grew uneasy, and exclaimed that the island had not been mentioned in the Treaty of Fontainebleau. But the Emperor took no notice of his objections.[1]

* * * * *

The Mulini palace was scarcely finished when the

[1] Campbell, 210; Pons de l'H., 278, 296, 299.
[2] Pon de l'H., 304; Campbell, 163; *Ile d'Elbe et Cent Jours*, 27.

Emperor wished for a house in the country free from the noise of the town. Moreover the hot weather had come, and some provision must be made against the high temperature of these latitudes.

For these reasons the Emperor built the house at San Martino.

About three miles from Porto Ferraio on the Marciana road, another path branches off through a valley, leading to an amphitheatre, like that at Monserrat, formed by a steep mountain side, planted at its base with vines, higher up with oaks and brushwood. The road winds slowly half way up the hill, and from there, on turning, is an admirable view of Porto Ferraio, and its fort, with the semi-circle of its roadstead. It seems like a picture expressly arranged to give pleasure to the eye. This site on the hill side has not the Virgilian charm of Monserrat, but it has a beauty of its own, and by its proximity to the capital was peculiarly suitable for the "Imperial Saint Cloud" as the veterans speedily christened it.

The house is a sylvan retreat à la Jean Jacques Rousseau, a fit home for Philemon and Baucis, such as one sees in old eighteenth century prints. Four white walls, a roof of tiles, a ground floor with a narrow door, and one story above it. At the back of the house, by reason of the slope of the ground, there is only one floor. All round are trees—ilexes, nettle-trees, magnolias with their polished leaves and waxy flowers; in the garden are shady alleys with box hedges and borders of periwinkles.

On entering is the *Salle des Pyramides*, measuring nearly 8 ft. 9 in. by 9 ft. 10 in. In the centre is a stone basin and fountain—both dry.[1] The ceiling is painted with the signs of the Zodiac, and on the walls are represented Egyptian columns, minarets, palm trees, and charges of mamelukes, in memory of past victories. In spite of the audacious assertions in the *Mémorial de Sainte Hélène* "that the best Italian painters competed for the honour of decorating the Imperial residences,"[2] the paintings on these walls remind one of a common café. They are in the base realistic style of a theatre-scene, which the Romans latterly affected, and Italians of the present day love to decorate their houses. The chimney piece, a flat marble slab, supported by two slender columns, is very pretty. A whole epoch is represented by this room, and on one of the painted columns on the wall one reads these words, "*Ubicunque felix Napoleon.*" The Emperor wished to prove by assertion that he was contented on his island, and never wished to leave it.

The *Salon* comes next. Here on the ceiling are two doves, united by a ribbon, flying in an azure sky. "The loop tightens as they seem to fly further asunder." These two doves represent Marie Louise and Napoleon. The Emperor expressed his wishes to the artist, desiring that his wife should see on her arrival that she had not been forgotten.

[1] Reg. de l'I. d'E., No. 53. "The large hall is to be paved with marble, having an octagonal basin in the centre, with a fountain in the middle, as in Egypt."

[2] Mém. Ste. Hel., Feb, 20, 1806.

Marie Louise never came, but the doves and their blue ribbon still flutter in the sky.

On the right of the *Salon* is the Emperor's room, in the angle of the house. The bed is shaped like a boat, of mahogany. There is also a rocking chair, and a guéridon with china toilet set. The porter in charge declares the bed to have belonged to the Emperor, but another story gives it to General Bertrand. Both assertions are probably untrue. The original furniture at San Martino, like that of the Mulini, was dispersed, and the bed belonged probably to Jerôme, taken to San Martino in 1859 by Prince Demidoff.[1] The rocking chair, made for the garden or deck, has no history, and the guéridon and its china were simply placed here by the proprietor. They may have formed part of the furniture of either house, as the inhabitants of the island bought up much that remained.[2]

The Emperor collected at San Martino all the souvenirs he possessed of Marie Louise and the King of Rome. In place of pictures he covered the walls of the rooms with engravings from an illustrated book on Egypt.[3]

[1] The descriptive catalogue of the Museo di San Martino, published by Demidoff, states expressly that Demidoff found the room empty. "Room of the Emperor. The furniture in this room presents fine specimens of the work of the Bros. Jacob, famous cabinet makers of the Empire period. They have no dynastic associations." (These articles, as mentioned in the catalogue, and introduced by Demidoff, have since been dispersed. See p. 269.) In the same catalogue we find: "No. 260. In the room of the Grand Maréchal is a mahogany bed that belonged to H.I.H. Prince Jerome." This is the so-called Bertrand's bed, introduced by Demidoff, that still remains.

[2] See p. 270.

[3] Larabit, 69; Peyrusse, 250. This was the work in 12 folio vols.,

THE "SALLE DES PYRAMIDES" IN THE HOUSE AT SAN MARTINO.

The upper and lower floors of the house are connected by a steep and narrow staircase, that of a windmill. The Emperor scarcely made use of it, as the first floor, where all his rooms were situated, was, as we have described, on a level at the back, with the garden. The ground floor was reserved for the household, and the kitchen, with the exception of the Emperor's bathroom, where he bathed every morning.

The stone bath still exists. On the damp stained walls is a fresco, faded like a painting at Pompeii, representing the nude figure of a woman, reclining, and holding the mirror of Truth, as we are told by the inscription, "*Qui odit Veritatem, odit Lucem.*" The melancholy Naiad is still there, with the graceful gesture she made long ago to the Imperial bather, who, if he loved to get the truth from others, had no particular love for speaking it himself.

* * * * *

In order to pay for the construction and maintenance of San Martino,[1] the Emperor decided to cultivate the greater part of the land and produce corn as well as vines and vegetables, "of which every leaf, every bunch of grapes" were to be accounted for in the budget.[2] San Martino was to become a model of agriculture.

published 1809–1822 by the savants who took part in the Egyptian expedition.

[1] Pauline defrayed the cost of acquiring the property. Peyrusse, 251, 257.

[2] Corres. Imp., xxi. 567.

The Emperor sent for his Chamberlain, Traditi, who was an agriculturist, and explained his views, with the conviction of an experienced landlord. But, unfortunately, San Martino was richer in stones than in productive soil. Signor Traditi was silent as the Emperor spoke, letting him pile up, in imagination, sacks of corn in hundreds to feed all the island in case of siege. When his Majesty had finished he exclaimed in Italian, forgetting that the Emperor could understand, "*O questa, si, che è grossa!*" ("Oh what tall talk!")[1] The Emperor's face fell, his breath fairly taken away by this plain-speaking. But quickly commanding himself, he smiled, and put his chamberlain at his ease, who had realised his mistake by the terrified faces of the attendants.

Since the departure from Fontainebleau, the Austrian Commissioner had frequently said, "Your Majesty is mistaken. Your Majesty is wrong." The Emperor was not accustomed to contradiction, and replied sharply, "You are always telling me I am wrong. Is that the way you speak to your own Emperor?" General Koller assured him that his Sovereign would be much vexed if he did not always say what he thought, and the Emperor, hiding his annoyance, said, "In that case he is better served than I have been."[2]

Another time, at Elba, he asked a man at Piombino what his sister Elisa did while she

[1] Pons de l'H., 306, 309, 310; Reg. de l'I. d'E., No. 128.

[2] Gen. Durand, 257; Waldbourg-Truchsess, 55.

governed the country. The man replied, without lowering his eyes, "She made love." The Emperor cut him short to prevent his saying anything further.

Major Gottmann (who had been sent to Pianosa to live with his family in a cave) came back to complain of his quarters, and also of Lieutenant Larabit's treatment. His complaints took the form of standing in the road and raving at the Emperor in public like a maniac. This scandalous behaviour was only stopped when General Bertrand threatened to arrest him.[1]

Taillade, the commander of the Imperial brig, discussing a mathematical problem which the Emperor found difficult, snatched the paper from his hands, exclaiming, "It is perfectly simple, a child could understand it."[2]

General Dalesme, the former Governor of Porto Ferraio, a worthy man, "who would die," he said, "a hundred times for the Emperor," but who boasted he always "called a spade a spade," gave his opinion so rudely when consulted that the Emperor would have much preferred to be without his advice.[3]

Once at Rio Marina, an Elban sergeant-major, a powerful fellow, seeing the Emperor (now growing stout) hesitate before mounting his horse, seized him from behind, lifted him into the air, and threw him into the saddle. The Emperor resisted

[1] Pons de l'H., 256, 267.
[2] *Ibid.*, 49.
[3] *Ibid.*, 58, 64, 134.

and struggled somewhat ludicrously, but he had to submit to brute force. Some days later, the hero of this exploit received a second lieutenant's epaulettes, so that it might not be said that the Emperor had received such familiar treatment from a common soldier.[1]

On another occasion, the fête day of San Cristino, the patron of Porto Ferraio, at the banquet attended by the Guards, Pons proposed a toast to "Liberty, sun of the universe." Also on his study table he left a copy of Fenélon's *Télémaque*, with the following passage underlined in pencil, "The King ought to be more free from ostentation and pride than any other man. . . . Minos loved his people more than his own family. . . . I was reduced simply to being thankful, that with a small number of soldiers and friends who followed me in my misfortunes, I possessed even this barbarous country, adopting it as my own, and having lost all hope of ever seeing again the happy land which the gods had bestowed on me. So fall those kings who give way to their desires and their flatterers' counsels." The little daughter of Pons, who had been brought up in strong Republican principles, was presented to the Emperor, and replied, on being asked by her mother if she were not pleased to have seen the great man so near, "Yes, mother, but I think I courtesied too low, and I am sorry."

The father, unable to conceal his admiration for

[1] Pons de l'H., 69, 284.

such precocious wisdom, repeated the answer to the Emperor.[1]

Finally, the Emperor demanded the inflexible Minister of Mines to hand over the 229,000 francs, the remainder of the profits obtained from them before his possession of Elba. Pons, who considered that this fund belonged to the French Government, refused to obey, "as he would do nothing against his conscience." Interminable discussion followed, and after two months the Emperor lost patience, and went himself to Rio. Having hitherto boasted that no one had ever said *no* to him, he now heard the outrageous word repeated to his face, and could not restrain himself from shouting, with such violence that the windows shook, "after all, I am the Emperor." But he had to leave without obtaining anything. The Financial Minister, Peyrusse, was sent to Pons with a message, that if he did not give way, the Emperor would send his grenadiers to him. Pons replied that "three hundred thousand bayonets should not force him to give up the money," and that if the grenadiers came he should pitch them out of the window. He only yielded after referring the matter to Paris when "his conscience allowed him." [2]

The Emperor seemed to take no notice of these rebuffs, some of them unconscious, others cold-blooded and intentional. They were none the less bitter insults, and wounded him deeply, reminding

[1] Pons de l'H., 230, 235, 237, 257.
[2] Peyrusse, 241; Pons de l'H., 85, 109; Campbell, 109.

him at every moment on what a frail footing his sovereignty stood.

* * * * *

When first the Emperor took possession of his property at San Martino, he found a half-ruined house, scarcely better than a hovel, occupied by a farmer, and a shed for storing wine. Everything had to be freshly constructed from the beginning, and the only approach was by a narrow, steep path, cut out from the rock in steps. Twenty-four grenadiers were employed to help twenty stone-masons in their work of construction, and also in making a more practicable road for carts; nevertheless the new "Saint Cloud" could not be ready for some time. To avoid having to import tiles and bricks from the mainland, the Emperor had established a kiln, where they could be made on the spot. The work was constantly interrupted and retarded by discussions, failures, and fresh trials.[1]

Meanwhile the heat was increasing daily at Porto Ferraio, and the Emperor suffered greatly from it. As soon as two or three rooms at San Martino were habitable, he departed there with an aide-de-camp and a servant, taking also three iron bedsteads. But here, also, the heat was almost overwhelming. Encircled by mountains, which radiated the heat, San Martino was sheltered from wind, and the air was stifling. There was hardly any shade. The trees, which later grew so luxuriantly, were at that time mere skeletons. The Emperor, overcome by

[1] Reg. de l'I. d'E., Nos. 16, 24, 34; Corres. Imp., xxi. 617.

the heat, would sit by the side of a little stream, drinking from it out of a leather cup.

He came to the conclusion that San Martino would be a charming residence for spring and autumn, but that another retreat must be chosen for the summer; and his thoughts turned to Marciana Alta and Monte Giove. That glorious summit seemed to touch infinity, and he had stood wrapt in wonder at the incomparable prospect from it. His imagination was perhaps fired at the thought of the marvellous palace which might stand on the peak of Volterraio, but, alas, the dream was not to be realised by the poor King of Elba!

He was satisfied, however, with much less, and pitched his military tent near the Madonna's chapel, where, "like the ancient kings, he set up his traveller's throne."[1] He took in addition the house belonging to the hermit, who removed himself to his stable. Two or three other tents were put up under the chestnuts, for two orderly officers, who used the chapel as a dressing room, and for some servants.[2] This was all the Emperor's suite. Madame Mère also left Porto Ferraio and settled down in the village of Marciana Alta, with her chamberlain, her steward, two ladies in waiting, two maids, a cook, and four other servants.[3]

The Emperor, also after the manner of the kings of old, arranged all the household details himself.

[1] Pons de l'H., 211, 212.
[2] Foresi, *N. all' Is. dell' Elba*, 64.
[3] The house which Madame Mère inhabited at Marciana Alta still exists, and has a commemorative slab on the façade.

He wrote from La Madone, on August 23, to the General at Porto Ferraio, " M. Le Comte Bertrand, —I require two shutters for the windows of my room. The third window has some already. Please try to send them to-morrow. Also send me two lamps to hang at my tent door, and a lantern. I have brought my three iron bedsteads with me, and one is to be sent down to Marciana for Madame Mère. She will be quite comfortable in the deputy's house, and may go there on Thursday. She will have a room for herself, and three for her household. The necessary furniture is already in the house, and I will add a wardrobe. I also think she will find enough kitchen utensils, candles and lamps. Send up three curtains for her room ; the rods are all ready. Also send me some fire-irons, shovels and tongs, as the evenings are cold."[1] " I do not expect to stay here more than four or five days," wrote the Emperor to Bertrand, the day after his arrival.[2]

He stayed nearly a fortnight, however, and did not leave La Madone until the fourth or fifth of September. No doubt the presence of Monte Giove fascinated him (as well as the expectation of a visitor), and also the rugged village of Marciana, which apparently had the same attraction for Madame Mère. Both mother and son here found an echo of Corsica.

In the grim forbidding-looking houses, the intoxicating air, the pure beauty of mountain tops, in the fragrance of the maquis, the long distant past

[1] Corres. Imp., xxi. 615. [2] Corres. Imp., xxi. 617.

seemed to live again for them both. From the rock where, with his feet in the heather, he sat to rest, his gun between his knees, not only did he breathe this native perfume, which at St. Helena recalled Corsica to him "with his eyes closed," but he could actually see it on the horizon, in the flame of the setting sun. What were his feelings as he looked at his native land over the sea at the close of day, and the close of his own life? Corsica and Elba! The opposite extremities of his glory! There, it had not begun, here, it was nearly over. All his life lay between these two summits.

At Corte over there, the old Gaffori house (riddled with Genoese bullets, and quite impregnable) had been the home of his mother, married at fourteen and celebrated in the island for her beauty.

During the last struggle of Corsica against France for independence, Madame Bonaparte, three months before her son's birth, travelled on horseback with her husband across the plains and valleys of Nebbio, to fight for her country's freedom. The unborn child made this first acquaintance with powder and the hiss of musket balls. Next came the memory of the old house at Ajaccio, burned and pillaged by envious rivals, when the Bonaparte family joined issues with France. There was the memory of little Giacominetta, his eight year old love, and Pauline his merry little sister and playmate, whose stockings always fell down over her shoes. Then there was his uncle, the archdeacon Lucien, a patriarch in a cloak of goatskin, following the goats over the mountains, and scolding the shepherds for feeding their flocks on the fresh grass of the forests, which they turned into deserts. Next the departure for Brienne, the return, in artillery lieutenant's uniform, then the second departure to fame and Empire.

All this must have passed through his mind as he gazed from Monte Giove, or when alone with his mother, as they looked in each other's eyes, reading the same thoughts: the mother whose energy was untiring, and whose austere tenderness was the only affection left him. The news of Josephine's death had reached him at the Mulini, causing him real sorrow, and his other wife, the Empress, was absent, he knew not where.[1]

* * * * *

Marie Louise still delayed her coming. Her rooms at Porto Ferraio waited for her in vain. In vain the doves on the ceiling at San Martino began, under the painter's brush, to tie their lovers' knot. The symbol became day by day more bitterly ironic.

The Emperor did not try to conceal his vexation and disappointment. In his own way he loved Marie Louise.[2] He loved her from a sense of duty,

1 Pons de l'H., 206; *Mém. aux Puiss.* All., 36, 37. Josephine had died at Malmaison, May 29.

2 Besides his connection with Countess Walewska, which did not cease after his marriage to Marie Louise, Constant affirms that he had another *liaison* soon after, with the daughter of a major, who lived at Bourg la Reine, and was pointed out to him by an official "protector." This lady was a brunette of seventeen, with pretty hands and feet, a fascinating coquette, who was received by Napoleon at St. Cloud at 11 p.m., when she was introduced into the Orangery, where she remained with him three hours (Constant, VI., 94).

THE CHAPEL OF THE MADONNA.

THE HOUSE INHABITED BY MADAME MÈRE AT MARCIANA ALTA.

NAPOLEON'S SEAT (SEDIA DI NAPOLEONE) ON MONTE GIOVE.

because he had married her, and his whole being, even his heart, went by rule. Already a mature man, he had been sensually attracted to the timid child; she had learnt life through him, and been dazzled by the diamonds he had showered on her. His pride, moreover, was flattered and fed by this union of the successful soldier with the descendant of emperors. Now that he was at Elba, a solitary exile, thrown back on himself and his own thoughts in long hours of enforced idleness, these various feelings were resolved into one, the desire to have his wife near him: Emperor though he was, he wished for his home, another caress beside his mother's, a companion for his intimate feelings: perhaps not of his thoughts, for these she had always been incapable of understanding, and he kept them to himself.

On their change of destiny, the Emperor had endeavoured to obtain Tuscany for her, or at least the territories of Lucca and Piombino, added to Parma and Placentia; thus their lands would have been next each other, with only the strip of sea in between. The allied Powers refused to allow this, partly to separate him from Marie Louise (a separation desired by Austria), and also fearing that, in exercising his right to see his wife, he would be continually travelling to the mainland.[1]

From the time of the abdication the idea of a complete separation between the Empress and her husband had been considered. On the 10th of April

[1] Meneval, II., 147–214.

Meneval, Marie Louise's secretary, in reply to the Emperor, said that he feared the Empress was not free to follow him, in spite of her desire to do so, but that she had every confidence in her father's kindness. Three days before, Cambacéres, Jerome, and Joseph had gone to Blois, to endeavour to persuade the unhappy woman to fly as quickly as possible. Marie Louise drew back. She feared to make a mistake without a direct order from the Emperor, and became so frightened at the persistence of the three men, that she cried out for help, bringing in the officers in the house to her rescue. Two hours afterwards, a Russian Commissioner arrived to secure herself and her son. From that moment she was a prisoner.

The Emperor made another attempt. He asked her to rejoin him at Gien or Briare. They would travel together, she to Parma, and he to the island of Elba. The Emperor of Austria replied, however, that Parma and Placentia were disturbed by war, and that Marie Louise could not go there without a properly organised government. The doctor, Corvisart, declared, also, that the climate of Elba would be hurtful to the Empress in her present state of health, and that she must go to Aix[1] for the waters there. Corvisart had no real knowledge of the climate of Elba, and his declaration seems not to be trusted. The Emperor protested, "that the best thing for his wife's health, was to be with him." Corvisart, an idiot, or an

[1] Aix in Savoy.

accomplice, was determined neither to exile himself to Elba, nor to appear to desert the Empress, and remained obstinate in his opinion.

The Emperor, however, continued to dispute the ground, inch by inch. "There are many places in Italy as healthy as Aix." Corvisart maintained his first opinion, "the waters of Aix alone would suit the Empress."

The Emperor finally understood that he would gain nothing, at the present at least, against so much opposition. He agreed on the waters of Aix for Marie Louise, fearing, moreover, something worse, viz., that she might be sent to Vienna. (As a matter of fact this course had already been decided on by the Emperor of Austria.) Moreover, Napoleon was ignorant, at that time, of the resources of the island of Elba, and of how the Empress could be housed, or of whether he should have to fight for his landing, and time was short. He decided to go alone, hoping, or pretending to hope, that when the political crisis was over, and feeling ran less high, Marie Louise would be restored to him.

* * * * *

On the evening before his departure from Fontainebleau, at 8 o'clock, the Emperor wrote to his wife, with a polite message to Corvisart, who it was important to pacify. The next day, before leaving, he wrote a second letter, saying good-bye, and sending "a kiss to the little king."[1] At 10

[1] Corres. Imp., xxi. 560, 562. Marie Louise only received the first of these letters. Beausset, Préfet du Palais, who was charged to deliver the second, refused to do so (Note to Corres. Imp.).

o'clock, when the horses were ready to start, and the luggage packed, he told the foreign commissioners that he refused to go. Since he was to be separated from Marie Louise, an infraction of the Treaty, he revoked his assent to the Treaty, and also his abdication.[1] This protestation was quite useless, as go he must.

At Fréjus, he wrote to the Empress on April 28, and received news of her by Meneval on the next day, as the Undaunted was on the point of sailing.[2] He wrote again from Porto Ferraio, on May 9th, with an attractive description of Elba, giving the letter to Field-Marshal Koller, who was returning. Three days later he informed her, through Bertrand, that when she left Aix she would find at Parma 50 of the Polish Light Cavalry and 100 horses, which he would send for her.[3]

On May 25 a letter came from France.[4] But instead of being a reply to his three letters it was a month old, dated from Provins, April 26. It informed the Emperor that his wife, instead of going to Aix, had decided to leave for Vienna, and to rest with her son and her relations after all her trouble and excitement. What he so much dreaded had come to pass. After that, no more news.

[1] Waldbourg-Truchsess, 9.

[2] Meneval, II., 242, *et seq.*; Helfert, 69. In the 1844 edition of Meneval, the letter in which Bertrand informs Meneval that the Emperor has written to Marie Louise is erroneously dated: *Fréjus, April* 26. April 28 is the correct date.

[3] Corres. Imp., xxi., 569. Fifty-four Polish Lancers had been detached from Napoleon's Guard at Savona (*see* Campbell, *Napoleon at Fontainebleau and Elba*, 306, 308).

[4] Meneval, II., 217.

There was still no news by the 25th June. Bertrand wrote to Meneval, from the Emperor, to ask for explanations, laying the blame on the irregularities of the post. During the early part of July, that is, after two months of complete silence, five letters came, one after the other, two from Meneval and three from the Empress, the latter having written four besides—which were either intercepted or lost.

The news so eagerly expected, was bad. After staying five weeks in Vienna, Marie Louise was leaving, but not for Parma. She was to go to Aix for the course of waters ordered by Corvisart, without taking her son.

Without her son! The Emperor was stupefied, and that very day wrote to his wife that "he desired her not to go to Aix, or if she were there already, she must leave at once." He reminded her of the waters in Tuscany "which have the same quality as those of Aix. They are close to Parma, and to Elba, and there she could have her son with her. When M. Corvisart recommended Aix he did not know of the Tuscany waters, whose properties were identical. Moreover, Aix did not satisfy the Emperor as there were probably no Austrian troops in the town, and the Empress might be exposed to the insults of adventurers. In Tuscany there are none of these drawbacks."

Insults, however, were not what the Emperor feared at Aix for Marie Louise. For the woman whom he had kept so jealously in a kind of Oriental retirement, and who was now free to do as she pleased, without even the safeguard of her child, he feared the gay cosmopolitan life of the fashionable watering place, and the society which would pay court to her, and distract her thoughts from the husband waiting for her. It almost seemed in the desperate effort of the letter to keep her from this journey, that the Emperor foresaw Neipperg.

The letter was sent; and precautions taken that it should arrive safely. No answer—and again there was silence.[1]

* * * * *

If the Emperor's feelings suffered so much by the absence of Marie Louise, how much more must he have suffered through his *amour propre?* He who had once dictated to Europe, who was still King, although a little one, to have his wife disposed of without reference to himself! What of her arrival solemnly announced, the preparations for her reception, the illuminations prepared by the Elbans for months! What of the deputations arriving to inquire anxiously the reason of the Empress's delay, expressing their desire to see their Majesties united, and the warm welcome they would give her! His position was ridiculous.

The disappointment and anxiety which weighed on him and broke his rest were frequently expressed by exclamations before his attendants, or by those

1 This letter was sent in duplicate—to the Empress direct from Napoleon, to Meneval from Bertrand (Meneval, 248). The Emperor adopted this mode of correspondence in all the letters he wrote from Elba to Marie Louise.

theatrical displays of feeling, which he often loved to exhibit in public.

On one of his snuff boxes was a miniature portrait of his son. He would often take out the box, gaze at the portrait, and kiss it earnestly, saying, audibly to those present. "Poor dear child! darling boy."[1]

One day he was sitting at a table, turning over a number of engravings sent from Rome. "Suddenly," says Pons, who was present, "he stopped, exclaiming with a shudder, 'There is Marie Louise.' We all looked at him anxiously. He tried to command himself, and closely examining the picture of the Empress he carefully noted every feature. The next engraving was a portrait of the King of Rome. Words cannot describe the intense feeling the Emperor put into the words 'My son!' The memory of it is constantly in my thoughts. It was not an exclamation, we could scarcely hear him, as covering his face with the picture, he murmured 'My son!' We hardly dared to breathe."[2]

In this theatrical display of sentiment there was, as in all his actions, a mixture of sincerity and calculation. The exhibition of his sufferings as husband and father worked on the public sympathy. Even if he were unsuccessful in getting his wife and son from his enemies, who thereby showed their continued hostility to him, his determined attempts were further proofs to his people that he had no

[1] Campbell, 52; Pons de l'H., 69.
[2] Pons de l'H., 217.

intention of leaving the island, and that his only desire was to end his days there with his family.

But as time went on, the chance of seeing his wife grew less, although a small remnant of hope still remained. Marie Louise was at any rate better at Aix than at Vienna, and her cure at an end, she might perhaps come to Elba by way of Parma. A letter from her on August 10, sent by a pretended Italian commercial traveller, said that this was not impossible.[1]

The festival of August 15 was celebrated, however, without the Empress. Balls and public fêtes took place, and horse races on the San Martino road, presided over by the Emperor. Seated on a platform made of planks, and covered with green foliage, he presented prizes to the winners.[2] On the next day was a display of fireworks by the artillery of the Guards. A set-piece represented portraits of his Majesty and Marie Louise.

> "*Sa Majesté Napoléon*
> *A mis le feu au Dragon*
> *Ah! quelle belle fête*
> *Du voir le portrait de Marie Louise paraître.*"[3]

The Elbans, who had the Emperor's promise that Marie Louise should certainly come "during the month of September," and quite unaware of the gloomy domestic drama being enacted, were de-

[1] Beausset, III., 48.
[2] Pons de l'H., 231; Monier, 71; Arch. Aff. Et. Letter from Porto Ferraio, Aug. 23.
[3] *Gazette rimée*, Adjutant Labadie, 50. "Dragon" was the name given to the fusee that lights everything else in set pieces.

lighted by the apparition of the two heads. But a high wind rose during the evening, spoiling the fête and extinguishing the illuminations.

The Emperor was now determined to learn the truth about Marie Louise, and whether she was being forced against her inclination, as he hoped and believed, in which case, she ought to be able to overcome all the obstacles and join him; or whether on the other hand, a want of feeling on her side was separating them. On August 20, therefore, he received in a private audience Hurault de Sorbée, a captain in the Guards, who had just obtained a month's leave "to visit his wife," one of Marie Louise's ladies in waiting. The Emperor explained his mission, viz., to approach the Empress through his wife and Meneval, accredited by a letter, and offer to conduct her by way of Genoa to Elba. The Emperor was to be kept informed of Captain de Sorbée's movements from four different sources.[1]

Such was the condition of affairs when the Emperor went on August 23 to Monte Marciana, where he experienced quiet and peace from its beautiful situation, and also terrible sadness during his solitary evenings. Restless and miserable, he wrote on the 28th to Marie Louise from the Madonna Hermitage, that she might write safely to him, addressing him as M. Senno, and sending the letters by way of Genoa under cover to M. Constantino Gatelli.[2]

[1] Corres. Imp., xxi. 611; Meneval, 257, 283.

[2] *Ibid.*, 624.

The necessity of taking shelter behind "M. Constantino Gatelli," and the disguise of his name as "M. Senno," was a piteous humiliation for one who had been the Emperor Napoleon.[1]

On September 1 or 2, at nightfall, a vessel entered the harbour of Porto Ferraio, and without being stopped by the coastguards, instead of resting at the quay, headed towards the end of the bay, and anchored at San Giovanni.[2]

A lady and a child were on the deck, accompanied by another lady and a tall man in uniform wearing gold-rimmed spectacles. The lady asked for the Emperor, and Marshal Bertrand talked to her, his head uncovered. An order was sent to the Imperial stables to prepare a carriage, harness two saddle horses, and two mules. The unknown lady with her companion, the tall gentleman with gold rimmed spectacles, and the child, took their place in the carriage, followed by the horses and mules, to be used when the road to Marciana became too steep for driving.

The sailors on board the vessel reported that, during the crossing, the lady, who had come on board on the Italian coast, sometimes called the child "my son," and sometimes the "Emperor's son." The conclusion that she was the Empress was therefore safe. The grooms and coachmen,

[1] Signor Constantino Gatelli was a Genoese trader with whom the Emperor corresponded in relation to his farmyard and dairy at San Martino, and his purchases of olives and mulberries. Signor Senno was the lessee of the tunny fishery in Elba.

[2] A small chapel near the Roman remains.

THE MADONNA'S HERMITAGE ON MONTE GIOVE, WHERE THE EMPEROR RECEIVED MADAME WALEWSKA.

ONE OF THE FOUR ROOMS IN THE HERMITAGE.

who had all been at the Tuileries, asserted that they had recognised the child's clothes, a little military uniform that the King of Rome often wore. The lady was perhaps not quite so tall as Marie Louise, but they had only seen her by moonlight. Besides, both on land and on the boat she had repeatedly used expressions to her son which the public had always attributed to the Royal child. Moreover, the saddle on the unknown lady's horse was the saddle expressly made for the Empress. Her companion was a lady-in-waiting, and the tall gentleman in gold spectacles was Prince Eugène de Beauharnais. The whole island was roused to enthusiasm.

But the lady was not Marie Louise; she was the Countess Walewska.[1]

* * * * *

The very few who were in the Emperor's confidence in this attachment called her his "La Vallière." She was a blonde, with blue eyes and a fair complexion, small and well made, in temperament both gay and melancholy. The Emperor first met her in Warsaw, early in the year 1807, when she was barely twenty years old, and married to Don Ruy Gomez, an old man of stern temper. The Emperor admired her and made love to her, asking her at once, as was his invariable custom, for an assignation. He was at that time at the

[1] Foresi, 61; Pons de l'H., 212, 378; Sellier Vincent, 369; Peyrusse, 259; Gen. Durand, 100; Campbell, 156; Constant, III., 267, *et seq.*; VI., p. 92.

height of his glory, having entered Poland as a saviour, defeated Russia (for the time), and crushed Prussia, but in spite of this, the Countess resisted for four days, an absolutely unheard-of proceeding. As a rule, as soon as the Emperor deigned to honour any girls with his notice, their mothers, bursting with pride, would send them, decked out by their own hands. The Emperor was astounded at this rebuff; but the Countess shrank at the prospect of her probable future, at the shame of abandonment on the succeeding day, at the torture of her real religious scruples, and at the thought of losing not only her husband, but also her child. She finally made a compromise, so dear to the feminine heart, by considering the interest of her country, listening to those who told her she would be the instrument of its salvation, and gave herself to the man and deliverer.

Afterwards, as the old Count did not seem to value divided honours, she followed her Imperial lover, who, far from tiring of her, grew more attached to her every day.

He kept her with him at his headquarters at Finkenstein. Constant says, "They took all their meals together. When the Emperor was away from her she occupied herself in reading, or in looking through her window-blinds at the parades and drilling in the courtyard of the castle, where the Emperor was often commanding in person. She was an angelic woman."

From that time she continued to form part of

his life, although history in its falsehood and hypocrisy is silent regarding her. She went to Paris with him, and followed him to Austria in 1809. After the battle of Wagram she lived in a small house in the suburbs of Vienna, where Constant used to fetch her every evening in a carriage to take her to the Emperor in the palace at Schoenbrunn. The roads were torn up by artillery, and, when it rained, were absolute bogs. "Take great care, Constant," the Emperor would say to his valet, "are you sure I can rely on the coachman and carriage?" One evening, indeed, the carriage overturned, but happily Walewska escaped unhurt. She had a child by him that same year, and it was this fact more than any other which decided his divorce, proving to him, as no other *liaison* had done, that he was able to be a father.

They were not separated by his marriage with Marie Louise. Walewska continued to receive his visits, or to come secretly to the Tuileries. The dark staircase was open to her, leading her to the Emperor after the official wife had retired to her apartment. "All my thoughts and inspirations come from him," she said. "He is my future, my life." It is said that she gave him a hollow gold ring, with a lock of her hair inside, and with these words engraved "*Quand tu cesseras de m'aimer, n'oublie pas que je t'aime.*"

After the abdication, she hastened to Fontainebleau, and on one of the following nights, about ten o'clock, presented herself to be received. She arrived at the door of his room, and found Constant there, watching; he went to inform his master, but the Emperor was plunged in a sort of stupor, and appeared not to hear. After waiting a little while Constant went to him again, but without success. They could hear him walking up and down in the room; his steps resounding in the silence of the sleeping palace. Then he stopped, hummed an air, and talked to himself. Walewska waited on, hoping against hope that he would send for her, chilled by the night air, motionless and shivering in her cloak until the dawn began to whiten the windows. The palace would soon be awake, and terrible events again take their course. This was no place for her, and she went away without seeing him.

But she could not forget, and her whole mind was set on finding the man she loved.

She knew the obstinacy of the Emperor, and she thought it wise to keep for a time in the background. She waited till Marie Louise had gone to Vienna, putting off definitively her journey to Elba, and then by degrees she travelled to Italy, stopping at Genoa and Florence, when she wrote to the Emperor, who answered, asking for news of her, on July 27th.[1]

Having thus allowed sufficient time and opportunity to the ex-Empress, thinking that the exile was ready for her again, she asked for permission to

[1] Reg. de l'I. d'E., No. 38.

come, giving as a pretext the necessity of arranging for her future, and that of her child. The Emperor consented, and she came.[1]

* * * * *

She came, rejoicing in her pride as woman and mistress. The lawful wife had denied her duties, but she was faithful, and not only was she in a morally superior position to her crowned rival, but in the sole possession of his love.

The Emperor was much annoyed, however, the next day, to hear from Porto Ferraio that she had been taken for Marie Louise. He had wished her journey to be made secretly, and his nerves being set on edge by his misfortunes, the adventure was like a mockery of his conjugal humiliation. She had seemed to play with his Imperial dignity.

But when Cæsar's anger had passed away the man conquered the Emperor, and fell into the arms held out to him. When she reproached him for having repulsed her at Fontainebleau, for refusing to be comforted by her tenderness, he replied, touching his forehead, "I had so many things here."

They stayed for two days in his tent, lulled by the breeze, and the distant murmur of the sea. He pointed out Corsica, his country, to her. They played with the child, taken care of by Walewska's

[1] The young woman accompanying her was her sister, and the big man with gold eye-glasses her brother. He remained at Marciana Marina. The sister rode up with her and the boy to the Hermitage, under the escort of one of the Emperor's orderlies. Napoleon came down halfway to meet the two women.

sister, in the hermit's little house, where they all slept at night. The Emperor put himself in "quarantine," and received no one during these days. They talked, no doubt, of serious matters, Walewska relating what had happened on the Continent, and what was being said of Marie Louise.

On the evening of the second day, he said that they must part. The times had changed. In his splendid days, a powerful conqueror, filling the world with his exploits, he was at liberty to impose his mistresses (though always discreetly) on the two Empresses who had shared his throne. Now that he was dethroned and banished, with the whole of Europe standing by hostile, while endeavouring to recover Marie Louise, he could not risk any scandal. He was responsible for his actions, also, to the Elbans, in the tiny circle of his court. Porto Ferraio was like a glass-house, where every step and gesture were seen and known. He was the representative of public morality, so difficult to maintain in this country where the soldiers seduced all the girls; and having refused the *entrée* of the Mulini to the officers' irregular connections, he must show an example of an irreproachable private life. Thus, in this respect, as in many others, he had to obey the ordinary laws.

His decision had to be carried out at once, without discussion; the vessel which was to take her away was ready anchored at the foot of the mountain. She must on no account go back to

Porto Ferraio, where preparations were being made to receive the Empress. He would escort her part of the way, and the orderly officer who had come with her would take her to the shore. The horses were saddled ready.

She had hoped to stay longer—perhaps for always—and for the Emperor it was another wrench. Love was departing, like everything else.

And as if to sadden the farewell still more, nature seemed to be weighed down by approaching disaster. The heat was oppressive, the sea shrouded in fog. Heavy white clouds hung over Monte Giove, veiling the sun, and gusts of wind shook the tent.

In this storm the Emperor and Walewska parted. He turned away, and rode rapidly towards La Madone, while she went down to the sea.

Her brother and the boat were waiting for her at Marciana Marina, but in this exposed place it was impossible to embark, and as the Emperor had forbidden Porto Ferraio, the vessel must go round to Porto Longone, at the other side of the island, and must be reached by land.

As soon as the Emperor reached the Hermitage, he was alarmed by the fury of the wind, and sent his second orderly officer to Marciana, to postpone the departure. When he arrived, Walewska was already on the way to Porto Longone. The officer sheltered and went no further.

One can scarcely imagine how terrible that night-journey must have been to the woman and child, over hills and through ravines, half battered by the storm. They arrived at last at Porto Longone, and found the vessel waiting. But the authorities at the harbour refused to let them go, seeing the state of the sea. Walewska persisted, saying the Emperor had commanded it. They dared not disobey or show less courage than a woman. She embarked in a little neighbouring bay, at Mola, and the vessel, braving the storm, bore her away.

The Emperor endured tortures, and only felt relieved when he heard of her safety.

Impending misfortune was to come otherwise.

* * * * *

While Napoleon, under the tent on Monte Giove, lived in memory the hours of love spent with Walewska, Marie Louise had allowed herself to slip almost imperceptibly into the position of Neipperg's mistress. She had refused to follow Hurault de Sorbée, and she received a letter which Metternich dared to write to her, absolutely forbidding her to go to Parma, *i.e.*, to be anywhere near Elba. She was taken to Switzerland by Neipperg, amongst the Oberland glaciers.[1]

The Emperor now felt more lonely than ever, hearing moreover, "that an Austrian officer whom he would recognise from description, was continually with his wife." He asked Colonel Campbell to induce England and Lord Castlereagh to intervene so that his wife and child should be restored to him,

[1] Meneval, 283, 291, 292.

and on October 10 he wrote to the Grand Duke of Tuscany, begging him "to help him in corresponding with Marie Louise, to send him news of her regularly every week."[1]

But Marie Louise wrote no more, and the Emperor gradually ceased to talk of her, understanding that only on the day when he recovered his crown would he see her again.[2]

The Elbans made up their minds that they would not see their true Empress on the island, although they were never quite persuaded that she had not paid a visit incognito to Marciana. The remains of the fireworks from the fête of August 15 were kept for the arrival of Princess Pauline, and the Mayor of Marciana, who, mistaken like everyone else, had joyfully set going his illuminations, after receiving an order to extinguish them at once, received a sharp reprimand, warning him not to meddle in future in what did not concern him.

*   *   *   *   *

[1] Campbell, 152; Corres. Imp., xxi. 657.

[2] While at Elba Napoleon also received a visit from the brunette of Bourg la Reine, who arrived at Porto Ferraio with her mother. Constant affirms that the Emperor married her there to an artillery officer (Constant, VI., 96). But there is no evidence of any *liaison* between them. Such a connection would surely have been known at Porto Ferraio, whereas no one alludes to it.

IV

THE LION IN THE FOX'S SKIN

After the departure of Countess Walewska the Emperor left Monte Giove and went to live at Porto Longone, where he was in residence by September 6th. He installed himself in the Spanish Citadel, which had also been proclaimed a "Palace," and where accommodation in a wing of six rooms had awaited Marie Louise since the month of June. The Mayor of Porto Longone was appointed "Governor" of the said Palace, with the functions of "Major-domo, Groom of the Chambers, and Superintendent of the Gardens"; he had a gardener and porter under his orders, and an annual salary of 600 francs.

"Major-domo" was a figure of speech, for the vast old fortress had been entirely dismantled. The Emperor brought his three iron beds from Marciana, ordered two carpets and a pair of alabaster vases to be sent from Porto Ferraio, and commanded chairs to be procured from Pisa "of the most approved pattern at five francs each, with arm-chairs and sofas at corresponding prices." Some more elegant furniture from a firm at Leghorn was returned as too expensive.

The arrangements for Marie Louise remained visionary; 8,277 francs were allotted for general expenses and for the Emperor's household, 497 francs for that of Madame Mère, 376 francs for that of the Grand Maréchal, and 250 francs for the stables. This amounted to a total of 9,400 francs for the entire establishment at the Palace.[1]

The Emperor took possession of a lantern turret overhanging the sea, and spent hours there, gazing at the waves. In the far distance he could see the Coast of Italy vanishing towards Rome and Ostia.[2]

During his residence at Porto Longone (which he left between September 20 and 25) Napoleon found some entertainment in the Fête of the Chapel of Monserrat, to which annual pilgrimages were made from all the Communes of the island, and even from the mainland of Italy.

As the season advanced, and the temperature became more equable, he returned to his capital, first, however, sending masons to prepare a fifth "palace" for him at Rio. This was the house belonging to the Administration of Mines, one of the most comfortable in the island. The Emperor appropriated it from motives of economy, and

[1] Corres. Imp., xxi. 575, 584, 617, 630, 633, 635, 648; Registre de l'I. d'E., No. 75; Gen. Durand, 253.

[2] None of the Imperial arrangements are left at Porto Longone. The Emperor's turret was one of those in the angles of the citadel, which now encloses a prison within its walls.

appointed Pons to be its Governor. "Governor of my own house!" the poor man exclaimed, on hearing that he was turned out of his home. The Emperor assured him that he might stay there until he could find other quarters, and need be in no hurry to leave. But after a brief delay, an army of workmen arrived one morning to reconstruct the house from cellar to garret, altering all the doors, and throwing down partitions. Pons and his family had to decamp as best they could, amid the confusion.[1]

Other cares now began to preoccupy the Emperor, and the horizon was darkened by grave anxieties.

In the first place the French Government did not pay over the promised pension of 2,000,000 francs. The 350,000 francs that the income from the Domain amounted to were inadequate to meet the Budget on its present scale; 109,600 francs had already been expended on the Mulini and on San Martino (where the works were still in progress), while the Army Estimates for the current year bid fair to exceed the half-million by 200,000 francs.[2] In order to defray expenses, cost of roads, officials, public functions, all that was comprised in what really amounted to a very expensive style of living—the Emperor was obliged to draw on his reserves. If this state of things went on much longer, the exchequer would be emptied. He expostulated vainly. France no more replied to

1 Pons de l'H., 253–275.
2 Corres. Imp., xxi. 631, 648; Reg. de l'I. d'E., Nos. 33, 139.

RIO MONTAGNA.

PORTO LONGONE AND ITS CITADEL.

him on this point, than did Austria on the subject of Marie Louise.

Sinister rumours, moreover, were in the air. It was said that Europe, now she had set her own affairs in order, was busying herself once more with Napoleon, and regretted that she had not put him more completely out of the running. Elba was too near, and admitted of his taking the offensive again. He must be "removed," and transported to a greater distance. These were but empty rumours, and highly improbable, but the outlook was not reassuring.

* * * * *

It was amid such preoccupations that official life was resumed at Porto Ferraio.

Pauline Borghese had meantime returned from Naples, on November 1, the Emperor having sent his brig to Civita Vecchia for her. She lavished tender caresses on her brother, and bright smiles on all her surroundings.[1]

She delighted in making everyone who lived with her happy, and seemed, like the legendary woman of the poets, to have descended to earth for the seduction of mankind. The surliest critics proclaimed her "*une pâte humaine de perfection.*[2]

Prompt in apology to her waiting-women for her fits of nervous bad temper, generous of the money she scattered to the winds of heaven, she was

[1] Corres. Imp., xxi. 633; Peyrusse, 261; Letter from Madame Mère to Lucien Bonaparte, quoted by Larrey, II., 86; Pons de l'H., 353.

[2] Pons de l'H., 242.

prodigal to a degree of her physical charms. When sitting to a sculptor, she felt no shame in letting her tunic slip away like some antique model, and the medal struck in her honour at the Paris Mint symbolised her under the form of the Three Graces, nude and encircled with the inscription, "*Pauline, Sœur d'Auguste, Notre Belle Reine.*" She was the gentle and capricious Astarte, prone both to excite and to calm desire, at once the author and the consoler of all sorrows.

"If he wanted to beat me," she would say, "I should resign myself with a good grace. It would be painful of course, but I should bear it, if it gave him pleasure."[1] She was a valuable ambassador, and had, it was believed, succeeded in reconciling her brother with Murat.[2]

Pauline's return, and the pleasure of admiring this illustrious beauty at close quarters, consoled the Elbans for the absence of Marie Louise, whose apartments on the first story of the Mulini were occupied by the Princess.[3]

While here she was obliged to conform to a more chastened mode of life, in accordance with the dignity of a Court in exile, and the life of a home that had known misfortune.

The evenings were devoted to games of chess, cards, or dominoes, and were presided over by Madame Mère, who busied herself in the day with

[1] Pons de l'H., 238.

[2] Corres. Imp., xxi. 633; Pons de l'H., 376; F. de Chaboulon, I., 128.

[3] Corres. Imp., xxi. 633; Pons de l'H., 137, 239.

woolwork, surrounded by skeins of worsted and the portraits of her children, which were set out before her on a guéridon. The Emperor usually played with Marshal Bertrand or Madame Mère, and exchanged frequent pinches of snuff with his mother. His intimates were occasionally allowed to take part in the game, but the stakes were never high, at most one or two napoleons.[1] The Emperor made a point of not losing. His superstition amounted to fatalism. The loss of a game amounted to the loss of a battle, and was a bad omen. So he cheated. No one dared complain. Madame Mère alone, who was not above pocketing her winnings, and saw them eluding her, fidgeted in her chair, and pursed up her lips. The Emperor, amused, would cheat more and more openly, till in defiance of etiquette she would exclaim, with the quaint accent she was never able to get rid of, "Napoleone! I protest that you are cheating." Then the Emperor would sweep his hand over the table, shuffle all the cards, pick up the coins, and retire to his room. Next day he gave the money back to those from whom he had stolen it. Madame Mère alone was never paid, said the gossips, the Emperor's sole answer to her protests being, "But you are richer than I, Mother!"[2]

As a rule the Emperor retired at nine.[3] The

[1] Peyrusse, 239; Campbell, 89; Pons de l'H., 191, 207.

[2] Madame Bonaparte had prudently saved up a fairly large fortune during the years of her son's prosperity, and put it at his disposal several times in his dark hours. When she died this fortune amounted to about three millions (Larrey, II., p. 495).

[3] As stated above (p. 103), Napoleon rose before daybreak.

moment the clock struck he got up, went to the piano, and played the following notes: do, do, sol, sol, la, la, sol, fa, fa, mi, mi, re, re, do. At the end of this tune he bowed, and left the room.

Sometimes Napoleon threw off the lethargy of these family gatherings, and began to discuss some event in his career, some battle of the French Campaign. He used to explain his defeats and the mistakes and errors of judgment that led to them. He would bring the scene to life again with such animation that he got quite carried away, appealing to the centuries to come, and ending "It was written." Everyone shuddered while he was speaking. Campbell saw him once more upon the field of battle, issuing orders to his generals, urging on his soldiers, and staking all on victory: or, with his fleet assembled at Boulogne, successfully crossing the Channel, and invading England. Sometimes the Emperor appeared to invite discussion, but if anyone contradicted him he grew angry, and used opprobrious language. A general silence then ensued, after which he gradually calmed down, and before retiring would hold out his hand to whoever he had quarrelled with, saying, "We have behaved like lovers; we have fallen out with each other. But lovers make it up again, and are all the better friends afterwards. Good-night, and do not let us bear malice." Some of the suite accepted this apology for the hard things that had been said to them; others were less forgiving, and bore him a grudge in secret.[1]

[1] Campbell, 67, 77, 159; Pons de l'H., 59, 128, 192.

Monsieur le Comte Drouot, j'ai projetté de former une nouvelle compagnie de cannonniers, dans la quelle on ferait entrer, comme élément, tous les chevau-légers polonais qui ne sont pas montés. je pense que 15 chevau-légers polonais, mamelucks et chasseurs, avec un officier, me suffiront. comme il y en a 50, ce sera donc 35 hommes qui entreront dans la nouvelle compagnie. on pourra y mettre un officier polonais qu'on instruira des manœuvres. il y aurait une économie dans l'équipement puisqu'on ne leur donnera pas de bottes. = chacun de ces 50 hommes ayant ses selles et son équipement, il faudrait les mettre de côté = faites moi un rapport là dessus. = Sur ce, je prie Dieu qu'il vous ait en sa sainte garde — Porto ferrajo le 2 juillet 1814.

Napol

le 4 juillet fait le rapport demandé

FACSIMILE OF ONE OF NAPOLEON'S ORDERS WITH HIS SIGNATURE.

MEDAL FOR PAULINE BORGHESE.

Save for these transitory flashes, the evenings passed in frigid monotony. Pauline enlivened the scene with her admirable *joie de vivre,* in defiance of Imperial conventions. Like all nervous natures, she swung from one extreme to the other, from depression to excitement, with equal facility . . . one day carried to her chair, the next afoot, and exhausting herself with pleasure till she collapsed. The Emperor gave a ball for her return, when the Guards' band played the Marseillaise, and as Pauline adored dancing other receptions followed.

The Emperor forbade her to bedeck herself with diamonds and jewellery, lest the Elban ladies should be unduly eclipsed. The little she wore sufficed to dazzle all eyes.[1] She organised society comedies, which were performed in the large hall on the ground-floor of the Mulini. This was partitioned by a folding screen, and served as theatre, billiard-room, and dining-hall. Officers and subalterns volunteered with a good grace to make up the company, and the most lively of them were selected. Pauline loved to surround herself with pretty women, and numbered several among her ladies-in-waiting whom she enrolled as actresses, taking a part herself. Among other pieces *Les Fausses Infidelités,* and *Les Folies Amoureuses* were represented at the Théâtre du Palais; and the hearty laugh of Princess Borghese rang through the sombre dwelling, and infected her companions.[2]

[1] Labadie, 54; Pons de l'H., 262; Laborde, 41.

[2] Monier, 56; Pons de l'H., 239; Corres. Imp., xxi. 578; Registre de l'I d'E., Nos. 27, 113.

Next, in the spirit of imitation, Porto Ferraio wanted its own theatre. A petition was addressed to the Sovereign, begging him to endow his capital with a building for this purpose. The Emperor, unwilling to tax his finances, handed over a former church, which had been secularised, and was used as a military storehouse. In order to pay the costs of transforming the church, the theatre was made proprietary. The richer families of Porto Ferraio bought the boxes, which were eagerly vied for, and became the life property of the holders. "There were not enough for all who wanted them." The Members of the Society called themselves Academicians, with this motto, *A Noi la Sorte* (Luck go with us). Masons, carpenters, joiners, decorators, and locksmiths set to at once, and the installation was completed by the early days of 1815.[1] The Emperor, absorbed in the political situation, soon handed over the supervision of all these distractions to his sister.

* * * * *

The Congress of Vienna opened on November 1, but Talleyrand had not waited for this to tackle each of its members separately on the measure which he deemed of supreme importance, the capture of the Emperor and his deportation to a securer spot than Elba.

The idea was in the air. Talleyrand did good service in formulating it. The statesmen of other countries felt a certain reluctance in putting it

[1] Pons de l'H., 244.

forward, but when it originated with a Frenchman, it was natural they should act in concert. Talleyrand suggested the Azores, in the Atlantic. These islands, as he pointed out, are more than 1,200 miles from any land. The Portuguese, who owned them, might be induced to agree to the arrangement. Other propositions were the American Antilles, Santa Lucia, or Trinidad, Santa Margherita, or still better, St. Helena. The unhealthiest of these islands would be the most advantageous, as its fatal climate might be expected to relieve its inhabitants from the guest who was foisted on them.[1]

Intelligence of all this reached Elba by letter, by chance visitors, and by the Emperor's secret messengers. He affected not to believe it, and replied to those who inquired in consternation if the news were true, "Europe will not act thus. More especially from the English point of view, St. Helena is impossible. I should be too near India. Besides, we could defend ourselves here for two years." What danger there could be to England and India in Napoleon's incarceration at St. Helena is far from obvious. This was one of the phrases he employed to shut the mouth of his interlocutors when he did not know what else to say to them.

[1] *Corresp. de Tall. et de Louis XVIII.*, Oct. 13 and 21, and Dec. 7, 1814. . . . Prussia and England approved warmly; Austria protested; the Tsar was silent. Louis commended the idea as "excellent," but conscientious scruples interfered with his satisfaction. "Between ourselves," he replied to Talleyrand, "I should exceed the stipulations of the Treaty of Fontainebleau if the plan were put into execution."

St. Michael, the nearest of the Azores, is 900 miles from Lisbon.

He may still have been hesitating when, in the early days of December, an unknown stranger disembarked, and was mysteriously introduced into his presence. They conversed for an hour or two, after which the stranger rejoined his ship and sailed away. "From that day," says Peyrusse, "His Majesty's character altered. His words were few, his moody temper evident. The arrival of this stranger, and the moral effect of his visit, gave alarming support to the current rumours."[1]

The Emperor complained loudly to Campbell of the perfidy that was being plotted. But he now had no illusions as to the part Campbell was playing in the island of Elba, nor could he hope to obtain the least real help, if the situation became serious, in exchange for the espionage he was subjected to. Their relations had become embittered. Campbell endeavoured to suborn the Emperor's servants, one after the other,—Bertrand, Drouot, even the incorruptible Pons, whom he recommended to return to France, promising his own good offices and those of the English Government to obtain a post for him.[2]

He advised the Grenadiers of the Guard to desert. Some sham malcontents from their ranks were sent to him, and he fell into the trap.[3] The

[1] Pons de l'H., 371 ; Peyrusse, 262 ; Campbell, 172, 209.

[2] Pons, who "shuddered" at these advances, no doubt repelled them with his customary rudeness, for in the list of persons who had sailed with the Emperor, drawn up by Campbell after February 26, 1815, Pons is described as "a violent, intriguing fellow" (Campbell, *Napoleon at Fontainebleau and Elba*, p. 382, 1869 edition).

[2] *Ile d'Elbe et Cent Jours*, 27 ; Pons de l'H., 152.

Emperor had soon discovered that his frequent coming and going between the island and the continent, his disappearances on the plea of wanting rest, of health, of visits to the art treasures of Italy, and private affairs at Lucca and Florence, had no object other than that of drawing in the network of hostile combinations and intrigues that surrounded him. After this, fearing that the positive mischief done by Campbell would exceed the advantages of his presence, Napoleon tried to get rid of him, and to oust him little by little. Barriers of etiquette, coolness, delays in the ante-room, studied insults, infrequent audiences, systematic exclusion from the receptions at the Mulini when other English travelling through the island were invited . . . nothing was omitted under a specious cordiality to impress upon him that he was no longer *persona grata*, to wound his personal dignity, and compel him to take his departure.[1]

Campbell understood, but did not budge. "He was determined to sacrifice his feelings to the duty that was incumbent on him," and hoped the Congress of Vienna would free him from his anomalous and undignified position by settling the fate of Napoleon in one way or the other. Whenever the suppression of the English battleship stationed at Elba was mooted, Campbell opposed the measure, and won his point by showing that whether he was present or absent, it was the sole

[1] Campbell, 113, 114, 135, 168, 202, 205; Corres. Imp., xxi, 608, 642; Pons de l'H., 212.

effectual guarantee against the escape of the Emperor.

The Undaunted had been succeeded by the frigate Curaçoa, the brig Swallow, and then the sloop Partridge under the command of Captain Adye, whom Campbell presented at the Mulini on December 5.[1] Officially, of course, it was for the Emperor's benefit that England kept a warship lying off Porto Ferraio.

* * * * *

How and by whom was this abduction (the imminence and probability of which was much exaggerated) to be accomplished? Would any European Power dare to attempt it?

It seemed more probable that the enterprise would be undertaken by the Barbary corsairs, whose light barks, flying the Standard of the Prophet, hovered incessantly round the island. Had not these pirates hatched a project of capturing the Emperor during his passage from Fréjus to Elba, in hopes of sending him with a rope round his neck to the Dey of Algiers, who would have gloried in making a Christian of this rank row in his galleys, or till his gardens? Was it not they who in June or July had prevented Madame Mère from embarking at Ostia, and had it not been necessary for the protection of the Elban trading vessels and coasters to give chase to them in the Inconstant, manned for this emergency with

[1] Campbell, 85, 89, 99, 193, 197, 199.

fifty soldiers who were proof against sea-sickness ?[1]

The Emperor had traded on these legends after signing the Treaty of Fontainebleau, when he insisted on Elba being handed over to him, with its guns and stores, and the forts which the French Government wanted to disarm. But what if the stories of piracy were true ? What if they fell on him during one of his rambles along the shore, carried him off in some expedition to Pianosa, or kidnapped him at the Mulini, scaling the cliff under cover of a moonless night ?

An unexpected event had to some degree rehabilitated the rascals. A corsair from Tunis anchored at Porto Longone, taking up her moorings beneath the guns of the Citadel. Her *rais* or captain, clad in ceremonial garments, and wearing his most gorgeous turban, with two renegades as interpreters, inquired, "if the Great Lord of the Earth were there ?" as he wished to do homage to him. He then bought an Elban flag, for which he paid without bargaining, and ran it up to his yard-arm, saluting with five guns—which were returned. The Port Officer sent information to the Emperor, who was in the Citadel. The Moor was told that the sanitary regulations imposed on all vessels from the East forbade his reception by the Emperor, but that His Majesty was shortly going out for a walk, and might then be viewed from a distance.

[1] Reg. de l'I. d'E., 43 ; Corres. Imp., xxi. 598, 632 ; Pons de l'H., 311 ; Campbell, 16, 18, 149 ; Letter to Mme. d'Arbouville (*Archives Etrangères*).

Some treachery on the part of the *rais* was apprehended.

The Emperor sallied forth with his escort, and stopped to wave his hand amicably to the *rais*, who prostrated himself with his arms crossed upon his breast. Before he re-embarked, the crowd who had flocked round him asked what he thought of the hero he had had the good fortune to contemplate. He replied that "his eyes shone like crystals." He was further asked if it were his intention to make war upon Napoleon. He answered, "I do not fight with God," adding, "It is not the weak ones who betray, but the mighty." The Emperor sent some provisions and sundry gifts to his ship, and the Moor departed, saluting everyone with "*Addio! Addio! Moussiou!*"[1]

The Emperor would have liked to extract more information from him, to ascertain if his conduct were merely personal. His last speech seemed to imply that more powerful chieftains might think and act differently.

The three States of Tunis, Algiers, and Tripoli, moreover, were not united, so this visit really proved nothing. Napoleon took advantage of it to reassure his suite, saying, "There is one thorn the less in our path." But none the less he kept up his precautions.[2]

When news of this episode spread to Genoa, Livorno, Piombino, Civita Vecchia, and Naples,

[1] Campbell, 173; Pons de l'H., 312; Laborde, 42; Chautard, 88; Marchand d'Huiles, 140.

[2] Reg. de l'I. d'E., cxxxvii.

the merchant vessels of these ports craved permission of the Emperor to fly the Elban flag, as protection against the Algerines, and more fame accrued in consequence to the Sovereign of Elba.

The most entertaining aspect of the adventure was, that Campbell, who was duly informed of the incident, took it into his head that the Barbary corsairs (suspected at Elba of being in the pay of the Congress of Vienna or of Louis XVIII) were in amicable relations with Napoleon, and brought him secret messages . . . . transmitting his to Genoa and Corsica, as well as to Murat at Naples; and that he communicated through them with unknown conspirators, the island of Pianosa being the *rendez-vous*.

Campbell bade his agents investigate the nature and extent "of the amicable understanding between Elba and the Tunisian corsair," and being unable to verify his surmises, betook himself to Leghorn, to interrogate the French Consul, Mariotti, and his police spies. Mariotti was as uneasy as Campbell; he proposed to write to Talleyrand that the Tunisians were welcomed at Porto Ferraio, and that one of the corsairs, under cover of this harbour, was maintaining a flotilla of pirates that terrorised the entire coast. Campbell pursued his investigations as far as Florence, where he consulted with the Austrian Governor. He also met Baron Hyde de Neuville there, sent from Paris on a secret mission to obtain precise information about

Bonaparte, and his movements in the island. The conversation between these two men confirmed their suspicions, and they concluded that a plot was on foot between the Tunisian corsairs and the Emperor, for the transport of Napoleon to Toulon, where some treachery would deliver the Mediterranean Fleet, with the City and Arsenal, into his hands. Hyde de Neuville returned post-haste to Paris the following day, to warn the King of this alarming discovery.[1]

* * * * *

It was obvious that any plan adopted for the abduction of the Emperor would be difficult to carry into execution, and would encounter desperate resistance. Napoleon impressed this upon Campbell, in order that he might repeat it to all concerned.[2]

A more feasible way of getting rid of the Emperor would be by assassination. Even during his stay at Marciana "friendly voices advised him not to wander alone among the branching chestnuts," and more than once during his reveries on Monte Giove hc looked round mechanically to see that muskets were not pointing at him from the brushwood. His safety there could only have been assured if a detachment of soldiers had followed him everywhere, with arms in their hands, and he had preferred liberty of thought and action, at the

[1] Campbell, 323; Letter from Mariotti to Talleyrand, Nov. 15, 1814 (Correspondence de Talleyrand, 172); Hyde de Neuville, II., i.

[2] Campbell, 174, 176; Fleury de Chaboulon, I., 106.

PORTO FERRAIO AND ITS GULF, SEEN FROM THE GARDENS OF SAN MARTINO.

THE HOUSE AT SAN MARTINO, IN ITS ACTUAL STATE.

risk of death.[1] After his return to Porto Longone, however, the vague rumours of assault became more definite, and the Emperor no longer went out alone. "All my Cavalry, Poles, Light Horse, and Mamelukes shall be at the disposition of my First Orderly. He is to accompany me everywhere on horseback, and shall be allowed a horse from my stables, with two pistols; he will command the escorts, and take suitable measures of precaution; he will arrange with the Head of the Police that gendarmes be placed along my route. My carriage shall be followed daily by five attendants with loaded carabines and pistols."[2]

The warnings were many—many, too, the "bravos" who, it was asserted, were sharpening their daggers in dark corners, and had vowed to purge the world of the still redoubtable monster.

One warning came from the ex-King Joseph, who received intelligence through Madame de Stael in his retreat at Prangins in Switzerland, that two men, financed by the Royalists of France, were starting for Elba, to assassinate the Emperor. Madame de Stael, nobly oblivious of past injustice, and Talma, who was breakfasting with Joseph when the letter came, volunteered to go in person to Porto Ferraio, and warn Napoleon of his danger. An old retainer of the family eventually undertook the mission.[3]

Another warning was from a Prussian visitor, who

[1] Pons de l'H., 211. [2] Reg. de l'I. d'E., 73.
[3] Mémoires de Joseph, X., 209, 315.

informed the Emperor when admitted to pay his respects, that the Society of the Tugendbund, who had co-operated in his downfall, were now determined to kill him, and "were despatching three well-disguised bravos to the island with that object." The good offices of this Prussian were open to suspicion. Since he was a member of the Society, he might even be one of the three assassins. The police took extra precautions until he left the island.[1] In Rome, fanatical monks were brooding over the same deed in their convents, and, still nearer the island of Elba, Bruslart, the Governor of Corsica, had official instructions "to get rid of Bonaparte at any price." Assassins were sent to him, and he passed them on to Elba.[2]

For Bruslart, the public vendetta was complicated by a private grudge which dated back to the Consulate . . . a misunderstanding had cost the life of one of his friends, a former *émigré* like himself, to whom a pardon had been promised, and his blood still cried for vengeance.

A highly suspicious character was discovered one night by the sentinels in the maquis of San Martino. He was arrested and searched. His papers were not in order, and he was carrying a dagger. Undoubtedly this was an emissary from Bruslart. He was identified as a Corsican, who had been convicted

1 Marchand d'H., 145.

2 *Ile d'Elbe et Cent Jours*, 26; Fleury de Chaboulon, I., 111; Pons de l'H., 160; Laborde, 43; Letter from Comte de C. to the Comte d'Artois, *Miscellanea Napoleonica*, II., 160: "The public weal demands the suppression of this monster, and I believe it will be found possible to accomplish it."

of several crimes, and must have landed at some deserted spot along the coast. The news of the arrest spread, and it was generally expected that the man would be handed over to justice, or shot without trial. Still, as he denied the charge, there was only moral evidence against him, that is, none at all. The Emperor feared that if the culprit were executed "for an example," as he was advised, he would himself be accused of assassination, which would furnish a pretext for reprisals. He ordered him to be put on board ship again, and sent back to Corsica.

Imagination evoked the wildest chimæras. Marshal Soult sent a confidential note to the Emperor, to put him on his guard against one of the superior officers, mentioned by name, who, since the restitution of the Bourbons, had showered torrents of abuse upon him. Next came a triple warning, "from three different sources, and from safe persons, to the effect that a one-eyed Jew, a bookseller of Leipzig, had consented, for payment of a considerable sum, to despatch the Emperor while he offered him his wares." From that moment, one-eyed people were tabooed on the island. Old Colonel Tavelle (who had obtained his epaulettes by a mistake, and made it his business to deserve them) flew into a rage directly he descried one. He was sent on duty to Rio Marina. The Mayor of Rio Montagna had a bad record, and was, moreover, blind of one eye. The Colonel met him at Rio Marina, and accosted him furiously: "What are you doing here,

Sirrah! This is not your place. Go at once." The Mayor protested. He was a citizen, mayor, chamberlain to his Majesty. Tavelle would not listen. "You are branded," he said, "like the accursed offspring of those who sold our Lord, like the man who wants to murder the Emperor. It is an evil sign." The Mayor was obliged to withdraw, although he called in the Mayor of Rio Marina to support him. "I should have treated him," the brave Colonel boasted afterwards, "like the Jew, neither worse nor better." At the smallest provocation he would have carried his bed to the shore, to keep an eye on the horizon even in his slumbers.[1]

Everyone in the Army resembled him, and gory phantoms were conjured up freely. The swords that surrounded the Emperor chafed at this perpetual menace of unknown and intangible dangers. Cambronne was beside himself. The old mastiff showed his teeth, and sprang at the shins of all whom he suspected. And he was suspicious of everybody.

A Neapolitan warship appeared in the roadstead of Porto Ferraio, and ran up the Elban flag, giving the regulation salute of twenty-one guns, with three cheers for "the Emperor Napoleon."

A boat put off, with the officers of the vessel. The Commander, a Rear-Admiral, requested permission to land, and present his homage to the Emperor, if admitted, at the Mulini. Cambronne hurried to the scene. His blood boiled at the sight

[1] Pons de l'H., 164, 165, 180.

of the Neapolitan uniform, and the subjects of King Murat—Murat, who had been a traitor, and was capable of any fresh ruse. While the Commander was repeating his request urbanely, Cambronne roundly swore at him and his staff as bandits and scoundrels, who would be fired at, if they did not decamp with the utmost promptitude. He ordered the gunners of the Port to load their pieces, and would have opened fire if the boat had not promptly put off to sea. A quick transformation followed. In the belief that the fort was going to fire on him, the Commander took down the Elban banner, spread his sails, and made for the open seas. The town was thunderstruck.[1]

No new arrival could escape Cambronne. One day, while reviewing the Guard, he detected a stranger in the crowd, whose keen attention and evident emotion boded no good. Cambronne flew at him, asking in a voice of thunder who he was, and what he wanted. The unfortunate man was paralysed with terror. He lost the faculty of speech, and mumbled incomprehensible excuses. The greater his distress, the more Cambronne suspected him. The populace collected round them. Finally, the stranger obtained grace of being marched off to Bertrand, between two soldiers, when the Grand Maréchal recognised him as a former Commissioner of War, who had served under his orders. He was a good Frenchman, devoted to the Emperor, who had found himself out of place in the Bourbon

[1] Pons de l'H., 167.

Reaction, and had come in quest of employment to Elba. Bertrand apologised to him and assured him of his protection. But he could not get over his fright, and left the island by the next boat.[1]

On another occasion, an ex-Chouan, on his way to Corsica to take service with Bruslart, with a big white cockade in his hat, and a coat embroidered with a crop of fleur-de-lys, who had been forced by contrary winds to put into Porto Ferraio, created such a scandal by walking about the town in this costume that Drouot was obliged to give him an officer for his protection. The whole garrison wanted to buffet him, and provoke a duel. The old Vendéan watched the Guard defiling to parade, to the sound of the Marseillaise, each morning, and said to the officer who accompanied him, "But you are living in '93. Porto Ferraio is a dreadful place." He re-embarked as soon as the winds permitted, vowing not to come back there.[2]

The Emperor feigned annoyance on hearing of these incidents, some of which, *e.g.*, the affront to the Neapolitan vessel, put him in the wrong. But he could not be seriously displeased at the fanatical devotion that was watching over him.

* * * * *

Nor was it this alone that preserved him.

The announcement of his moral decrepitude, of the premature collapse of this proud spirit, rather than his war budget, or the guns of his forts, or the

[1] Fleury de Chaboulon, 103; Pons de l'H., 170.
[2] *Ile d'Elbe et Cent Jours*, 25; Pons de l'H., 159, 375.

AN AUDIENCE WITH THE KING OF THE MINES, OR NAPOLEON'S COURT IN THE ISLAND OF ELBA.
From a contemporary Caricature.

heroic adoration of his faithful servants, disarmed the implacable hatred of his foes, for the moment at any rate. Whether it was the effect of the immense catastrophe that had befallen him—the exhaustion of a brain too sorely tried,—or the torture of all these rumours of abduction and assassination,—or the cruel separation from his wife and child, and their subsequent and total disappearance,—there could be no doubt that more than one notable symptom betrayed the general depression from which the Emperor was suffering, the atrophy of his mind and intellect,—in a word his decadence.

Nor did this manifest itself merely in the ridiculous Court that he had instituted, in the parody of Government in whose child's play this former King of Kings now seemed to find satisfaction, writing gravely, without a smile, at the head of his decrees: "Napoleon, Emperor, Sovereign of the Isle of Elba, commands the following";[1]—nor in the promotion to be Admiral of his fleet of Lieutenant Taillade, who could not set foot upon a vessel without sacrificing to Neptune; nor in the toy army, the marches and counter-marches of which across the Island in which it was incarcerated resembled the antics of a circus horse going through his paces; nor the physician who seemed to have stepped out of one of Molière's comedies, nor the one-eyed chamberlain, nor all the high dignitaries who never succeeded in

[1] Decrees nominating Cambronne to be Military Commandant at Porto Ferraio; Captain Combes to be Captain of the Guard; Signor Catalani to be Port Lieutenant at Porto Longone (Peyrusse, Appendix, Nos. 20, 28, 34).

gloving their horny hands; nor from his habit of leaving the company every night as the clock struck nine, to go to bed like a child, after playing the fourteen notes on the piano that signalled his departure; nor his mania of cheating at cards, of being determined not to lose, even when he had lost, of walking off with other people's winnings . . . .—there were other and far worse things than these, of quite another category.

In the first place—his strange and repulsive horror of black (an aversion of which his intimates had always been aware, without inquiring into its causes), was becoming more and more intensified. When Princess Pauline appeared at a ball in a black velvet gown, which she had taken care to cover with pink flounces, because the Emperor liked that colour, she had no sooner made her *entrée* than he gave the order in public bidding her retire, and put on another costume. On another occasion, when he happened at dinner to be next the wife of an official who was unacquainted with his idiosyncrasy, and was dressed in mourning, the sight of her black robes threw the Emperor "into sudden gloom, which did not relax for an instant during the whole of the meal. It was not temper. It was a sad obsession that weighed on him." "He must," we are assured by Drouot, "have made a great effort to stay a whole hour in the company of this lady."[1]

This aversion to black was complemented by his

[1] Pons de l'H., 260, 261; Campbell, 110.

hatred of white. "When Pauline one day received a white gown from Paris, the Emperor remarked as she entered the salon: "Ah, Madame! You are dressed *à la victime!* And the Princess was forced, on this occasion also, to withdraw and put on different garments."[1]

"Napoleon," wrote Campbell, "seems to have lost all habits of study and sedentary application. He has four places of residence in different parts of the island, and the improvements and changes of these form his sole occupation. His mental agitations and uncertainties, however, do not admit of his continuing to take interest in them when the charm of novelty has worn off. He then falls into a state of complete inactivity."[2]

During one such fit of depression, he was reported as "sitting in his uniform of Colonel of the National Guard, at the bottom of a ditch, with water up to his middle." After this bath, he got on his horse again, wet through, and then went out in a boat. A few hours later he remarked: "I will go back to the Palace now, and change, for my feet are rather damp."[3]

He was also, it was said, subject to fits of rage for the most futile motives. Pauline, in one of her

[1] The so-called robes *à la victime*, and coiffure of the same name, invented by Duplan, Talma's coiffeur, were in fashion after Thermidor. The hair, simply drawn up from the nape, and the gown falling in straight folds, recalled the costume of those who were condemned to the guillotine.

[2] Campbell, *Napoleon at Fontainebleau and Elba*, 305.

[3] Reports presented by spies to the Leghorn Consulate, quoted by M. Pellet, 54. The agent who is responsible for this absurd story means the uniform of Colonel of the Chasseurs de la Garde.

expeditions to Leghorn, had gone to the bookseller whose business it was to bind the Emperor's library. As she did not approve of the bindings, she took upon herself to alter them. When the books arrived at Porto Ferraio, the Emperor was so infuriated that he summoned the Body Guard, and bade them slash up the morocco with their bayonets ![1]

Other whispers circulated confidentially about the terrors of his nights. One November night the mameluke went into his room to feed the lamp that was kept alight till morning: the Emperor awoke with a start, jumped from his couch, and blew the man's brains out, taking him for a thief or assassin.[2] Napoleon's three iron beds were dragged from place to place about the island, in a vain search for the repose that eluded him! The vulture of remorse was gnawing at his heart. The torrent of blood which "Attila" had shed was rising in floods around him. The skulls on which "this modern Tamerlane" had propped his throne grinned at him from their empty orbits in the night-watches. And since black reminded him of these things, he hated it. Bonaparte's punishment for the human butcheries in which he had revelled was just: no man may be the "Commander-in-Chief of skeletons," "the first grave-digger in the world" with impunity.[3]

[1] Local tradition, cited by M. Pellet, 44. Pauline never visited Leghorn during her residence in Elba.

[2] Spies' Reports in State Archives of Florence, published by G. Livi, Milan, 1888. Ali, of course, followed the Emperor to St. Helena. He was still living, at Sens, in 1847.

[3] Cochemare de Buonoparte à l'Ile d'Elbe on l'Apparition du Petit

These and similar ideas of the Emperor's state of mind were taking shape upon the Continent. They were founded on the "facts" communicated by the swarm of spies that hovered about the island and the coast of Italy. These spies were in the pay of England and Austria, and still more of Mariotti, the French Consul at Leghorn, whose post had been reconstituted by Talleyrand for the express purpose of bringing all these reports to a focus upon the Continent, as Campbell focussed them within the Island of Elba. These police spies were so numerous (some being sent direct from Paris, Vienna, or London) that they often shadowed each other, under a mutual misapprehension of being the agents of Napoleon. Those who were on active duty in Elba borrowed various disguises, coming as old soldiers to offer their services or seek relief,—as merchants, artisans, or traders in oil and butter. They were sometimes detected and expelled by the Imperial police as soon as they arrived at Porto Ferraio, but were often clever enough to produce reputable securities, and succeeded in passing themselves off as admirers of the Emperor, and in acquiring the confidence of Cambronne, who served as their cicerone. They crept in among the grooms and lackeys at the Mulini. One of Pauline's

Homme Rouge, Paris, 1814; Collection of French and German Prints, Biblio. Nationale, 1814–1815; *Parallèle de St. Louis et de Gengis-Kan*, Paris, 1814. "Bonaparte came down like Genseric, whither the anger of the Lord awaited him," wrote Chateaubriand after the return from Elba.

waiting-women was financed by the Préfecture of the Police in Paris, and many an intruding Aspasia was bribed to get information from her lovers, and report what she had learned to Leghorn or Florence.[1]

* * * * *

These spies were for the most part starving rascals, devoid of conscience and credentials, who doubtless invented, or at any rate exaggerated, what they retailed, the better to fill their report and swell their salary. After Countess Walewska's visit to the Emperor, they had not failed to report duly to their chiefs (who knew nothing of the kind had occurred) that Marie Louise had come to see her husband, in defiance of the embargo laid upon her, and they revived the subject four months later, adding, to make the information more definite, that the Empress had departed *enceinte!*[2] Such was the character of their meretricious information. Public opinion also tended to justify their reports, and confirmed what they related of the Emperor's disorder.

[1] Marchand d'Huiles, pp. 118, 120, 127, 128, 129, 132, 134, 149. The file of reports (some illegible, others in cipher, others written in secret ink, and corroded by reagents) which exists at the French Consulate in Livorno has been partially returned by M. Pellet. Among these is the journal of the Marchand d'Huiles (the "Oil Merchant") which, save for two gaps, continues day by day, from Nov. 30, 1814, down to the departure of the Emperor. This agent of Mariotti does not seem to be of a higher order of intelligence than his fellows. Like them he retails, indiscriminately, whatever comes under the scope of his pen. He is only interesting when his notebook records, not the information he is ostensibly giving, but the circumstances of which his stay in the island made him a witness, and in which he finally became an actor.

[2] Marchand d'Huiles, 137.

A crowd of visitors daily arrived at the Island of Elba. They came from all countries of Europe, from Italy, Germany, Norway. French mothers flocked with their first-born to show them the "hero of heroes," without knowing a soul in Elba, almost without resources. By dint of perseverance they obtained audience of the Emperor, and won some small gratuity by their touching supplications. Regardless of their advancing years, enthusiastic ladies who were unable to endure the banishment of "the Glory of France," renounced their homes, their families, and their daily life, and committed themselves with just sufficient money to pay the expenses of the journey to an unknown future in exile.[1]

The majority of the visitors were English, who professed an admiration for their former enemy which was the more sincere inasmuch as they had conquered him. Some came unconventionally as tourists; others who were personages—peers, politicians, aristocratic damsels, half in love with the hero, were presented according to the rules of the protocol, and claimed the honour, usually conceded, of an invitation to the Mulini and a seat at the Imperial table. The officers of the English squadron in the Mediterranean absented themselves from their ships in order to visit the Island of Elba, although the Admiral expressed strong disapproval of "the voluntary court and unnecessary visits paid by naval officers at Porto

[1] Campbell, 207; Pons de l'H., 221, 222.

Ferraio.[1] Captain Usher, who brought Napoleon to Elba, said the voyage "would immortalise the Undaunted." Nor was the Emperor behindhand in compliments and courtesies. He told them "their nation was the most polite and powerful, and the most generous of all, the most esteemed by himself, superior even to the French nation. No one, no Power, was capable of fighting against her. He had been England's most implacable foe, but was so no longer. Was he not under her protection at Elba, almost an English subject? All islands belonged by right to England. If he were ever, in the future, to leave Elba, he should retire to the banks of the Thames." When Colonel Campbell came to present a country-man at the Mulini, the officials would exclaim, "Ah! it is you, Colonel! What a regard the Emperor has for you, and how he honours the English nation."[2] After visiting the Undaunted and making a speech to the crew, Napoleon sent them "a thousand bottles of wine, and a thousand dollars, and presented Captain Usher with a gold snuff-box, with his portrait set in fine diamonds."

On the anniversary of George III's birthday, celebrated by the two captains of the British ships, Curaçoa and Swallow, in the harbour of Porto Ferraio, Napoleon went to the ball given on board the Curaçoa. The guns were shifted to the hold

[1] Pons de l'H., 149, 276; Marchand d'H., 135, 151, 155, 156; Campbell, *Napoleon at Fontainebleau and Elba*, 288.

[2] Gen. Durand, 204; Gen. Vincent, 198; Campbell, 15, 73, 93, 136, 327.

of the ship to make room for dancing, and the Emperor sat on the bridge, beneath the flags of England and Elba.[1]

Some of the English abused the cordiality shown to all British subjects, and took advantage of the permission given them to roam about the island, to map out the roads, and make plans of the forts, the topography of the coast, and the various strategic positions. They were watched, or requested to return to the Continent, without further penalty.[2]

All arrivals had to satisfy the sanitary authorities on first landing, and then presented themselves before Cambronne, to show their passports, which were subsequently endorsed, and they received a permit to remain. A hotel (Hotel Bouroux) had supplemented the one inn kept by Mlle. Sauvage, but the beds were packed as close as in a hospital, for the crowd was considerable, and the Inconstant sometimes disembarked a hundred passengers in one day. People lodged where they could, at the restaurants, or with the inhabitants, who let and sub-let the greater part of their houses, furnished, at exorbitant prices.[3]

[1] Campbell, *Napoleon at Fontainebleau and Elba*, 269; Campbell, French ed., 94, 99; Peyrusse, Appendix, 33; Gen. Durand, 254; Pons de l'H., 233; Gen. Vincent, 203. Snuffboxes, rings, and watches were the Emperor's customary gifts. *See* Peyrusse, "His Majesty's Accounts (May 12—April, 1814): 22 snuffboxes with portraits, from 5,600—10,300 francs; 40 with monogram, from 635—4,600 francs; 28 rings and 21 watches with monogram, 530—4,600 francs." Peyrusse, Appendix, 119.

[2] March. d'H., 122; Mém. aux Puiss. All., 112.

[3] Reg. de l'I. d'E., 2; Marchand d'H., 118, 129; Corres. Imp., xxi. 644; Peyrusse (Appendix), 66; Labadie, 383.

Distinguished visitors obtained audience of the Emperor, and one of his carriages was exclusively reserved for them. The rest endeavoured to see him when he went out. They would wait about for him, near the Mulini, or along the road to San Martino, for five or six hours at a time. Many, on leaving the island, crossed to Ajaccio, where they made a pilgrimage to the Casa Buonaparte, and carried off fragments of stone and mortar. In Elba they loaded themselves with little souvenirs, busts of the Emperor, columns, and marble paper-weights from the island quarries, the manufacture of which was highly lucrative to the sculptors.[1]

With one accord they flocked over the seas, panting to inspect the glory that had filled the world, the fallen demi-god, whom they imagined solitary and sublime, crowned with a dazzling aureole, finger on chin, eye darting lightning flashes, delivering himself from time to time of weighty utterances.

Instead, what did they find? A thick-set, corpulent little man, with the profile of an Italian Polichinello, and nostrils stained with snuff, sharing a *bouillabaisse* cooked in their saucepans on the beach with the tunny-fishers, and apparently enjoying it. Or they espied him in his garden-plot at San Martino, absorbed in quoits with the worthy dames of the Elban bourgeoisie, badly-dressed and unintellectual provincials . . . his mistresses, doubt-

[1] Reg. de l'I. d'E., 5; Labadie, 49; Monier, 68; Pons de l'H., 144; Mém. aux Puiss. All., 70.

less, to whose noisy chatter he listened complacently. The lorgnettes of the astounded tourists discovered the Emperor running after his fowls in the vineyard, or playing innocent games in a field with the same good ladies and their daughters. *What will you put in my basket? Hot Cockles, Chevalier Cornard* with twisted horns of paper in his ear, *Kiss in the Ring*, or *Blind Man's Buff*, running with eyes bandaged to catch hold of any one he could, or tumbling over some obstacle, amid the blandishments of the sportive seraglio. On one occasion he was seen, before the whole Court, to pick up a handful of little fish that had been thrown out of the nets on to the sand, and to slip them into Bertrand's pocket . . . after which he begged the loan of the General's handkerchief. Bertrand immediately put his hand into his pocket, and drew it out still more quickly when his fingers came in contact with the wet and sticky mass. The Emperor, delighted with his practical joke, was convulsed with laughter, while the Grand Maréchal, the eternal butt of his jesting, emptied his pockets, grumbling the while, and wiping the salt water-stains from his uniform.

When scenes such as these succeeded those of the Court at the Mulini, with its receptions by the one-eyed chamberlain in the saloons of the Palace (where folding partitions shut off the bath-tubs, and pitiful amateurs made fools of themselves on tottering trestles), the aristocrats stood aghast, the tourists sneered, and not a few went back to the Continent with a smile of pity for this worse decadence than that of Fontainebleau, this painful spectacle of the moral humiliation of the hero of Austerlitz, fallen so low beneath the burden of ennui and misfortune.[1]

And yet the sword of Damocles, the sentence of deportation and exile, was kept suspended over the head of the Emperor by these very reports, which penetrated to official circles. What advantage was there, under these conditions, in risking an undignified violation of treaties and abuse of the rights of man, and all the perils of a forcible abduction, when Napoleon was already assailed by dementia, and launched on the road to speedy self-destruction?

* * * * *

On January 1, 1815, there was a reception at the Mulini, as had formerly been the custom at the Tuileries.

The passing of one year and birthday of the next is always an affecting moment, and how much keener must the emotion have been for the little Imperial circle! Behind them lay the first completed year of exile, the year of disaster, of accumulated ruin. Before them, the uncertainty of a morrow that was felt to be lowering with tempests.

1 Pons de l'H., 248 ff.; Mém. aux Puiss. All., 55; Laborde, 46; Marchand d'Huiles, 155; Archives Étrangères. (Open letter to the Paris Post: "Have seen an Englishman who says that Napoleon might be permitted to return, and would be dangerous no longer. He is brought too low.") Fleury de Chaboulon, 106.

To-day they were at Elba. Where would the next year find them?

The Emperor, on whom this thought must have weighed more heavily than on anyone else, accepted and returned the greetings of all with a serene and smiling countenance. He again declared that he was satisfied with his lot, and ready to devote himself as in the past to the happiness of his Elban subjects. He spoke of the possible advent of Marie Louise, who would occupy Pauline's apartments on the first floor of the Mulini. Everyone took his cue from the Emperor, and, whether from indifference in some, or from confidence in others, were gay and light-hearted, after his example.[1]

The outlook had never appeared more ominous. On this very 1st of January two French warships, a brig and a frigate, were seen cruising round the island, and on the next day a third appeared. Throughout the day they were watched from the forts, as they tacked and fired broadsides. The inhabitants grew uneasy, and the Emperor, who was no less anxious, sent orders to Drouot to keep himself vigilantly informed as to these vessels and their designs. "You must find out what is going on all over the island. The police patrols must interrogate the inhabitants of the houses situated near the shore to ascertain that no suspicious

[1] Peyrusse, 263; Labadie, 53; Marchand d'H., 139, 141, 143; Corres. Imp., xxi. 661. The Emperor clung for some days, at the end of December, to a vague expectation of Marie Louise's arrival, and made inquiries about hiring "the Maison Lafargue," to which he would have transported Pauline and her furniture.

character has landed. You must keep a watch on the whole coast, on the capes, rocks, and inhabited islands. Pretend you are going to sell salt in the adjacent islands so that you may observe the French ships and pass near them without being suspected. Establish signals between the forts. See that the look-out men are provided with good glasses, and do not let these vessels out of their sight. Let no one leave his post day or night."[1]

Porto Ferraio could, if necessary, be declared in a state of siege from one day to another. The forts had been placed beyond the reach of a surprise by new defences; houses which were too near and would have interfered with the cannon had been bought from their owners, and levelled to the ground. The artillery were practising with red-hot shells. Twenty field-guns were mounted on their carriages so that they could be brought to bear on any threatened point. The bombs were ready, and the garrisons of the smaller forts were doubled.[2]

* * * * *

Even if these vessels were not preparing to attack and capture the Emperor, their arrival intimated a more active surveillance, and intention of

1 Corres. Imp., xxi. 663; Marchand d'H., 143, 144; Campbell (Report from Chevalier Garet), 250. The first frigate was the Melpomene, and the brig, the Zephyr, belonging to the Naval Station of Corsica. Hyde de Neuville gave such alarmist reports, on his return to Paris, that the third vessel, a frigate, the Fleur de Lys, commanded by Chevalier Garet, was sent from Toulon to reinforce the squadron.

2 Corres. Imp., xxi. 656. 660; Reg. de l'I. d'E., 149; Peyrusse, 262; Marchand d'Huiles, 127, 131, 139, 141, 145, 146, 148; Campbell, 209.

incarcerating Napoleon definitively within his island. This second alternative was not much better, for tied up as he was by the fatal question of money, the Sovereign of Elba was threatened with famine.

The pension of two millions had now been obstinately withheld for nearly nine months. The Emperor had never cherished hopes that the Bourbons would voluntarily pay one centime of what they owed him. But he had reckoned on their being forced to do so by Europe.[1]

He reiterated his claims at the Congress of Vienna, backed up by Campbell, to whom he complained of his penury on every available occasion, and to whom Madame Bertrand declared that the Emperor "had scarcely a shilling, not even a ring to present to any one, and that his situation is frightful."[2]

The Allied Sovereigns, fearing that the Emperor would avail himself of the non-execution of this clause of the Treaty to leave his island, had transmitted the claim to Talleyrand, who had been obliged, sorely against his will, to write to Louis XVIII: "There is much inquiry on every side, and Lord Castlereagh has frequently asked me directly, whether the Treaty of April 11th is to be put in execution. The silence of the budget on this point has been noticed by the Emperor of Russia. In short, this matter is constantly turning up under

[1] Meneval, II., 185.

[2] Campbell, *Napoleon at Fontainebleau and Elba*, 319. Countess Bertrand joined her husband in Elba at the beginning of August.

different forms, and nearly always in a disagreeable connection. Painful as it is to insist on details of this kind, I cannot avoid pointing out to your Majesty that it is desirable that something should be done in the matter. A letter bringing me this assurance would produce a good effect." Louis XVIII conformed to these representations. He promised Talleyrand to write, by his Minister of the Interior, a letter, of which it was understood that not a word was to be taken seriously, but which Talleyrand would be able to show to the Members of the Congress, and in which the King of France would pledge his word that he was honest, and had not forgotten his obligations. This was all that Talleyrand required, as he could make shift with the letter. And it was all that reached the Emperor.[1]

As to Napoleon, when the expenses of 1814 had been defrayed, he would have not "one shilling" but a little more than two millions of the 3,811,615 francs he had brought with him, that is to say, enough to last for perhaps a year. After that, *nil.* He would have to meet his public and private estimates out of the 300,000 francs of revenue from the mine, and 50,000 francs from the tunny fishery and salines. Now the budget of the Imperial household alone, which had swallowed up 479,987 francs in 1814, required for 1815 a minimum of 380,000 francs, and that of the War Estimates,

[1] Corr. between Talleyrand and Louis XVIII, Oct. 13 and 21, 1814.

1,015,000 francs.[1] It was becoming of urgent importance that economic measures should be inaugurated.

From the 1st of January, the Mailboat Service was suppressed. Its receipts did not cover expenses, for, since most of the letters sent *viâ* Piombino or Livorno were intercepted by the Austrian Police, a great deal of correspondence was forwarded by private messengers. The despatch-boats Mouche and Abeille now undertook the service, with five Marines of the Guard . . . . and thus effected an annual saving of 4,300 francs. The postmen within the town were replaced by orderlies on foot, the rural messengers by mounted orderlies. Expenses were cut down for the Engineers, Navy, provisioning of Pianosa, clothing of the troops, and various items of the Military Budget. Saving of 47,905 francs. From November 1 the officers' mess was suppressed. General Drouot took his meals with the Emperor. The household table at the Mulini was abolished, with the allowance to its members for firing, light, and washing. Saving of 40,000 francs. Stable expenses were reduced. Eight carriage-horses were sold, with a reduction of 1,912 francs on the monthly charges for fodder and bedding, and fewer stablemen. The stables were not to cost more than 75,000 to 80,000 francs all told, in 1815. Minor posts which were superflous, or deemed to be so, coast-guards near the mine of Rio, accoun-

[1] Corres. Imp., xxi. 662 ; Reg. de l'I. d'E., 111 ; Peyrusse, 265.

tants at Porto Ferraio, and office clerks, were suppressed. One of the two Imperial architects, at a salary of 3,000 francs per annum, was dismissed. The suite and officials retained were to receive only half their former salary in cash. The rest would be paid them in I.O.U.'s upon the French Treasury, which was in the Emperor's debt for the two millions pension. During the course of January the officers were to be mulcted of their allowance for lodging as they had already been of that for board. In future they would have to put up in the barracks.[1]

These economies harrowed the susceptibilities of the Emperor. They humiliated and enraged him, and were useless. They were the merest drop in the ocean. Far more radical measures were necessary, namely, that he should renounce the rights of a crowned head, and consent to be no more than a substantial bourgeois, and homely magistrate, as he had promised to consider himself in the Island of Elba. But Napoleon was unable to submit to this ultimate humiliation in the eyes of his subjects. How, if he consented, could he keep up the Army, his only safeguard? His Military Estimates, on the contrary, needed to be augmented. Hardly did he achieve a reduction on the one hand, than he restored the funds which he had alienated, on the other.[2]

He set himself to minor economies. He wept

[1] Reg. de l'I. d'E., 66, 116, 117, 119, 142, 143, 144, 150, 157, 170; Peyrusse, 262, 263 (Appendix) 129, 130; Pons de l'H., 101; Marchand d'H., 152.

[2] Registre de l'I. d'E., 180.

over the loss of a mule that was drowned. He hectored his mother and Pauline, who, like himself, had not received one sou of the 300,000 francs apportioned to them respectively by the Treaty of Fontainebleau (Article VI), but possessed substantial residues of the fortunes with which he had formerly endowed them. He refused to pay for the trifling decorations they ordered in their apartments. "It is only proper that the account of the expenses incurred by Madame Mère in the Vantini house should be sent in to her. This is the only way to prevent further extravagance, since nothing could be less essential than these items." Pauline put up eight blinds in her drawing-room. She provided the linen. The making-up and hanging cost 6 francs 50 centimes. Marshal Bertrand presented the bill to the Emperor, who wrote upon the margin: "This expense not having been ordered, and not relating to the estimates, must be defrayed by the Princess." This was not on account of the cost, which was minimal. It was intended as a lesson to the Princess and Madame Mère. They must needs understand that the well they had so long been drawing from was dried up. Pauline did not take offence, but helped him covertly with her money and jewels. He prescribed a limited expenditure of funds for the six balls announced at the Mulini for the season, in terms that recall Harpagon. "The total cost for each ball shall not exceed 1,000 francs. There will be refreshments but no ices, in view of the difficulty of providing these. Invitations for nine o'clock. Supper not before midnight." At Marciana there was an ice-house where snow could be procured for the manufacture of ices and sherbets, but the Emperor had let it out to Signor Senno, proprietor of the tunny fishery. He was bent on distributing the spoiled flour from the disused stores at the Fort, which the soldiers declined, to the labourers in the iron mine. Pons protested that the stomach of a labourer was worth as much as that of a soldier, and that it was an injustice that poor wretches who ate nothing but bread, while three-fourths of them drank only water, should be condemned to poison themselves with this bread. The Emperor insisted. A first distribution was made, and then a second, and in twenty-four hours' time some hundred of the miners were on the sick-list. The flour was then sold on the Continent. The Emperor wished, as an economy, to turn off some of these miners, without lessening the yield of work. Fresh protests were made by the overseer. "Such a measure would lead to a riot. The lot of these unfortunate people was so hard already." "But I, too, am poor!" exclaimed the Emperor. Pons vainly pointed out that "this poverty was one of the most splendid rays of his aureole." He remained "sullen and silent." "I am poorer than Job," he repeated to all who approached him, and who did not fail to see in this another sign of a weak brain, profoundly affected.[1]

[1] Reg. de l'I. d'E., 64; Corres. Imp., xxi. 622, 665, 667, 670; *Ile d'Elbe et Cent Jours*, 18; Pons de l'H., 94, 101, 102, 256.

PORTO FERRAIO: THE SOUTHERN ASPECT OF THE CITY, AND FORTE FALCONE.

As an added worry, the municipal and land taxes were not returned, or came in badly. One of the pleasantest of the illusions cherished by the Elbans had been the notion that there would be no more fiscal charges under the rule of "Napoleon the Great." They were soon disillusioned. The arrears of contributions went back as far as September, 1813. The Emperor bade the tax-gatherers call them in by gentle means. The Elbans paid no attention. Napoleon insisted. Riots then broke out in all the villages, and the collectors were insulted with shouting and blasts from horns which drowned all attempts to read their summons. August 1 was then fixed as the latest date for payment of the contributions, under pain of military execution. But the Emperor wished first to try if the clergy had not some influence. The Curés were bidden to address their flock from the pulpit and exhort them to obey the law and give no further distress to the "paternal heart of their Sovereign." The Curés were hissed out of the churches, and not one *paolo*[1] had been collected by September 7.

There was no pretext, no subterfuge, to which the Elbans did not resort to escape payment. In the idea that English influence was paramount at the Mulini, the priests inquired whether a memorial might not be addressed to Campbell, requesting England to interfere, to prevent the exactions of Napoleon![2] When every dilatory expedient had

[1] A *paolo* in former Tuscan coinage was worth 56 centimes.
[2] Campbell, *Napoleon at Fontainebleau et Elba*, 279.

been exhausted, Marciana, Poggio, Campo, and Porto Longone decided to discharge their arrears, and to deposit partial payments for the current year. At Rio Montagna and Rio Marina, where the entire population worked in the mines, the collectors accepted the slightest sign of goodwill; they even advanced the wages to the poorer members of the community, in order that they might contribute something. The main point was to disabuse the Elbans of the notion that they were dispensed from their obligations to the State.[1]

Capoliveri held out. Here the tax-gatherers met with armed resistance. Two Imperial Commissioners had been sent, with a party of gendarmes, to enforce the arrears of contributions. Riots and insurrection broke out. The Commissioners and gendarmes were attacked at the instance of a priest, disgracefully handled, routed, and disabled. Capoliveri had once more justified its infamous reputation.

The Emperor lost patience, and announced that Capoliveri must expect retribution.

The inhabitants were summoned through the Mayor to give up three of the insurgents, the priest among them, and to acquit themselves of their obligations within four-and-twenty hours. The Mayor assembled the Municipal Council, who replied that they would neither pay nor give hostages. Drouot then received orders to draft out 200 men and twenty gendarmes, each provided with three packets of cartridges, and to march them

[1] Peyrusse, 239, 255; Reg. de l'I. d'E., Nos. 66, 67; Campbell, 101, 127, 134, 140; Pons de l'H., 202.

against the rebels. Alarmed at last, Capoliveri surrendered. The priests and some of the principal inhabitants were imprisoned for a few days and then pardoned.[1] Bloodshed had been avoided, and victory remained with the law. But these disturbances were ominous for the future collection of the same taxes, and still more for the harvesting of those which the Emperor contemplated. The subsidies from the mine were also returned with difficulty. Since the suppression of the two coastguards and their boat, smugglers had come in the night to steal the minerals. The Emperor already foresaw the necessity of parting with 20,000 francs worth of houses and lands belonging to the Domain, in 1815, and of raising 150,000 francs on the scrap-iron still left in the forts, 210,000 francs on the old timber, 50,000 francs on the damaged commissariat, and of selling some of his horses and carriages for 10,000 francs.[2]

Meantime, alas! the loyalty of his followers was declining before this want of funds and the monotony of exile. Troopers recalled, as they declared, by family claims, demanded to be released and allowed to return to France. They left, loaded with certificates of valour and parchment attestations.[3] It was a question how many others would be found to replace them, when all the pay they received, like the Household at the Mulini, was an I.O.U. on the Bourbon Treasury.

* * * * *

[1] Pons de l'H., 201; Reg. de l'I. d'E., 129; March. d'H., 122.

[2] Reg. de l'I. d'E., 66 and 134, 76 and 160; Pons de l'H., 101, 210; Peyrusse, 267.

[3] Campbell, 204; Reg. de l'I. d'E., 135, 166; Corres. Imp., xxi. 658; March. d'H., 122, 141.

Month by month the Emperor watched the melting of his little army. It was the enforced idleness that demoralised the veterans of the Guard. These men, accustomed to the active life of camps, to improvised marches on a campaign, to the tragic vibration of combat, succumbed to ennui in "the fox's earth," as they dubbed Elba. They would unflinchingly have continued to shed their blood; they flinched from doing nothing.

For pocket-money the troopers and light horse received 1 fr. 16 centimes *per diem;* the Corporals, 1 fr. 66 c., the Sergeants, 2 fr. 22 c.; *plus* their rations. The distractions to be obtained at this cost were mediocre, and they no longer had the looting and other emoluments of life in a hostile country. They amused themselves as best they could, in drinking and getting tipsy, in dancing and flirting with the women of the town. This was harmless enough, even when they scaled the enclosures of San Martino and harvested the Emperor's grapes for him. "They belong to our little Father," said they. "The Emperor and our little Father are one. What belongs to him belongs to us." If the Emperor met them he took them by the ear and laughed. Sometimes, unfortunately, their conduct was scandalous, when they molested the civilians, and incurred military reprimands for breach of discipline. As punishment they were then sent without wages to Pianosa, and put to hard labour for a month or two. If they did not mend their ways they were sent back to the Continent.

These bad characters were, happily, the exception among the Guard, and the thirty or forty vacancies caused by those who departed or were dismissed from the ranks, were filled by the admission of Tyrolese, Piedmontese, Bohemians, Hungarians, and a few Frenchmen who had come to Elba asking to be enrolled. Bearskins alone were wanting.[1]

Indiscipline and desertion were rampant in the Corsican Battalion. All these "cronies" of the Emperor (on pretext that the recruiting officers who enrolled them had promised "ready-roasted quails," and put them off with a bare pittance of 45 centimes a day) turned the island upside down, and streamed over the country-side levying contributions from the peasants, who were obliged to defend themselves with guns and forks. They deserted *en masse*, with their arms and uniform, firing on the officers who pounced on them just as they were embarking, and endeavoured to hold them back. It was necessary to make an example. When five of them were taken in the act of flagrant desertion and revolt, the Emperor commanded them to draw lots for the one who should expiate the fault of all, and that he should be shot. At the last moment the Emperor granted a pardon. He declared that he wished to keep no one by force, that all who preferred to return to their own country were free to go. The disturbances

[1] Peyrusse, 254; Corres. Imp., xxi. 599; Monier, 71; Mém. aux Puiss. All., 84; Reg. de l'I. d'E., 47, 121, 181; Corres. Imp., xxi., 658.

diminished, but desertion still flourished, despite the court-martials and sentences to five years in irons and the dungeons of Fort Falcone.[1]

The Emperor sought fresh recruits in Italy and Corsica to take the place of these deserters. But the recruiting officers were seized and shot by order of Stahremberg and Bruslart. Napoleon sent a protest to Stahremberg, and made Drouot write that he was merely desirous of keeping up the ranks of his army, and was not levying regiments for an attack on Europe. The Austrian Government vouchsafed no reply, and continued to shoot "all the rabble," recruiters and recruited, that fell into its hands.[2]

As to the Elban Battalion, its uniform had ceased to charm. This unmilitary militia was pleased enough to parade on Sundays on the Piazza d'Arme in gold trappings and plumes, but claimed the right of attending to its own affairs and tilling its fields throughout the week. On January 19th, the Emperor decided that the Elban Battalion should be disbanded on the 1st of February.[3]

The most faithful regiment was that of the 109th Polish Lancers, dismounted cavalry for the most part, since their steeds had been transported to Pianosa for lack of forage in the Isle of Elba. These Poles were employed as gunners or stable-helps, wherever they were wanted. They were the

1 Pons de l'H., 341, 342; Reg. de l'I. d'E., 55, 65, 176, 181; March. d'H., 160.

2 Campbell, 121, 127, 128, 145, 164; Peyrusse (Appendix), 35.

3 Corres. Imp., xxi. 669.

first to forgo their pay, which was suspended at the same time as that of the military pensions of the Legion of Honour.[1]

If the Emperor lacked soldiers, he was overdone with officers, who arrived in crowds, French or Italian, discharged as suspects by Austria or the Bourbons, and demanding position and rations in Elba. He kept them, though they were a superfluous drain upon his resources. The emoluments of the Staff, which amounted to 30,000 francs in the last seven months of 1814, rose to 107,000 francs in the Provisory Budget of 1815. Imaginary emoluments, be it said, since the funds were lacking. These officers received fifty francs a month and their rations as maintenance for themselves and for the family who, in many cases, had accompanied them. It was starvation.[2]

"I know not what the future has in store for us," said Bertrand, "but be our fate what it may, it can hardly be worse than what we are now enduring. If we were not borne up by hopes of better days I do not know what would become of us. For my own part, I do not regret having followed the Emperor. My duty made it incumbent on me. But I grieve for France, like a child that has lost its mother, a lover mourning for his mistress." And when he spoke thus his eyes filled with tears.[3]

[1] Reg. de l'I. d'E., 13, 17, 86, 184.
[2] Corres. Imp., xxi. 607; Campbell, 145; Fleury de Chaboulon, 105; Peyrusse, 246, 264.
[3] Fleury de Chaboulon, 117.

One last catastrophe was conceivable, and it duly came about. On the night of January 11–12, Commander Taillade, who cruised about perpetually in the Inconstant in order to obey the Emperor's orders (which took no more account of the resistance of the elements than of that of man), was caught in a sudden squall, and wrecked.

The winter months, in which flights of migratory birds settled to rest their wings upon the snow-covered and misty heights of Monte Giove, loosed a series of incessant tempests upon the shores of Elba, which vented their fury on her rugged cliffs, and dashed the waves against her.

During the night of January 5-6, the Inconstant encountered a gale from the N.E. She was returning from Civita Vecchia, whither she had carried letters and despatches, taking in a load of corn. On making Elba, running before the wind, she had to pass the Island without being able to put in, and was beaten back on Corsica, which she doubled at the northern end, then, flying for safety, took refuge on the western coast, in the Golfe de St. Florent. In these moorings she fell in with one of the frigates of the French Squadron. But this shelter was inadequate. The wind veered round to the Gulf, and completed the disablement of the vessel. It took five days to make good the damage, under Bruslart's surveillance, and almost broadside on with the French frigate, which had also not escaped without damage.

Although the two commanders exchanged visits,

the vicinity of the frigate was disquieting for the brig, whose crew were confined to the ship, with orders on no account to land.

On the 11th the Inconstant put to sea again in fine weather, with a fair breeze from the N.W. Midway to Elba the wind changed suddenly, began to blow, and drove the brig towards Capraia. Taillade, however, succeeded by tacking in approaching Elba, but the night was dark and the sea was running higher every moment when he found himself off Porto Ferraio. He hugged the coast in order to elude the squalls, and passed between the reef of the Scoglietto and the shore, reckoning on a last tack to make the passage, which was indicated in the darkness by the lighthouse. Whether he manœuvred too abruptly, or was too late, the brig refused to go about. There was nothing for it but to lower the sails with all speed and cast anchor, in order to prevent her from crashing on to the rocks on which the waves were breaking round her. The anchors held for part of the night, but the wind grew more and more violent, and the strain became excessive. At 4 A.M., Porto Ferraio, which was sleeping through the hurricane, with doors and windows shut, was awakened with a start by the distress signals of the Inconstant. The populace rushed out of their houses, with torches, and ran to the scene of the disaster. The Emperor was out of bed in a second, and dashed off on horseback. Relief was organised under his direction, and an attempt made to launch boats into the stormy sea.

The raging waves frustrated every endeavour, and it seemed inevitable that the brig must founder with all on board, when Taillade, taking advantage of a moment at which he found himself opposite a little sandy cove, slipped his anchors and ran the vessel aground, saving her by this manœuvre.

The dawn saw a lamentable spectacle. "The Inconstant was cast up on the beach, her masts entangled with the rigging. Her jib seemed to defy the winds, beating them with its tattered ribbons. The waves leapt upon the flanks of the brig, forbidding any approach to her, and threatening to tear her in pieces." An old gentleman, with white hair, was seen on board, who uttered cries of despair and made frantic gesticulations. A lull permitted of some traffic with the ship, and the disembarkation of crew and passengers. The Emperor encouraged the rescue party with voice and gesture. The old gentleman knelt down on the shore, giving thanks to Heaven. He was a blood-relation of the Emperor, a Ramolino, who had retained his post as Director of Finance at Ajaccio despite the changes in the Government. He was coming to pay a visit to Napoleon, and to present him with a horse. But less fortunate than himself, the horse was drowned in leaving the vessel.

The Emperor summoned all available vessels to tow the wreck into port, where she was to be rehabilitated.

The Inconstant was the sole link between Elba

and the mainland, the only vessel that was really equipped on which the Emperor might attempt to escape from his prison with any prospect of success. And it was upon this very ship that he embarked for France a month later—so slender are the threads on which history hangs. If the brig had foundered on a reef, or had been demolished by the gale after her disaster before it became calm enough to get her into port, the Emperor would have been reduced to small boats, which would have been inadequate for the transport of his little fleet, left defenceless in case of attack. What new situations might not have been developed, how different a trend might not have been given to Napoleon's history during the time that must then have elapsed before he could replace the Inconstant, supposing even that Europe permitted this, and did not seize the opportunity of blockading the island. It was observed that the Emperor retired without making any comment on the catastrophe.[1]

Public opinion was hostile to Taillade, who was accused of only going on the bridge in last resort, and of having left a midshipman named Sarri to wrestle with the tempest; and a court martial was expected. The Emperor contented himself with depriving him of his command. He replaced him by one Chautard, a former pilot of the Royal Navy, who had emigrated in 1793, had commanded a naval division on the Lago di Garda in 1798, and

[1] Pons de l'H., 354 ff. ; Reg. de l'I. d'E., pp. 4–5 (note) ; Sellier Vincent, 223 ; March. d'H., 149, 150.

had arrived at Elba from Toulon within the last month. He was a worn-out man, who did not appear particularly capable. But the Emperor had no one else to whom he could give the appointment.[1]

* * * * *

What was the "hope of better days" of which Bertrand spoke?

No one knew, and yet it was in the air. Everyone felt it to be inevitable. The situation was intolerable, and could not possibly continue. Want of funds, disorganisation of the army, perpetual fears of abduction and assassination—nothing could be worse than the prolongation of this existence from day to day. Some definite issue there must be. Everyone was full of it. But what would be its character?

Would Murat come from Naples to receive the Emperor in Tuscany, or would the Emperor rejoin him at Naples, and proclaim himself King of Italy, with his support? The Peninsula, oppressed by Austrian tyranny, was ready to revolt. Milan, Piedmont, a portion of Liguria, Modena, the Legations, the Marches, Venetia, a part of Tuscany, the whole of Romagna, were only awaiting his landing in order to offer him an army of 110,000 men and subsidies. The maritime towns alone, save for some few priests and sexagenarians, were hostile to him. Or would Massena attempt a coup

[1] Pons de l'H., 359; March. d'H., 152.

in his favour, and connive at his direct return to France, "where the ashes were being secretly fanned to rekindle the fire!" where the Revolutionary Party and all the malcontents were calling for the Emperor, and where the majority of the officers had sworn only to draw their swords with the object of replacing him on the Throne? Massena, who was at Toulon with 10,000 men and eighteen battle ships, was reported to have already hoisted the tricolor flag with that of Elba, making his soldiers and marines shout, "*Vive la République! Vive Napoléon!*" The cocked hat of His Majesty, set up on the shore, upon a pole, would suffice to attract the whole of France. Would Marie Louise, whose clandestine correspondence with her husband apparently still continued, deliver him, in spite of Austria, or even with her compliance? The world would soon hear of any "plan" she formed. Or would England, whose acts betrayed her sympathy, facilitate the flight of the Emperor? Commercial matters had caused this avaricious nation to fall out with the Bourbons. Would the Emperor go over to Corsica, which was in a state of revolution, over a hundred soldiers having been killed in a single skirmish—or would it not rather be the Sultan of Turkey, to whom emissaries had been sent at Constantinople, and who was disquieted at the increase of Russia's power, who would inaugurate the war? He would attack the Allies from the rear, while the Emperor would go by Italy and the Rhine to Mayence, and towards Flanders. Whatever the chosen path, the Jews would provide the funds, and would be repaid at exorbitant interest after the Restoration of the Empire.[1]

Such was the gossip in the streets and cafés of Porto Ferraio. In the barracks and guard-houses these things were proclaimed aloud in a Babel of voices and the smoke of many pipes, with emphatic gestures, and banging of fists on tables. All these plans were discussed. Others more extravagant still were suggested. A Marseillais Corporal of the Guard, nicknamed the Scholar, explained to his comrades that the Emperor would make them embark for Malta, so that they might reach Egypt, pick up recruits there, and then effect a landing again in Europe, at the mouth of the Danube: "The Hungarians are waiting till we come, to rise against Austria, for, look you, Austria and Hungary are like fire and water. Good! Our army has swelled, and we go up the Danube. The Polish army has started from Warsaw, and comes to meet us. This army, you know, is the sister of ours. We find us ourselves together beneath the walls of Vienna. Good. Vienna is surrounded, and falls into our hands. Good again. From the Austrian capital to our own . . . we know the way! We could find it with our eyes bandaged. Good. We reach Paris again. The rats have escaped from the Tuileries, and the Parisians cry: '*Vive l'Empereur!*' Good." The start! Every

[1] March. d'H., 111, 112, 118, 120, 123, 130, 132, 133, 135, 136, 144, 146, 147, 148, 149, 155, 159, 161.

conversation came back to that. Each day's delay was a fresh disappointment.[1]

The start? It was only the chief actor concerned who never alluded to it. Nothing in the behaviour, words, or orders of Napoleon, which all referred to defensive precaution, and not to plans for a sortie from the island, and attack, gave ground for supposing that he was thinking of it. Quite the contrary. He insisted with all his might on not thinking of it, repeating "The Emperor is dead. I am a dead man. I am worth nothing now!" "They may spy out the land," he said to Campbell, "intercept my correspondence, arrest and interrogate whomsoever they suspect, they will find nothing against me. As regards Murat, he acts only in concert with Austria. He would be a fool to do otherwise, for he would infallibly court disaster. They may assassinate me. I shall uncover my breast to receive the blow." To the Italian patriots who sounded him, he replied or made others reply that "he wanted no conspiracies." He took them to San Martino, made them admire his six milch cows and the two calves, and read them the inscription in the Salle des Pyramides, "Napoleon finds happiness everywhere." At Porto Longone, he showed them his belvedere overhanging the waves, like some hermit cell, which the country-folk had dubbed "The Retreat of Socrates."

What did the French people want of him? "They have another sovereign. Their duty now

[1] Pons de l'H., 369; March. d'H., 145.

is to think only of him." And when letters came expatiating on the situation in the country, and the desire of his former subjects to resume relations with him, the Emperor read them aloud to all, exclaiming, "If they love me so dearly, let them come and fetch me."[1]

The spring was close at hand. Napoleon gave orders to resume the work on the roads of the island, and in San Martino, which had been interrupted by the winter. He set grass-plots in front of the barracks, and planted 600 mulberry trees along the road to San Martino and that to Fort Falcone, "which will in a few years facilitate the cultivation of the silkworm." He studied botany with a herbarium under his arm, and became an enthusiast over agricultural works. His bedside book was *La Maison Rustique*. Combining practice with theory, he roamed over the island with his escort, bestriding a mule and holding forth to the peasants on "cabbages, turnips, and onions." He taught how they ought to set about having good radishes and good salad. He was not above putting his own hand to the plough, and learning to trace a furrow. When he went into the cottages he praised up a vegetable unknown in the island—a tuber, which he called *parmentière*, and which we know as the potato.[2]

[1] Campbell, 93, 151, 172, 184, 209; Larabit, 64; Peyrusse (Appendix), 144; Gen. Durand, 253; Fleury de Chaboulon, 105; March. d'H., 134; Pons de l'H., 351.

[2] Reg. de l'I. d'E., 163; March. d'Huiles, 152; *Ile d'Elbe et Cent Jours*, 12; Pons de l'H., 280, 290, 291. The following inscription may be read upon the villa of Mario Foresi, at Ancona, not far from

THE CURTAIN OF THE THEATRE AT PORTO FERRAIO: NAPOLEON, UNDER THE GUISE OF APOLLO, WATCHING HIS SHEEP.

Now that Pianosa was capable of defence, he fell back on his grand schemes in regard to this islet of some twelve and a half miles in circumference. The programme of colonisation included:

"The reconstitution of a vineyard and the cultivation of olives.

"The planting of mulberry trees wherever practicable, making it obligatory on the proprietors to use them to delimitate the boundaries of their properties.

"Fruit trees, as many as possible, particularly stone fruits and red fruits.

"Preference for wheat fields.

"The breeding of a race of horses.

"A public institution for the training of domestic animals.

"Absolute prohibition against introducing dangerous beasts to the island.[1]

"Ewes and sheep.

"Fir plantations, and the planting of an oak forest, the acorns to be brought from the Black Forest."

Lastly, a portion of the island was to be consecrated to a pious object.

It was to be a national endowment, a retreat for

Cape Stella (the original being in Italian): "Napoleon—passing by, in MDCCCXIV—took the plough from a peasant, in a neighbouring field—and tried to guide it—but the oxen rebelled against the hands—which had bridled Europe—and broke away from the furrow." Charlet's drawing of "the Emperor at the plough" represents a similar scene at St. Helena (*see* Memorial, December 30, 1815).

[1] Pons de l'H., 305. In "dangerous beasts," the Emperor doubtless alluded to badgers and foxes, also goats, on account of the mischief done by their depredations.

Elbans grown old in their country's service, who would end their days, like the Emperor himself, at San Martino, amid the delights of gardening.[1]

A sergeant, a carabineer, a trooper, and a Polish lancer each applied for a concession in Pianosa, which was granted them. Those veterans who preferred to have property in Elba and had not been included in previous distributions, received an allotment near Porto Ferraio. The Emperor encouraged them in the cultivation of flowers and vegetables. These donations were made to the officers *in perpetuo*, so that the owners might rest assured that the works they were engaged on would "be to the advantage of themselves and their children."[2]

In order to create a diversion and to enjoy the pleasures of sport without fatigue, the Emperor enclosed Cape Stella with a stone wall and ditch, and ordered that all the hares and rabbits in the island should be driven into this enclosure. "Three pointers, as many for badger drawing in the mountains of the island, and six hounds, will with a whip and two or three horns represent the hunting equipage."[3] In order to keep up this pack, and the park and equipment, a supplement of 100 francs per month was added to the budget of 1815. Napoleon was also negotiating for the purchase of

1 Pons de l'H., 306.

2 Reg. de l'I. d'E., 181 ; Corres. Imp., xxi. 610, 650 ; Labadie, 54 ; Pons de l'H., 380.

3 Corres. Imp., xxi. 640, 668 ; Reg. de l'I. d'E., 78 ; Pons de l'H., 247 ; Labadie, 52. Cape Stella is situated on the south side of the island, between Capoliveri and Campo. It is a narrow neck of land about 1½ mile long and half a mile wide.

a movable wooden house, containing five rooms, which could be put up in two hours and taken down in one, and which had just been brought to Porto Ferraio by an engineer from Lyons. The Emperor proposed to camp out in this portable abode, on the pointed peaks of Volterraio, or any other part of the island to which his fancy led him.[1]

None of the more serious-minded, therefore, were carried away by the tide of popular imagination, which set in the direction of an immediate departure from Elba. Neither Bertrand nor Drouot believed this departure to be probable or even possible. Drouot, encouraged by the Emperor, was proposing to wed an Elban maiden, who was in love with his glory and his fine qualities. Other marriages were about to be arranged.[2]

Nor did the Emperor's gaolers, the spies who dogged his actions, know what to make of him. They were bewildered by what they saw, and understood nothing. At times Campbell was afraid, at times he felt reassured. The more carefully he considered the Emperor, the more did he regard him as one who had come down to the common level of mankind, and the less did Napoleon appear to him under a favourable aspect.

At some moments the Emperor seemed to be "perfectly resigned." The understanding with Murat was surely a fable: the whole scare had originated in the old guns and worn-out pieces of

[1] Pons de l'H., 288 ; March. d'H., 154.
[2] Reg. de l'I. d'E., 118, 139 ; Pons de l'H., 171, 174.

artillery which the Emperor had put on board ship, in order to sell them at Civita Vecchia. The Marchand d'Huiles, for his part, writes: "Many things give an aspect of veracity to the news of an approaching departure. Nevertheless, the works recently undertaken in the island, and the plantations commenced by the soldiers and officers of the Guard on the land allotted them by the Emperor, should be taken into consideration. Judging by this sight, there is more of installation than of departure in the wind." How could any one suppose that this model gardener, planting his acorns, did not consider himself the guest in perpetuity of the Island of Elba? All he desired was to be left in peace to shear his sheep and shoot his rabbits. And when the Emperor declared to Campbell, looking him straight in the face, that he knew he had been summoned, that there was growing discontent in Europe . . . . in Italy and Germany, where Würtemberg and Bavaria could no longer dissimulate their uneasiness; that in France, Louis XVIII and his ministers had misunderstood the national character ("I am informed by correspondents from the Capital that the French are greatly resenting their present humiliation; the Bourbon Party are few in number, and nothing but a war could save them, by rallying the army; they are afraid of a Revolution originating with the émigrés, hence a new 'Reign of Terror'! It is a torrent of opinion that will carry all before it"); when he asked Drouot in public,

"What do you think about it, Drouot? Would it be too soon to start during the Carnival? Drouot and Campbell took his words for bravado, too audacious to be genuine.[1]

*   *   *   *   *

The inauguration of the Théâtre de l'Académie, which was completed in three months, coincided at Porto Ferraio with the beginning of the Carnival. The centre box was reserved for the Emperor, who was depicted on the curtain as Apollo banished from Heaven, keeping the flocks of Admetus, and giving instruction to the shepherds. A thunder of applause saluted this touching allegory. The arch was adorned with a painting set in a medallion of Fortuna in a chariot. The chariot was the Isle of Elba, and Fortuna symbolised the "hero of the century," bringing prosperity to the island. The comedians had arrived at the appointed time—a troupe of *cabotins*, "not first class, nor even second." To be too exacting would however, have been in bad taste, and his Majesty gave the signal to applaud.

After the performance there was a fancy ball which lasted till seven next morning. Pauline appeared as a Neapolitan, and at the next dance (for the gaieties increased) she figured as a shepherdess from the Isle of Procida. An emporium of the latest fashions was opened in the town. Never had there been such gaiety. The Théâtre

[1] Campbell, 111, 161, 171, 185, 198, 203; March. d'H., 120, 159.

du Palais was finally organised, and painted with frescoes by the Emperor's orders.[1]

Threats of assassination, nevertheless, were frequent. When the Inconstant was in danger of shipwreck, the midshipman Sarri flung a letter into the sea, wrapped up in tarpaulin, which had been entrusted to him in Corsica, warning the Emperor to keep up his guard against Bruslart. Another note, addressed to the Chief Justice Poggi, advised him that a magistrate, whom the Emperor had deprived of his office two or three years before, was coming to Elba to revenge himself. Detailed particulars were given. The individual in question landed in Elba, and was immediately shadowed. It was supposed that he would carry out his nefarious scheme during the performance at the theatre. Long before the curtain went up the Hall was filled with the adherents of the Emperor. The military were armed to the teeth. The civil functionaries stuffed their pockets full of pistols and daggers. The assassin took his seat beside the Administrator of Mines, a former acquaintance. "Then," says Pons, "all eyes were turned upon us. Commander Mallet darted fiery glances at me. They signified, 'do not miss . . . . strike the instant he makes a movement," the Emperor did not appear at the Play, and the catastrophe was

[1] Laborde, 41; Pons de l'H., 243, 246; Labadie, 54; Corres. Imp., xxi. 665. The theatre of Porto Ferraio still exists, with the two frescoes, the curtain, and the arch. It comprises four tiers of boxes and a gallery, and holds nearly 1,000 spectators. The "Société de l'Académie" are still the proprietors of it.

averted. This denunciation was an infamous affair, which originated in a private quarrel, a vendetta between the incriminated magistrate and the accuser. The alarm had been keen, and it left a painful impression.[1]

None the less it was politic to let things run their course, to pursue diversion although unknown catastrophes might be stalking in the shadows, to practise a fatalism that constrains to present enjoyment of life, since the morrow may bring death; and the pass-word was, to shake care off.

At the once austere soirées of the Mulini, the wife of a Polish officer danced fandangoes to the accompaniment of castanets, while Cambronne, scarlet, and mopping his forehead, capered about with Pauline, enjoying the close proximity of the beautiful sister of the Emperor.

The Emperor proposed to add operatic representations to the comedies of the Théâtre de l'Académie. On February 3rd, he writes to Bertrand on the subject: "The expenses will amount to 40,000 francs a year, I will give a subsidy of 12,000 francs. An Italian company demands 12,000 francs for three months. This is very dear. If engaged by the year, one could doubtless have it for 36,000 francs. Another company asks 5,600 francs a month. You will offer 2,600 francs, or even 2,000 francs without orchestra. The memorandum only includes four men. Four men do not make a company. There must be women as well.

[1] Reg. de l'I. d'E., pp. 4–5 (Note); Pons de l'H., 162.

See that all this is plain." The orchestra was to be provided by the twenty musicians of the Guard, whose clarinets, horns, and flutes would play the accompaniment to the trills of Clorinda or Armida. A seat for this remarkable performance was to cost ten sous by subscription. Porto Ferraio bid fair to become "a second Capua."[1]

On the last days of the Carnival, Ash Wednesday, February 8, an extraordinary masquerade appeared in the streets of Porto Ferraio. The procession was headed by Commander Mallet, dressed as a Sultan in the cachemires of Pauline Borghese . . . as proud as Artaban, and riding the famous white charger of the Emperor, itself a demi-god of yesterday. With Commandant Mallet rode Captain Schultz, who represented Don Quixote to the life, since he was five feet nine inches in height and as thin as his steed, "which was the sorriest jade in the island." The entire staff followed, "clad in many other splendid costumes," while the tipsy Guards applauded from the doors of the drinking-booths.[2]

This affair was the last straw, the climax of the pitiful and grotesque. It was also, declared the

[1] Pons de l'H., 155 ; Mém. aux Puiss. All., 105 ; Corres. Imp., xxi. 671. The figures of the correspondence are erroneous. They should read, not 1,900 francs, but 1,000 francs, monthly subscription : *i.e.*, 12,000 francs per annum, or for each of the sixty-six boxes of the theatre 50 centimes a day. In addition to this, the receipts from the gallery were returned at 44 francs each evening.

[2] Pons de l'H., 244. As we have pointed out (p. 90), the Emperor's white charger represented two horses, Tauris and Intendant, or "Coco." It is evidently the latter, which did parade duty, that is alluded to here.

army of police spies, the acme of corruption and profligacy. They proclaimed the Emperor, "devoured by secret maladies," to be the incestuous lover of his sister Pauline, ever ready to yield herself, and the adorer of her brother. Submerged in these debauches, Napoleon was no more than a wreck of humanity, incapable of terrifying a child.[1]

The Bourbon journals and the libellists in the pay of the Bourbon Government seized triumphantly upon this intelligence. They invariably referred to "the man called Napoleon," "the parvenu of Ajaccio," as "an adventurer who had at one time been the oppressor of France, a charlatan who counterfeited Mohammed, and whose many victories had not been able to save him from disaster." Now "they likened him to the King of Haiti, who reigns over monkeys and negroes," and regales himself in his anthropophagistic paroxysms with the flesh of his own subjects. In order to allay the fears of the public, they added that the ocean round the rock on which this wretched and "rotten" creature dragged out his doomed existence was covered with French and English vessels that kept an eye on his every action, and would not allow a single boat to pass their cordon. The emissaries he attempted to send to the Continent were arrested and "shut up in walled

[1] Hérisson: *Cabinet Noir*, 131; Waldbourg-Truchsess, 34; Letter from Caroline to Cardinal Fesch, *Nouvelle Revue Rétrospective*, II., 150. There was a mania for providing Pauline with lovers. Even Drouot was assigned to her (St. Helena Memorial, March 11, 1816), and people vowed she had been met at Leghorn, on amorous expeditions, dressed up in man's clothes! (Report of Spies, quoted by M. Pellet, 68).

prisons." Opposite the sumptuous portraits of "the Glorious King of France," beneath which was inscribed the legend "God created Louis XVIII and then rested from his labours," caricatures were fastened up in the windows of the book shops, showing the "pursy Sovereign of the Isle of Mines" surrounded by cripples and hunchbacks, decreeing "mass-levies of thirty men," or wandering on the shore in the costume of Robinson Crusoe, with a fur cap on his head, a parasol in his hand, and his feathered eagle on his shoulder instead of a parrot.[1]

Talleyrand, who knew his former master, and was aware that he had more than one card up his sleeve, shook his head at these stories, and insisted that "the Man in the Island of Elba must be put out of the way." "Later on!" was all the answer he received. If he pressed the point, he was accused of pretensions to sharper sight than his colleagues, or charged with being in confidential relations with the Emperor, and asked if he were not "mixed up in this devil's play." In vain did Fouché, whose advice was asked by no one, write to the Comte d'Artois that Napoleon in the Isle of Elba was to France and Europe "what Vesuvius was to Naples." In vain did Hyde de Neuville protest that "even dead, the Emperor would be alarming," and propose to transport the Monarch of Elba to

[1] Journal des Débats, December 4, 13, 30, 1814, and *passim*; Fleury de Chaboulon, 101 (Note); Chautard, 87; March. d'H., 150; various pamphlets, *Constitution donnée par Buonaparte aux habitants de l'Isle d'Elbe*, *Robinson dans son Ile*, &c.; engravings.

America, to some asylum worthier of him, in hopes that he might there rest quiet; in vain did he asseverate that Napoleon's protests about Marie Louise and the King of Rome were only framed to cheat the public, and that in reality he had no desire to be hampered with the presence of his wife and son beside him. He was treated as a visionary, and assured that the Corsican squadron would be on the spot in any emergency.

On February 16, the Emperor audited the Army Estimates for the past year, and gave orders that the current budget should be drawn up.

On February 19 he opened a credit account of 40,000 francs for the roads and bridges, "which sum may be expended in the months of March, April, May, June, and July at 8,000 francs a month." He busied himself over his villeggiatura in the coming summer at Monte Giove, making improved arrangements at La Madonna, and increasing his Guard. A portion of the Court were to accompany him, and to live at Marciana Alta. "Monsieur le Comte de Bertrand, since it is my intention to go towards the middle of June or beginning of July to Marciana, it will be necessary to begin operations in the month of April, and to decide on the houses that can be occupied by Madame, Princess Pauline, Comtesse Bertrand, and Comte Drouot. A Commission will be appointed to select these houses, and hire them for the months of July, August, and September. You will draw up a list of desirable alterations. I shall live at the Hermitage. Enlarge the room that makes my study. Remove the kitchen to the other side of the chapel. A wooden shed will serve the purpose. I require a house for my suite, another for my stable, and another for the Guard, as I cannot do with less than fifty men. Get an estimate for all this."[1]

On February 21 he went to see the portable house, which was being publicly exhibited by its inventor. Napoleon examined it in detail, bargained over it, and had the mechanism explained to him.

On February 22 he busied himself with the accounts of the salt mines, and organised their direct administration by the State in future. He commanded contracts for the making of a road along the shore to Porto Longone, at a maximal cost of 2,500 francs. "There will have to be three small bridges near Capoliveri."[2]

Campbell had been absent from Elba since the 16th. He was feeling very uneasy. On the 15th he indited an alarming despatch to Lord Castlereagh, but hesitated to send it for fear of being laughed at. Moreover, Castlereagh had desired him to avoid "all superfluous expenses, and only to send off special couriers in case of urgency, when really worth while." Accordingly he betook himself to Leghorn, in H.M.S. Partridge, and thence to Florence to exchange ideas, as was his custom, with the Austrian Minister. At Florence he met

[1] Corres. Imp., xxi. 673, 676, 677.

[2] March. d'H., 159; Reg. de l'I. d'E., 183; Corres. Imp., xxi. 678.

SIGNORINA SQUARCI, IN WHITE SATIN GOWN WORN BY HER ANCESTRESS AT NAPOLEON'S COURT.

the English Under-Secretary of State, Mr. Cooke, who had just come from the Congress of Vienna, and confided to him the object of his journey—his uneasiness on the subject of the Emperor, and uncertainty as to the forwarding of his despatch to Lord Castlereagh. He took the document from his pocket and read it. The Under-Secretary ridiculed his fears, and replied sarcastically, "when you return to Elba, you may tell Bonaparte that he is quite forgotten in Europe; no one thinks of him now." And on another occasion, "*Nobody thinks of him at all. He is quite forgotten—as much as if he had never existed.*"

"I did," continues Campbell, "feel very uneasy at the position of Napoleon, and the seeming inconsistencies of his conduct; but after Mr. Cooke's remarks I began to feel that my near view of him and of the state of Elba had induced me to exaggerate circumstances."[1]

He stayed another week at Florence and Livorno. When, on February 28, he returned to the Island of Elba, Napoleon was there no longer.

* * * * *

The Fox had triumphed. The Lion, feeling his weakness, had assumed the fox's skin, and as the trapped wild animal follows the cord that drags it quietly enough till the moment the sportsman is off his guard, when with a sudden movement it makes away, so the Emperor, in pretending to yield, had cheated everyone, and outwitted Europe.

[1] Campbell, *Napoleon at Fontainebleau et Elba*, pp. 362, 363.

The first order relative to departure was in January, if the memory of the man to whom it was given was accurate. The saddler, Vincent, received orders in the course of that month to take to pieces two gilded berlines which had come from Fontainebleau with the Guard, and to pack them off "to Rome." He did as he was ordered, and deposited them, ready packed, after numbering each piece, in the warehouses of the Port, ready to be sent away. As these two carriages were not in daily use, the matter passed unnoticed. Vincent himself attached no importance to it.[1]

Next, the Mameluke Ali brought Pons a confidential letter from the Emperor, asking him to draw up a report on the "possibility of organising an expeditionary flotilla." "An expeditionary flotilla! That was as much as to say 'I am off!' I drew up the report, and His Majesty appealed to my Republican virtue to keep the matter absolutely secret." This first plan was not carried out.[2]

In the early days of February, the Treasurer, Peyrusse, was advised that he must transfer his

[1] Sellier Vincent, 369.

[2] Pons de l'H., 193, 373, 374; Mém. aux Puiss. All., 95, 109 (note). "I confided in no one but Pons, and that because his co-operation was indispensable in preparing the transports which were so necessary to my scheme," the Emperor said to Montholon (*Captivité de Sainte Hélène*, II., 195). This first conversation between the Emperor and Pons about departure, the date of which is not given by Pons, appears to have been held in January. Obviously it must have been connected with the order given to the saddler Vincent to pack up the carriages, and the shipwreck of the Inconstant, which took place in the same month. It is impossible to say whether the wreck interrupted the Emperor's projects, or whether it preceded the above order, and convinced Napoleon that it was time to escape, lest further catastrophes should befall him.

coffers to Fort Stella, which overlooked the straits, and whence in case of blockade, sudden attack, or hurried flight, it is possible to embark, by clambering down the face of the cliff, without passing the port or going through the town. "I knew enough," said Peyrusse, "to guess the motives of this move. I secretly laid in some provision of flour, wine, potatoes and salt beef, and awaited events."[1]

On February 16, the day that Campbell left for Florence, the Emperor, at the very moment of ordering the Army Estimates for 1815 to be prepared, wrote to Drouot: "Give orders for the brig to be careened, overhaul her copper, stop the leaks, see to the caulking, and do whatever is required to make her seaworthy. Let her be painted like an English brig. See that she is fully munitioned—victual her with biscuit, rice, vegetables, cheese, half supplies of wine, and half of brandy, water for 120 men for three months, salt meat for fifteen days. For the sake of economy the wine can be taken from my cellar. See to all these details and let her be ready to sail by the 24th or 25th of this month. Give me the estimate for all this to-morrow. Let me know how many boats the brig can carry. I wish to take as many as possible." The first part of this order, referring to the careening and general repair of the brig, was necessitated by the bad condition of the Inconstant. She had been severely damaged by the shipwreck, and was still leaking, although she had been put to rights, and handled as

[1] Peyrusse, 268.

carefully as possible, after the catastrophe. The operations referred to would not surprise Drouot, nor any one else concerned. The second half of the letter, commanding her to be painted like an English brig, provisioned for three months, and provided with boats in excess of the regulation number, was more mysterious. Drouot evidently understood that there was something in the wind, but since the Emperor gave no explanation it was not his business to ask for one. Two days later, February 18, the ship's carpenters and caulkers began operations on the brig, which had been beached for the purpose.[1]

On the same day, February 16, the Emperor ordered Pons to charter two large transport ships from Rio, "brigs or xebecs to be over 90 ton, the largest possible," and to bring them to Porto Ferraio, one with a cargo of timber from the base of Monte Giove, the other with all available ammunition from the citadel of Porto Longone. Pons, to whom Drouot transmitted the order, at once grasped that it had to do with the Emperor's departure, and the plan was this time put into execution.[2]

[1] Corres. Imp., xxi. 674; Pons de l'H., 361; Marchand d'H., 153, 158.

[2] Corres. Imp., xxi. 675; *Ile d'Elbe et Cent Jours*, 35; Mém. aux Puiss. All., 109. It was from the Rio side of Monte Giove, not from Marciana, that Pons was to take the timber. Wood was formerly carried by all vessels on active service. It was used for general repairs and for stopping of leaks on the vessel or the boats she carried. Timber still forms part of a ship's outfit, but is much less used owing to the predominance of steel or iron. It was also employed for rafts in case of shipwreck, and on battleships for the landing of troops.

On the 20th, a polacca from Marseilles, the Saint Esprit, carrying 200 tons, and crossing from Genoa to Naples, anchored at Porto Ferraio to shelter from a gale. She took on board "for Naples" the two berlines that had been packed up in January, the café-au-lait landau, cases of plate, and various packages.[1]

On the 21st, while the Emperor was looking at the portable house and Pauline was disporting herself on the Gulf with Madame Mère, in a gondola, the quartermasters gave out complete uniforms to the company, and two pair of shoes to each soldier.[2]

On the 22nd, the order was given to withdraw the horses of the Polish Cavalry from Pianosa. The Inconstant, now at sea again, and the Emperor's xebec L'Etoile, were cautiously loaded up with cases of cartridges, bales of stores, and different kinds of provisions. All this was done in the night.[3]

During the day the Emperor went to see Peyrusse. He entered unannounced, and walked to the window which looked on to the Guards' Barracks. He contemplated the plantations which the soldiers were making, the flower-beds they were laying out, and declared his satisfaction at seeing a

[1] Marchand d'H., 156, 159; *Ile d'Elbe et Cent Jours*, 35; Sellier Vincent, 370; Peyrusse, 271. This was the pinque or polacca of which Peyrusse, evidently making a mistake, announces the arrival on the night of the 24–25th. These vessels were large trading-boats, with two or three masts and lateen sails, and could be propelled by rowing. The transports Pons sent from Rio were feluccas.

[2] March. d'H., 158, 159.

[3] March. d'H., 160.

taste for horticulture developing in all these worthy fellows. Intendant Balbiani was in the room. He felt that his presence inconvenienced the Emperor, but did not dare withdraw, lest he should commit some breach of etiquette. The Emperor went out, and Peyrusse was shortly after summoned to the Mulini. The door of the Imperial Cabinet closed upon him. "Well! Peyrusse," the Emperor began, "What are they saying of us? What was the Intendant talking to you about?" "Sire, at the moment you did me the honour to call, we were discussing the rumours that are circulating in the town to the effect that your Majesty intends to join the King of Naples." "You are a couple of idiots." And walking up to his treasurer, he tapped him on the cheek: "Have you much money in hand, Peyrusse? What does a million in gold weigh? What do 100,000 francs weigh? What does a trunk of books weigh? Get hold of some trunks. Put the gold in, and some of the books from my library on the top. Send all your people away, do the packing yourself. Strap up your trunks. Be lavish with your cash. *Payez. . . . Mais ne payez pas. . . .* I need hardly tell you all this is confidential."

Peyrusse was astounded at this conversation, at the end of which the Emperor dismissed him without adding another word, and went to look for Drouot. Drouot was gloomy. "I tried to sound him as to our future destination. He stared at me, and kept his counsel." Peyrusse set to work to pack up the 1,863,500 francs remaining in his coffers.[1]

Even if Drouot had not been formally advised of his plans by the Emperor, he could have had no doubt about the departure, the more so as the embarkation of ammunition went on under his orders. He summoned the saddler, Vincent, and inquired if his saddles were in order. On receiving an affirmative answer, he bade him supply a saddle-cloth, straps for a portmanteau, and a portfolio case, "so that," as he said, "he might go to Marciana, to work with the Emperor, and draw up plans."[2]

On the 23rd, the provisions from the Continent and interior of the island arrived at Porto Ferraio. They were at once put on board the xebec and brig, along with the casks of fresh water.[3]

The preparations had reached this point when, on the 24th, at 10 A.M., the English sloop which had taken Campbell to Livorno a week before, and was to await him there to bring him back to Elba, appeared upon the horizon. A general alarm ensued. Would it be necessary to precipitate

[1] Peyrusse, 269, 334 (*Compte en Caisse*, Feb. 22). In addition to this sum, 387,880f. 87c. were left behind in running accounts, private and public, in the Island of Elba, at Rome, and Genoa.

[2] Sellier Vincent, 369.

[3] March. d'H., 161. We have seen that Napoleon had ordered the provisioning to be for "120 men during three months." In reality he was conveying not 120 men, but over 1,000, so that the provisions would barely suffice for ten days, and it was necessary to prepare for such contingencies as pursuit by the French squadron or by English vessels, when the Emperor would have been forced to run back to safety in Italy or Corsica.

events, to seize the enemy's ship, by force or strategy, and make the whole company prisoners, including Campbell, if he were on board? A terrible fight, with uncertain issues, a sure *casus belli* with England, seemed imminent. All suspicious movements in the Port were interdicted.

Campbell was not on the sloop. She brought six English tourists, whom Captain Adye escorted to the Mulini by the circuitous road along the edge of the ramparts, so as not to be discovered in this errand. After an hour's cordial talk with the Emperor, he went to see Marshal Bertrand, who made inquiries about Campbell and the exact date of his return, and then went back to the Port. He stopped to watch the soldiers of the Guard, who were "all busy in carrying earth and in planting trees in front of their barracks," after which the Captain rejoined his vessel, sailing with her in the course of the afternoon. Hardly had he reached the open, watched by the telescopes of the Fort, and by a little boat that followed in his wake on pretence of fishing, than Napoleon resumed his embarkation of artillery, shells, and provisions.[1]

Then came another *contretemps.* The Emperor sent a courier to Rio Marina, warning Pons that if the two transports which he was bringing to Porto Ferraio with ammunition from Porto Longone and timber from Monte Giove had completed their loading, he was not to sail till the morrow, for fear

1 Campbell, 227; Peyrusse, 271; March. d'H., 162. The shells were taken in case of an encounter during the voyage with another battleship.

of encountering the English vessel. The messenger arrived at the very moment when the transports had started. The sloop, which was concealed from them by the mountain, would meet them face to face, since she was making for Palmaiola.

To turn round and go back to Porto Longone or to Rio was no longer possible without arousing the suspicions of "the British Argus." Pons took another course. He wrote to Campbell, whom he, too, supposed to be on the sloop, "inviting him to a dinner he intended to give the following week." A shrewd man was despatched in a boat with the letter. He was received by Captain Adye, who promised to transmit it to Campbell, and thanked the writer in his name. He asked where the two transports were going, and what they contained? The question had been anticipated. The messenger replied that they were filled with minerals for the Romagna. The sloop continued her route, and wanted to put in at Palmaiola, but the authorities declared that this was contrary to regulations, so she proceeded to Livorno. The boats from Rio entered Porto Ferraio in the evening.[1] The Emperor still kept his own counsel. The Veterans, who had been re-formed into four companies, were firmly persuaded that he only intended at this juncture to "exercise them in the island," and that if they were going "it would be in a month's time."

[1] Pons de l'H., 380; Campbell, 228; Peyrusse, 271; *Isle d'Elbe et Cent Jours*, 35.

On the 25th the camping utensils were put together, the pouches of the soldiers were replenished with cartridges, the Corsican Battalion were drilled and sent to their barracks, to prevent any possibility of desertion. Commandant Mallet, at Fort Falcone, kept watch over the sea, to make sure that the English sloop did not return. An embargo was put upon the island.

The Emperor, feigning indisposition, did not appear during that day. He wished to avoid inconvenient questions. Porto Ferraio was growing excited. In the evening he received a delegation of the Corps Constitués in audience, who represented to him the sorrow and joy alike felt by his subjects, in seeing that he was about to abandon them "to tread again the path of glory." He thanked the delegates for their expression of sentiment, and contented himself with vague generalities.[1] His mother alone received his confidence.

After dinner he was playing cards with her and Pauline at the Mulini, and seemed in unusually good spirits. Suddenly he broke off the game and left the room. As he did not return Madame Mère got up, went to the door, and called him. The chamberlain told her the Emperor had gone down into the garden. She followed him.

The moon shone brightly between the trees, and Napoleon was walking rapidly up and down the paths, the gravel crackling under his feet. He stopped, and leaning his head against a fig-tree,

[1] Pons de l'H., 381 ; March. d'H., 163, 164, 165.

exclaimed, "But I must tell my mother!" At these words she came forward, and asked eagerly what was disturbing him. "Yes, *ma mère*, you have a right to know," he replied, after some real or feigned hesitation. "But I forbid you to repeat my words to anyone whomsoever, not even to Pauline. I am leaving to-morrow night." "And where are you going?" "To Paris. What do you think of that?" With a smile he kissed the heroic woman who had endured so much for him with such bitter anguish, while she bade him let her reflect a moment so that she might forget that she was a mother, and suppress all signs of weakness. "If you must die, my son," she said at length, "I trust that heaven, who would not sanction this in a repose unworthy of you, will suffer it to be not by poison, but with your sword in your hand." And that was all.[1]

The Emperor busied himself part of the night in drawing up and printing three proclamations, to be ready for the hour of his landing in France. Two were in his own name to the People and the Army; the third was to be signed by the Guard during the voyage, and circulated as a spontaneous manifesto to their brothers-in-arms, the Generals, Officers and soldiers of the Grand Army.[2]

[1] Account given by Madame Mère to Mlle. Rosa Mellini, lady-in-waiting, quoted by Larrey, II., 531.

[2] "Français, la défection du duc de Castiglione livra Lyon sans défense à nos ennemis. L'armée dont je lui avais confié le commandement était, par le nombre de ses bataillons, la bravoure et le patriotisme des troupes qui la composaient, à même de battre le corps d'armée autrichien qui lui était opposé. La trahison du duc de

On the next morning, the 26th, a Sunday, at the customary reception during the Emperor's levée, he spoke.

The civil and military authorities, down to the adjutants, were invited by Bertrand to present themselves at the Mulini. All etiquette was

Raguse livra la capitale. . . . Français, dons mon exil j'ai entendu vos plaintes et vos vœux. J'ai traversé les mers au milieu de périls de toute espèce. J'arrive parmi vous, reprendre mes droits qui sont les vôtres. . . ."—"Soldats, nous n'avons pas été vaincus. Deux hommes sortis de nos rangs ont trahi nos lauriers, leur pays, leur prince, leur bienfaiteur. . . . Reprenez ces aigles que vous aviez à Ulm, à Austerlitz, à Jena, à Eylau, à Friedland, à Eckmühl, à Essling, à Wagram, à Lützen, à Smolensk, à la Moskova, à Montmirail ! La victoire marchera au pas de charge. . . ."—"Soldats, camarades, nous vous avons conservé votre Empereur. Nous vous le ramenons au milieu de mille dangers. Foulez aux pieds la cocarde blanche, elle est le signe de la honte. . . ."

Translation.—"Frenchmen, the defection of the Duke de Castiglione delivered Lyons defenceless to our enemies. The army which I had entrusted to his command was in a position, from the number of its battalions, and the courage and patriotism of its troops, to defeat the Austrian corps d'armée that confronted it. The treachery of the Duke of Ragusa betrayed the capital. . . . Frenchmen, from my exile I have heard your laments and prayers. I have crossed the seas in the face of innumerable perils. I have appeared among you, to take up my rights, which are yours also. . . ."—"Soldiers, we have not been beaten. Two men from our own ranks betrayed our laurels, their country, their prince and benefactor. . . . Take up the standards you had at Ulm, at Austerlitz, at Jena, at Eylau, at Friedland, at Eckmühl, at Essling, at Wagram, at Lützen, at Smolensk, at the Moskva, at Montmirail ! Victory will follow your charge. . . ."—"Soldiers, comrades, we have guarded the Emperor for you. We bring him back in the midst of a thousand perils. Trample the white cockade under your feet. It is the badge of shame."

These fiery proclamations, in which the Emperor recapitulated events antecedent to his leaving France, and in which, letting his ideas outrun his acts, he announced that "he had crossed the seas," are dated March 1, 1815, Golfe Jouan, in the *Corr. Imp.*; and the Emperor denied that they were printed at Porto Ferraio (*Ile d'Elbe et Cent Jours*, 40). But they are to be found in the *Arch. Etrangères* with this note : "Porto Ferraio, Broglio, Government Printer" (Houssaye, *1815*, 192, 206). The torn scraps of paper found in Napoleon's room after his departure were in all probability the rough notes for these proclamations (*see* p. 234).

suspended. Even those who were usually refused the entrée found free admission on this occasion. The Emperor came in. He was transformed. It might have been his first appearance. His expression was grave but composed, his moving words penetrated to all hearts. A slight indication of fatigue betrayed that he had kept a long vigil. According to his custom on these occasions he began by trivial questions, then, without further preamble, announced that he was departing that very night. A thunderbolt would not have been more startling. The Emperor returned to his apartments, the crowd dispersed, and there was a general cry: "The Emperor is leaving!" Whither was he going? Would he reconquer Europe with an army of 673 men? He maintained the profoundest mystery as to his destination.[1]

At nine o'clock mass was said as usual. At 11 a boat put in under Fort Stella to land a special messenger who went up at once to the Mulini, bringing, doubtless, the latest information as to the

[1] Pons de l'H., 382; Labadie, 56. This total of 673 men given by Pons appears to be that of the Old Guard, soldiers, officers, and Imperial Staff. To these must be added 108 Polish Lancers, 300 Corsicans and Elban volunteers, and 50 gendarmes, besides civilians. This gives about 1,150 as the total of the army. Many of the Corsicans deserted at the last moment. Some gunners, including a few Poles, were left in the forts to keep up the embargo on the island and defend the exit (Campbell, *Napoleon at Fontainebleau and Elba*, 383; March. d'H., 167, 168, 170; *Moniteur*, March 23, 1815). According to the *Moniteur*, the Emperor reduced the number of the Guard to 400, the official figure according to the Treaty of Fontainebleau, which, by diminishing the number of troops, adds lustre to the enterprise.

movements of the English sloop and the French squadron. Out of prudence, however, the Emperor commanded "that the grenadiers who are working at the officers' garden shall continue their task till 3 in the afternoon. Then, and not before, they may break off."

At 4 o'clock the troops were served with soup. At 5 the drums beat to arms, and the bustle of embarkation followed.[1]

The embargo of the day before was doubled. No vessel was to be allowed to touch at the island, or to leave it, on pain of being fired on with red-hot cannon-balls from the forts, and sunk. For the last two days the police had not granted any passports, and had shadowed all suspicious characters, and not one of the many spies upon the island was able to get across to the Continent. They ran to and fro, in laughable despair, persistently framing their reports, begging, offering, imploring, and swearing by all their gods that commercial matters of the utmost importance called them to Piombino or Leghorn. The sentinels were ruthless. The "Marchand d'Huiles" induced the owner of a bark to put him across the Straits for 60 francs. Hardly had he started, however, when an officer hailed him from the Inconstant, and asked where he was going. The spy protested that his intentions were innocent. The beauty of the day had tempted him to go out sailing. The officer ordered him

[1] Laborde, 48; March. d'H., 166; Larabit, 71; Memorial from St. Helena, Feb. 24, 1816.

back to shore, on pain of being fired at. Some English tourists, consumed with curiosity, attempted to approach the brig. They were invited by the same arguments to return ashore. To crown his misery, the fellow encountered Cambronne, with whom he had often discoursed on his feelings of admiration and devotion to the Emperor. Cambronne made a feint of inscribing him on the roll of Elban volunteers. "Your place," he said to him, "is on Boat No. 5"! And if a mutual friend had not intervened, and gone bail for his rejoining the convoy in a few days, Cambronne would have forced a gun under his arm, a knapsack on his back, and would have insisted on his embarking.[1]

None of those who were leaving with the Emperor (except Bertrand and Drouot, who would have been insulted if there had been any further mystery) knew where he was taking them. No one troubled his head about it. Pons, the Robespierriste, went off with the rest. Commandant Cornuel got off his deathbed in order to breathe his last sighs in Paris. Cambronne marched with his eyes shut. When the Emperor asked him "Where are we going, Cambronne?" he replied: "I have never tried to penetrate the secrets of my Sovereign." Bertrand hoped and feared at once, and obeyed as usual, sad at leaving his wife behind him. Who could tell if they would ever meet again? Drouot alone was frankly averse to the

[1] March. d'H., 165, 166; Campbell, 230.

project, and had done all "that was humanly possible to turn the Emperor from it." But he was none the less resolute to do his duty to the end. Taillade had resumed command of the Inconstant in collaboration with Chautard, and the two were perpetually wrangling. The sons of the best families of Elba "cast in their lots with the man of destiny."[1]

Madame Mère set an example in her farewells. Madame Bertrand tried to show the same fortitude. Pauline, livid, with discoloured lips, wiped her eyes with her lace handkerchief, and embraced the veterans, laying her hand caressingly on theirs, as she conjured them to watch over the beloved head she was entrusting to them.[2]

Between seven and eight nearly everyone was on board. The stragglers, carrying four-pound loaves, with sausages, bottles of wine, and cutlery, put off to the ships in fishing boats. Many had to abandon the furniture they had acquired in the belief that they were settled in Elba, as the officers refused to accommodate such things on board.[3]

During the day the Emperor had ordered cash payment to be made to Captain Cardini for the cargo of the Marseilles polacca, which had received his carriages and effects on February 20, and had on divers pretexts been prevented from continuing

[1] Pons de l'H., 344, 382; Mém. aux Puiss. All., 131; Laborde, 51; Peyrusse, 278; March. d'H., 161; evidence given by Cambronne and Drouot at their trial.

[2] Pons de l'H., 383; Mém. aux Puiss. All., 119.

[3] Vincent, 371.

THE DEPARTURE FROM ELBA.
From a German Print.

THE GULF OF PORTO FERRAIO, WHENCE THE IMPERIAL FLOTILLA SAILED.

her voyage to Naples. Peyrusse paid 25,000 francs to the Captain. He wanted to reduce the charges, which seemed to him excessive. But the Emperor intervened, judging that it was no time to bargain, and to the horror of his treasurer, flung the bills, "that waste-paper," into the air. The Captain pocketed the money, and the Polish Lascars threw the cargo into the sea and installed themselves upon the ship. For lack of room, they had to leave the horses of the troopers behind, and take only the saddles. The officers alone took their chargers.[1]

The flotilla accordingly consisted of the brig Inconstant, armed with eighteen guns (ten with their carriages), laden with the Emperor's saddle-horses, and the trunks of gold, the Staff, and 400 to 500 Grenadiers, who were crowded together on the bridge and in the hold; the schooner Etoile, the felucca Caroline, Le Saint Esprit (the pinque from Marseilles), the two feluccas from Rio, and one other transport, the property of Signor Tonietti, a merchant of Elba. These three last vessels were chartered at a freight of 8,869 francs.[2]

[1] Peyrusse, 272; Vincent, 370. The vessels were uncomfortably crowded, for, besides the troops, they carried all the civil functionaries and the Imperial household, as well as the wives and children who had come to join the husbands in Elba, and embarked as best they could with the expedition.

[2] Campbell, *Napoleon at Fontanebleau and Elba*, 381–2; *Isle d'Elbe et Cent Jours*, 35, 36; Mém. aux Puiss. All. 129; Peyrusse, 274, 305. A sepia drawing by Major Mellini (Reg. de l'I. d'Elbe, 110), father of Mlle. Rosa Mellini, lady-in-waiting to Madame Mère, shows the departure of the flotilla by moonlight. An eighth sail is seen in the background, doubtless one of the despatch-boats, the Abeille or the Mouche, which does not seem to have gone any distance with the convoy. The original of this drawing is at the Municipio of Porto

Three other feluccas were to sail for Corsica in two or three days' time, each carrying fifteen or sixteen Corsicans, influential people in their own country, who were armed with manifestoes, and commissioned to raise the island in favour of the Emperor, whose escape they would proclaim, and to arrest and try Bruslart. They would prepare a refuge for the expeditionary flotilla, in the event of its being obliged by bad weather, or the cruisers of the Squadron, to fall back on that coast.[1]

The Emperor descended from the Mulini to the port, with Bertrand, in the little open carriage, drawn by two ponies, that belonged to Princess Borghese. He embarked in his barge, which was manned by the Marines of the Guard, to the strains of the Marseillaise, sung by the soldiers and taken up by the assembled populace.

Every heart beat fast when the Imperial barge left the shore. The Mayor, Traditi, was sobbing. The crowd clapped hands, with shouts of "*Evviva!*" in which, despite the outbursts of enthusiasm, a strain of indescribable melancholy was mingled: while the emerald-green night melted away into the distant heavens, and innumerable lights from the illuminated city were reflected in the mighty lake of the ocean, as on the evening of the day when the God-Emperor arrived.

Ferraio. There is a reproduction of it at the Biblio. Nat. in Paris (Prints, Collection Hennin). The St. Joseph was a two-masted brigantine of 80 tons.

[1] *Isle d'Elbe et Cent Jours*, 37; March. d'H. and Report of Spies, 117, 168, 170; Pons de l'H., 382.

He came at daybreak, he left in the mysterious gloaming, and his passing was so swift that it seemed to have lasted but one long day. The same splendid serenity of sky and waves prevailed, unruffled by the slightest breeze. The warm, pure air was impregnated with a scented fragrance, for an early spring had already burst the buds, and caressed the fields of flowers in the maquis into blossom.

Yet the calm of this divine night would, if it continued, be the ruin of all hope, and bring disaster from the outset. If the convoy had not progressed sufficiently far before dawn, which fortunately came late at this season, they would meet the English sloop returning from Livorno with Campbell on board, and fall an easy prey to her superior speed and big guns. The French squadron would hasten to the scene at the sound of the firing, and the only possible sequel would be to sell their lives dearly.

The Emperor said not a word. He paced up and down the quarter-deck of the Inconstant, in his grey overcoat, and waited, like the rest. The sails hung from the yards, and lapped the masts, in sullen inactivity.

Four mortal hours went by. At last, towards midnight, a slight breeze ruffled the waves. The sails filled. The watcher at the semaphore, and the fishermen sent out to reconnoitre, announced that the south wind, damped by the circle of mountains round the Gulf, was blowing strong outside. Wind from this quarter brought salvation. It blew the expedition along with a following gale, and held the English frigate stationary at Livorno. The crews and soldiers took oars to get out of the Gulf, and the flotilla, rallying round the lantern suspended from the mainmast of the brig, moved silently away in the moonlight.[1]

On the following day, some English tourists, detained at Elba by the embargo, begged leave to visit the Mulini.

The house was empty. Pauline had gone to join her mother. An old woman from Corsica, left as care-taker, bade them enter. They found the Emperor's bath still filled with the water he had used before leaving. On a table near his bed lay an open volume of a history of Charles V, marked at the page at which he had ceased to read it. The floor and furniture were strewn with bits of torn paper, covered with illegible pencil notes. A map of France was spread out on a table, with large-headed pins stuck into it in various places.[2]

[1] Owing to the moonlight, the flotilla could not count on slipping away unseen, under cover of darkness, from Elba. Accordingly there was no need to put out the fires, which, moreover, would have crowned the suspicions of the French squadron or English cruisers if they encountered them. It was the safest course to pass as a simple convoy of merchant boats escorted by the Inconstant as often happened. The vessels kept together till the next morning. After doubling Capraia, the Inconstant, which sailed faster, forged ahead, leaving the others behind till they caught her up in Golfe Jouan.

[2] March. d'H., 167 ; Campbell, 230 ; Peyrusse, 275 ; Monier, 101 ; Pons de l'H., 381, 383, 384 ; Gen. Durand, 261.

* * * * *

V

FROM THE EVASION TO OUR OWN DAY

In St. Helena, later on, the Emperor declared that the return from Elba had been planned as early as Fontainebleau.[1]

Among the many untrustworthy assertions incorporated in the Memorial, which was to bewilder posterity, this appears to be veracious.

Napoleon could no more confess himself beaten after the first fall, and consider his part in history ended for ever, than could an energetic wrestler, who has never yet been defeated, be thrown in the arena and vanquished at the first onset—or a man of robust health succumb to the first attack of a fatal malady. His return was the ricochet of the spring that has been pressed home, the rebound of the ball from the ground it is thrown on, before it comes to rest.

It is obvious that Napoleon had meditated on this return ever since he left Fontainebleau. Hardly had he quitted France, and recovered from the incidents of his tragic flight across the South; hardly

[1] Mémoriale de Ste. Hélène, April 17, 1816.

had the Undaunted weighed anchor, than he betrayed his secret feelings. "Although at Fontainebleau," writes Campbell, "he expressed his desire to pass the remainder of his life in retirement at Elba studying the arts and sciences, he inadvertently gave frequent proofs in his subsequent conversations on board the Undaunted of the active restlessness of his disposition, and indicated his expectation of opportunities arising which would once again afford scope for the exercise of his ambition.

"He evidently persuaded himself that the greatest portion of the population in France remained favourable to him.[1]

"'The Bourbons, *pauvres diables*,' he went on to say, 'are like great nobles, content as long as they enjoy their estates and their mansions. But if the people of France become dissatisfied with that, and find that they have not such encouragement for their manufactures in the interior as they ought to have, they will be driven out in six months.'"[2]

Nor had the Emperor been a week at Elba before he began again: "The French are unable to keep quiet. I don't give them more than six months' patience after the Allies have recrossed the frontier." At the time these remarks were taken for mere rodomontade by Napoleon's audience.[3]

Another proof of his preconceived notion of return, was the choice he made, after his abdication, of the Island of Elba. This "miserable little hole,"

[1] Campbell, *Napoleon at Fontainebleau and Elba*, 280.
[2] *Ibid.*, 204.
[3] Campbell, 44, 50, 73.

as he termed the island in his moments of bad temper or candour, had not been forced on him. He had been offered Corsica. He always said so, and it is not at all improbable. It would have been natural to send the ogre back to his lair, the Minotaur to the country that produced him. But it was Napoleon who refused.

And why? Why, instead of asking for the tiny islet, had he not thankfully accepted his own country, at which he used to gaze from the summit of Monte Giove, . . . an extended territory with many towns, a fragment of the Continent, where he would have been a real King of a real People? There he would have had nothing to fear from his enemies. He would have become impregnable. It would have been impossible there to carry him off by surprise, and if the attempt had been made by force of arms, he would have been able to revive the age-long tactics of the Corsican chiefs, and by turning "bandit," could have resisted 50,000 men, in his inaccessible gorges and forests. He was so well aware of this, that he had schemed to take refuge in Corsica, after quitting the Island of Elba, if he failed in his design of reaching France, while it was to Corsica again that he dreamed of flying after Waterloo.[1]

What then caused him to take a different line of action? Was it shame at returning vanquished to his birth-place, at coming back in last resort, to

[1] Peyrusse, 230; Campbell, 18; Meneval, II, 164; Mém. Ste. Hélène, November 18, 1815, May 29, 1816.

his starting point? The acclamations of his compatriots, who would have borne him on their shields, would soon have made him forget this hurt to his pride, and the remembrance of his hours of glory, in some congenial abode, would speedily have consoled him. If any implacable enemies of his race and family had declared against him, and refused to recognise him as their sovereign, a little fighting from time to time would have created an agreeable distraction.

Was his choice, as Las Cases makes him say, the result "of his mood at the moment"? What! This man who reasoned everything, down to his very gestures, who had never allowed the minutest of his actions to be governed by chance, had permitted himself to be swayed by a caprice at the hour on which his whole future depended?

No! If he selected Elba, it was because the larger Corsica was useless to him. Inasmuch as it was a real Sovereignty, it stood for the definite stability which he refused to consider. It represented the accomplished fact, the moral annihilation of the future, separation from the world by the thickets of his maquis, remoter isolation by the waves. Elba, on the other hand, was a transitory stage where there was nothing to distract him from his ends, a temporary foothold whence he viewed the Continent from his windows, from which, as he frankly avowed, "he could overlook France and the Bourbons," and recognise and seize the propitious hour for this very problematic return.[1]

[1] Fleury de Chaboulon, I, 110.

Napoleon was fully aware that the restoration which he so much desired, depended not on him, but on the course of events. He had no illusions as to the situation. "The Bourbons" (as he better than anyone else expressed it), "held my actions in their hand. If they realised that they had to inaugurate a new dynasty, and not to continue the old, there was nothing left for me to do, my political mission was concluded. I might remain in Elba. But their entourage, and the mistakes they committed, rendered me desirable. It was they who rehabilitated my popularity, and gave the word for my return. People may object that the Congress of Vienna would have deported me from my island, and I admit that this circumstance hastened my return. But if France had been well governed, my influence was a thing of the past, and no one would have thought of reinstating me. It was the course of events in Paris that made people think of the exile, and led to the whole affair."[1] The situation, for the rest, mastered Louis XVIII far more than he mastered the situation. Whatsoever he did, for good or evil, was turned against him.

* * * * *

It has been asked who gave the Emperor information whilst he was in Elba.

It came from all and everyone. Historians still appear to imagine, as was then believed in France, that Napoleon was buried in the depths of the sea.

In the first place there were the visitors. They

[1] Mém. Ste. Hélène, April, 17, 1816.

were legion on the island; their coming and going was perpetual: we have seen that the Inconstant would land as many as a hundred passengers on a single voyage. The obstacles which the Austrian police endeavoured to interpose were perfunctory. In the larger ports, such as Genoa or Leghorn, they exercised a brutal and tyrannical and quite useless supervision, as, for one person whom they detained, twenty would make good their escape. From every little port along the shore, the sailors and fishermen undertook to transport whoever would to the Island of Elba. The difficulties were lessened if the passage was made from Naples, especially if the traveller spoke Italian and could claim to be a Neapolitan subject. It was by Naples that Countess Walewska came to the island. As to the ocean, that was free enough. Once on board there was no more to fear. Everyone was free to enter and leave Porto Ferraio without encountering the slightest obstacle.[1]

These visitors did not all come to gaze. Bertrand's brother, travelling from France to Rome, touched

[1] Pons de l'H. 357; Mém. Aux. Puiss, All. 31; Peyrusse, 263, "the facility of our communications excited alarm at the Congress of Vienna"; March. d'H. 129, 137, "I have discovered that a Lucchese, named Luigi, engages for a small remuneration to take passengers across to the island, where they arrive without difficulty"; Campbell, *Napoleon at Fontainebleau and Elba*, 360, "Porto Ferraio is constantly filled with vessels from all parts of Italy"; Corres. Imp. xxi, 666 (Jan. 4, 1815): "M. le Comte de Bertrand, I beg you will submit to me the names of the foreign vessels now in the harbour of Porto Ferraio, their tonnage, and nationality. I think there have never been so many"; *Isle d'Elbe et Cent Jours*, 21, "All the boats from the Genoese shore are willing to ferry individuals across to Elba at their pleasure, even when papers and authorisation from the local authorities are wanting"; Fleury de Chaboulon, 85, 102 (note).

at the island of Elba, "with a full budget of news." Numbers of officers arrived, and gave information as to the temper of the army—Italian patriots, often in high social positions, whose advances were rejected by the Emperor, but whose words he gathered up—English peers, with whom he held long conversations. Pons crossed to Tuscany, and went unhindered as far as Florence, on a mission to the Grand Duke Ferdinand, and to the Italian Minister Fossombroni. Commercial travellers, embarking at Genoa or Marseilles, brought the opinions of the middle classes. There was not a café in Porto Ferraio where the latest gossip from Paris was not circulated.[1]

Next to the visitors, there were the letters. The Austrian police took the same precautions over the correspondence to or from the Isle of Elba as for the travellers, and they were equally superfluous. Theoretically all this correspondence passed through the secret bureau of Leghorn, where it was read, and intercepted if desirable. The Emperor complained of this, and as he still received letters with broken seals, or no letters at all, and as those which he sent never arrived at their destination, he organised special couriers at Piombino, to whom the boat from Elba transmitted the mails directly, twice in the week. Other postal stations were established at Civita Vecchia, at Genoa, or at Naples, and the Inconstant then undertook the transport. The

[1] Pons de l'H. 177 ff., 216, 351; Campbell, 215; Corres. Imp. xxi., 607; March. d'H. 123, 151, 155, 159; Laborde, 75.

R

letters addressed to the Island of Elba reached it by the same route and agencies, or by the ships that touched at Porto Ferraio with goods and passengers. Such occasions were frequent. "Our relations with France and with our families were never interrupted," says Peyrusse. Meneval never desisted from giving the Emperor news of his wife and son, after Marie Louise had ceased to write to him. "Notwithstanding the rigorous surveillance," he tells us, "that was kept up round me, I sent him news by every possible channel. I found facilities in the commercial traffic with Vienna. Kind merchants, whose hearts had not been hardened by politics, readily undertook to transmit my letters to General Bertrand by Leghorn and Florence. All over France and Italy similar pretexts of commerce marked the correspondence with the Isle of Elba. From time to time the Austrian police were permitted to open some letter, which whetted their curiosity. But Stahremberg was in despair, for he found nothing interesting in any of these, as though matters had been arranged expressly.[1]

[1] Corres. Imp., xxi, 595, 602, 629 ; Hyde du Neuville, II, 29 ; March. d'H. 136, 139 ; Reg. de l'I. d'E. 38, 56 ; Peyrusse, 255, 263 ; Pons de l'H., 352, 353 ; Meneval, II, 315 ; Larabit, 64 ; Campbell, 115, 145.—There were any number of commercial relations between Elba and the Continent, and they were absolutely unhampered. The Emperor bought all his fruit-trees in Genoa or Tuscany. He ordered 20—30,000 francs worth of clothing for his troops from Genoa. He was in constant communication with his uncle, Cardinal Fesch, and with Rome, chiefly over the purchase of oats and corn for the island. Everyone ordered what they wanted from Paris. Pauline had her gowns from the capital, or from Naples, and when Vincent, the saddler, made blue silk reins for Marie Louise's horse, he obtained his

Some that arrived were, however, most interesting, and after reading them "the Emperor was so content that he walked about the room, rubbing his hands and laughing to himself." Of the 5,000 letters which he received from officers or soldiers of different nations, who wrote to ask if he would engage them, 500 came from France. Nine-tenths of these were written by soldiers who had returned to their homes, either because they had been discharged, or because they had come from prisons in England, Germany, or Russia. Often before they reached home they had journeyed across several provinces, and gave descriptions of "the temper of the soldiers and peasants." When any of the Guard went on leave to France the Emperor gave orders to Commander Mallet that they "were to write the news of all kinds to their comrades." The veterans who stayed in Elba also received communications from their families. The mother of one of them addressed the following missive to him from Verdun: "I love you better since I have known you were with the Emperor. That is what all who are good for anything do. I well believe what you say, that people come from the four corners of the earth to see him, for here they come from the four corners of the town to read your letter, and one and all say you are a man of honour. The Bourbons have not got to the end yet, and

materials from Lyons (Corres. Imp. xxi., 587, 588, 602, 671 ; Reg. de l'Isle d'E., Nos. 21, 68, 78 ; Peyrusse, 263 ; Pons. de l'H., 261 ; Sellier Vincent, 366, 368 ; *Ile d'Elbe et Cent Jours*, 97).

we do not like them. I have no news to tell you, except that I pray to God, and make your sister pray, for the King and Emperor."[1]

This epistle "had the honours of fame. It was read and re-read, in the barracks and beyond them. The Emperor wished to see it for himself, and asked for it. It brought that veteran several napoleons." Masséna wrote Pons a letter of simple friendliness, but it ended with these words: "You are happy in that you can live in peace!" Pons brought the letter to the Emperor, who gave it back, with the remark: "That shows that the Prince of Essling is not content." Still more explicit was another letter to Pons, from Cambon, who was opposed to the Empire, but wrote "as a patriot with his soul on fire," saying: "We expelled the Bourbons from France. Now they are expelling themselves from the hearts of the French. They are slaves of England. They exist only in and for England. This cannot last." While more clearly still, Scitivaux, the Receiver of Treasure, replied, when Pons, after his dispute with the Emperor about the revenue from the Mines, inquired what line of conduct he ought to pursue: "Let Napoleon have what he requires. The matter is of no importance.

1 "Je t'aimons plus depuis que je te savons auprès de not'Empereur C'est comme ça que les honnêtes gens font. Je te croyons bien qu'on vient des quatre coins du monde pour le voir, car ici on est venu des quatre coins de la ville pour lire ta lettre, et qu'un chacun disiont que t'es un homme d'honneur. Les Bourbon ne sont pas au bout et nous n'aimions pas ces messieurs. Je n'avons rien a t'apprendre, sinon que je prions Dieu et que je faisions prier ta soeur, pour l'Empereur et Roi."

For there is every indication that he will soon return to Paris."[1]

All the letters, which eventually, by one means or another, came into the hands of the Emperor (to whom they were usually brought direct by those who received them) had in the majority of cases been read by him in the first instance. He examined the mail bags, and broke the seals, the more calmly since the outrage was subsequently attributed to the French or Austrian police.

With the letters came journals, pamphlets, and political papers, which the Emperor collected and arranged in files "for" and "against." He ordered Bertrand to subscribe under a feigned name to most of the principal newspapers of France, Germany, and Austria. These were addressed to Naples, whence a courier brought them to Piombino, to the mail-packet for the Island of Elba. Campbell procured an English paper for him every week, and those issued in Italy could be obtained from every Port along the coast. It was by means of the papers that the Emperor followed the journey of Marie Louise in detail, after her departure from Provins, and knew of her visit to Schaffhausen, and arrival at Vienna, before the postal communications had been re-established.[2]

[1] March. d'H., 142; *Ile d'Elbe et Cent Jours*, 21, 22; Reg. de l'I. d'E. No. 135; Pons. de l'H., 114, 364, 365, 367. Masséna was, of course, quite loyal to the Bourbons, and it was he who sent the first despatch from Marseilles to the Minister of War, announcing the landing of Napoleon. (Mém. Ste. Hélène, March 23, 1816).

[2] Corres. Imp. xxi, 633; Peyrusse, 263; Monier, 69; Campbell, 139, 319, 322, and quoted by M. Pellet, 113; Meneval, II, 246, 247, 249, 405.

Lastly, Napoleon obtained information from his police, and from the secret emissaries whom he despatched or received, for, in this business, oral transmission was preferable to written communications, in order that he might affirm that he "was not keeping up any political correspondence"—"that, search as they might, they would find nothing against him."

Items of expenses for the secret police are few in the ledgers of Peyrusse, and do not exceed some thousands of francs. It is, however, remarkable that the figure of 500 francs set down each month for the "Emperor's toilette" jumps suddenly, in January and February, to 2,999 francs, with no plausible motive save the unexplained necessity for an increased monthly expenditure of 1,500 francs. And, for payment of his agents, the Emperor possessed another fund, on which he was able to draw largely, that of the personal income and jewels of his mother and Pauline. Who, besides himself and these two women, knew what became of the resources which they constantly put at his disposal? The emissaries who came from France were sent and paid by his partisans and faithful friends who placed their hopes in him.

Other information, again, most probably reached him from the Préfecture of Police in Paris.

Pons, in reference still to "his deplorable financial disagreement with the Emperor," wrote to General Dalesme, after the latter had returned to France, begging him "to enlighten his conscience."

In his letter he complained in covert language of the Imperial rapacity, saying that "the shepherd did not spare his sheep." His letter, or, more exactly, a copy of his letter, came back to him, accompanied by an emphatic reprimand, advising him "in his own interests not to cavil at the great man, and under no consideration to send his grievances through the post." Letter and reprimand were alike despatched from the office of the Préfet of the Police. And when Pons, in amazement, thought the best thing he could do was to put the whole affair before the Emperor, Napoleon, without blaming him further, replied with marked emphasis: "I have partisans wherever there are right-minded people." So that even in the Island of Elba, "he maintained relations with the Lair of Cacus"?

Fouché, on his side, who was tired of inaction, and was safe "to put his dirty finger into every pie," Fouché, who passed on to Louis XVIII the offers he received for the assassination of the Emperor in Elba at the same time that he was writing to Vienna that there could not be a more favourable moment for the reinstitution of the Regency in France, and that if the son of the Emperor were to show himself in Strasburg, riding a donkey, led by a peasant, the first regiment before whom he presented himself would bring him to Paris without encountering a single obstacle, was not the most backward in playing to the future, and in expediting an intelligent emissary from time to time to Porto

Ferraio, as the bearer of some double-edged advice or useful suggestion.[1]

To make a long story short, it is certain that the Emperor, when in the Island of Elba, knew everything that it was to his interest to know, since every emissary and every letter that wanted to get in, got in, whether openly or with the aid of subterfuge. In October he knew of the project, hardly ventilated in Vienna and in Paris, of deporting him. From September 16, he knew that Neipperg was constantly with Marie Louise. He had been informed some little time later, that if the Emperor of Austria shrank from the scandal of a divorce, it was in self-defence, and against his secret inclinations; and on December 20, he spoke plainly with Campbell about the growing fears in France of a new White Terror.[2]

* * * * *

And thus by a regular and fatal development

[1] Peyrusse, 262, Appendix, 123, 132–3–4, 142–3; Labadie, 57; March. d'H. 154, 157; Campbell, 208; Pons de l'H. 44, 364, 366; Ste. Hélène Mém. April, 3, 1816 (note); Meneval, II, 313; *Ile d'Elbe et Cent Jours*, 92; Fouché, II, 286—312. Fouché had begun by making advances to the Bourbons which were not reciprocated. He then veered in favour of a project for a Regency, with Marie Louise at the head, from which the Emperor was to be excluded, and wrote Napoleon a long letter, a masterpiece of cunning and duplicity, in which he advised him to leave the Island of Elba and withdraw to America, "in the interests of France," as he said, "and to secure the peace of Europe." This oratorical precaution would, if the letter were intercepted, count in his favour with Louis XVIII. He subsequently approached the Bonapartist Committees which sent emissaries to the Isle of Elba, and worked for the Emperor's return. "I judged," said he, "that he would serve as a rallying point to the army, but that they would turn upon him afterwards."

[2] Campbell, 152, 172, 187, 203.

CEILING AT SAN MARTINO, WITH TWO DOVES SYMBOLISING NAPOLEON AND MARIE LOUISE.

THE EMPEROR'S BATH-ROOM AT SAN MARTINO.

the notion of return assumed the ascendant in the mind of the Emperor.

A preliminary period of lassitude, of temporary equilibrium and arrest, lasted until he took up his abode on Monte Giove. Once there he ceased to look back. When autumn came, he was launched on the other plane, which inclined towards France—down which Louis XVIII, by refusing him the means of existence, Austria, by separating him from wife and child, Europe, in threatening to deport him to some island of the Atlantic, were pressing him at the sword's point. By the last days of November his prospective embarkation was being toasted in all the wine shops of Porto Ferraio.[1]

He let the winter go by, to give the popular discontent time to ripen, to obtain the advantages of less stormy navigation, and to allow the road through the Alps, which he reckoned on taking, to become practicable. And he departed at the precise moment at which his resources were becoming daily more exhausted—when, with the dangers of abduction and blockade drawing closer round him, "it was becoming more dangerous to stay than to depart."[2]

[1] March. d'H., 118.

[2] One of the last emissaries received by the Emperor, before his departure, was Fleury de Chaboulon, former sous-préfet of Château-Salins and then of Reims, who landed at Porto Ferraio, about February 15, disguised as a sailor, on a smugglers' boat. When Fleury de Chaboulon had left Paris is not known. It is only clear that his journey was long and arduous, for he fell ill on the way, and knew no Italian, which complicated matters. In his Memoirs (published in London, in 1819, where he puts his narrative into the mouth of an officer who was killed at Waterloo) he describes the

Nor was it enough to know the hour at which it would be advantageous to tempt fortune. It was

vicissitudes of this journey . . . his preliminary understanding with Maret, Duke of Bassano, one of the most fervent partisans of the Emperor, his arrival at the Island of Elba, and his reception at the Mulini. The Emperor cross-questioned him at first in the abrupt manner which he used to disconcert people and read their inmost thoughts. Then, says Fleury de Chaboulon, he gradually relaxed into full confidence, indicting the Bourbons and Europe, discussing the situation and the chances of his return, explaining how he proposed to effect this great coup, his doubts, his scruples; and finally, convinced by Fleury's eloquence, he said to him "You are a fine fellow. Had it not been for you I should not known that the hour had struck, and I should have gone on raking the soil in my garden. No one will ever have received a greater proof of confidence than I am giving you, in deciding to leave Elba on your word alone, and in commissioning you to go and proclaim my approaching advent in France. I had intended not to meddle any further in politics. What you have told me has changed my resolution, I shall start from here on April 1, perhaps earlier." It must be admitted that the whole of this narrative is wanting in sincerity, and reads from one end to the other as if it had been drawn up after the event. Is it credible that, as stated subsequently, the Emperor should have presented Fleury, on February 15, with a plan of departure and of campaign that was not given to Drouot himself till the last moment, while the precise itinerary of the march, and wealth of details, prove it to have been edited after the event?

The information brought by Fleury de Chaboulon doubtless rejoiced the heart of the Emperor, and confirmed him in his idea of leaving. But to pretend, with Fleury: "that the departure was decided on from his report alone," that Napoleon made him "arbiter of his destiny, of the fate of the Bourbons, of France and Europe," and that "this astounding revolution was the work of two men" (Maret and himself) is an exaggeration that defeats itself. All one can say is that the visit of Fleury de Chaboulon (who for the rest gave unbridled rein to his imagination when he assured the Emperor "that the Kings of the Confederation were ready to become his allies, that Prussia and Russia would be silent, and that Austria would permit him to do what he would with the Bourbons") was one of the last drops that made the cup overflow. But it was already full. It is hard to determine whether there was a direct connection, or merely a coincidence, between the date of Fleury de Chaboulon's arrival and that of the orders for departure given by the Emperor on February 16. The one hypothesis or the other might be defended. In any case the Emperor, who could not well have started earlier, and to whom it was no advantage to wait longer himself, protested against the pretentious statements of Fleury de Chaboulon.

also needful to await it. The Emperor reflected that his enemies would speedily perceive that in asking for Elba instead of Corsica, he had obtained more in seeming to ask less, and would realise that in conceding it without due reflection, on the impulse of the moment, they had committed an imprudence which they might repent some day. It was necessary to prove to Europe that she was mistaken, that he was not a dangerous character, that he had given up his ambitions. He must let himself be forgotten.

So he pretended to be humble and resigned, and remembering the Italian strain that mingled with his Corsican blood, the wily and hypocritical strain of his Genoese ancestors, he acted for nearly a year, during each hour of his life. "*Commediante!*" exclaimed the Pope at Fontainebleau. Napoleon made it his business to justify this appellation beyond anything known of him up to that day.

The need of safeguarding his liberty and his head developed his innate dramatic instincts, and set them in the fore-front so that every action and every word at Elba were counterfeit. He pretended to take his Sancho Panza kingdom seriously; his cows, farmyard, pigs, and all the sops he flung to the thousand little ambitions that surrounded him. He lost no opportunity of proclaiming himself the contented King of his miniature people. He declared to everyone that he was happy, and inscribed it on the walls of his palace. Up to the last moment, he concealed the real under the fictitious, working at the estimates for the current year and commanding Bertrand to prepare his summer residence at Marciana, while Drouot was actually provisioning the ship that was to carry him away. He was prudent in all respects, taking characteristic precautions against unexpected factors. Departure, if no obstacle intervened, prolongation of his stay, if he were hindered . . . the one and the other alternative must be made equally certain.

The only flaw in his hopes and calculations had been the shipwreck of the Inconstant. This was owing not to himself nor to any human agency, but to Nature, which had conquered him in the steppes of Russia—to the sea and the winds, against which, from the dispersion of the conquerors of Troy to that of the Invincible Armada, have foundered all human previsions and human forces. That was only a check. His will carried him through to the end, and the comedy he played confused the ideas of everyone around him, and even lulled the hatred of his foes to sleep, like oil upon the waters.[1]

* * * * *

The hour once resolved on and arrived, Napoleon set out, as it were, destitute and unarmed, preceded

[1] No one having guessed anything, everyone discovered a mass of "combinations" on the part of the Emperor after the event. Pons asked if the arrival of Walewska at the island had been with the object of dulling Campbell's watchfulness (Pons de l'H., 379), and Peyrusse was naïf enough to feel convinced that "His Majesty had boldly given Taillade the order to wreck the Inconstant in order to facilitate the shipping of a larger quantity of provisions during her rehabilitation" (Peyrusse, 268, 269, 278).

by his fame alone, and holding his "Medusa's Head" as the Guard were called, in the hollow of his hand. The sole chance of success was that the enterprise might be reinforced along the route by the unknown factors to which it would give birth. This was no time for mathematical plotting out of battles and learned tactics. Boldness alone could carry the day. A plan prepared in advance would have been useless, with the added risk of its being sold to the enemy, and as the preparations for departure and for the expedition had been reduced to the strictest necessaries, the risks of betrayal were proportionately diminished.

In acting as he did, the Emperor once more disconcerted all previsions. His complicity with the corsairs had been contemplated; Stahremberg had been alarmed by the recruits enrolled in Tuscany; 50,000 Piedmontese and Milanese, declared Mariotti, were ready to rank themselves beneath the banner of the King of Elba on the day of his landing, and Louis XVIII had sententiously written to Talleyrand: "Never let us forget that if Napoleon has any last expedient, it will lie in Italy, through the medium of Murat, and in like manner *delenda est Carthago*."[1] The return of the Emperor direct to the soil of France, a stroke of genius which appears to us such a simple thing to-day, was the one possibility no one thought of.

And thus were disentangled and resolved the

[1] Mariotti to Talleyrand, November 15, 1814; Louis XVIII to Talleyrand, December 10.

various elements of what has been termed the "problem of the Island of Elba."

The return from Elba was foreseen, it was a fatality. Yet the rash adventure was doomed from the outset. Nothing stable could result from it. Hardly had France set eyes on him whom she desired from afar, and summoned to her rather from a revolting spirit and in order to terrorise the Bourbons than from conviction, than she took fright at his advent. At the news of the landing in Golfe Jouan, the stocks fell in Paris seven points in twenty-four hours, and the Bourse was smitten with panic.[1] A last flash of popularity carried the Emperor to the Tuileries, and if Europe had accepted him, the country must have submitted. But Europe, which had done so much to quell him, could not reasonably replace the man who had thus given one more proof of his redoubtable genius and indomitable audacity upon the throne. She rose in concert against him, and at the first defeat he fell. The France he had drained dry, in which there were left only cripples or women bereft of their husbands, had no more soldiers to give him for the butchery of battle. His task was accomplished, and the heart of the nation beat with his no longer. He felt this, and realised himself to

[1] "Cours du 5 per cent. : Ouverture, le 6 Mars, à 77 francs ; le 7 Mars, à 70 francs" (*Moniteur*, March 7, 8). After going up a little, the 5 per cent. were down to 50 francs on June 19. On June 21, when the news of the Waterloo disaster arrived, they went up to 55 francs. June 23, after Napoleon's abdication, they were 57 francs. June 30, after he had left La Malmaison, they reached 66 francs (*Moniteur*, June 20, 22, 24, and July 1).

be, as Fouché brutally expressed it, "a worn out character."[1]

Really exhausted and vanquished now, he pleaded after Waterloo to be allowed to end his days in peace in some quiet, homely resting-place. Once more he thought of Corsica or America. But no one now believed him, and the English, to whom he again addressed himself in flattering terms, and who were accused of having purposely or stupidly allowed him to slip out of Elba—furious at the trick he had played them—sent him 4,000 miles from Europe, to Longwood, where he thought remorsefully of his Mediterranean island. "Everything," he sighed, "is measured by degrees in this world. The Island of Elba, that seemed so abominable a year ago, was Paradise compared with St. Helena, and that again may challenge regrets that are yet to come."[2]

He could say for his consolation that the Bourbons might have shot him, and since facts in the long run explain each other, the polite but unlucky Campbell, about whom there has been an absurd mystery, elucidates Hudson Lowe, and justifies him.

* * * * *

When, on April 28, Campbell landed from the English sloop at Porto Ferraio, he had a sudden presentiment at not seeing the Inconstant any longer in the Port, and asked anxiously whether Napoleon was still there. He was informed that

[1] Mém. Ste. Hélène, May 20, 1816; Fouché, II., 303.
[2] Mém. Ste. Hélène, Feb. 20, 1816.

the Emperor had gone off by sea for an expedition. No doubt he would be found at Pianosa. He asked for the Grand Maréchal Bertrand. The Grand Maréchal was with the Emperor. He asked for General Drouot. No one knew where he was. Campbell saw that they were laughing at him.

He climbed up through the empty deserted city, where not a bearskin remained, to the Mulini. The Mulini was empty. He betook himself to the house of Madame Mère, and when received by Pauline cross-questioned her roughly, ordering her to tell him which direction her brother had taken. Pauline reminded him of his manners, and declared that she knew nothing. He went to Madame Bertrand, and tried to frighten her, saying that the Emperor and all who were accompanying him had been taken prisoners. Madame Bertrand changed colour, but remained silent. Campbell's discomfited aspect reassured her.

He asked who was in command in the island. They referred him to Signor Lapi, President of the Governmental Junta nominated by the Emperor.[1] Campbell announced that he should take possession of the island in the name of England, and should occupy the citadel the same day by a detachment of marines from the English vessel. Signor Lapi replied that the Island of Elba belonged to Napoleon,

[1] The Provisory Junta which Napoleon appointed a few hours before his departure consisted of the Vicar-General Arrighi, the Intendant of the Island, Balbiani, the Mayor Traditi, the Chamberlain Vantini, Signor Senno who farmed the tunny fishery, and Signor Bigeschi, under the presidency of Lapi, the Intendant des Domaines (Pons de l'H., 382; March. d'H., 166).

that the Elban National Guard, which was again under arms, would defend it against every attack, and that if the frigate attempted to land any troops, the fort would fire on her. Campbell was obliged to retire.

What was he to think? The Emperor might perhaps be concealed behind Capraia, from which base he could descend upon Livorno, so as to obtain provisions, troops, and ammunition. Campbell sailed for Capraia. The islanders had seen nothing. On the other hand, he despatched a courier to the English Consul in Sicily, with a notification of the Imperial flotilla and list of the troops embarked, which had been given him by his spies at Porto Ferraio. He begged the Consul to transmit this information immediately to the English squadron in the Mediterranean, so that they might arrest Napoleon, if he had taken flight towards the South. He himself departed again from Capraia with the intention of exploring the coast of France. By the time he landed at Antibes, the Emperor had reached Grenoble.[1]

During the campaign of 1815, Campbell re-entered the ranks of the English Army, and fought at Waterloo. He was subsequently appointed Governor of Sierra Leone in 1825, and was carried off in 1827 by the pestilential climate of that colony.[2]

Pauline had completed her preparations for departure by March 1, and left Elba for Lucca on the 2nd,

[1] Campbell, 229–235, *Napoleon at Fontainebleau and Elba*, 389–90; March. d'H., 169.

[2] Campbell, Memoir, *Napoleon at Fontainebleau and Elba*, 104–150.

hoping there to meet her sister. But on landing she fell ill at Viareggio, where she remained some time, and subsequently went to Naples, her delicate health obliging her to stay in the softer southern climates. Before parting with her brother, she had sent him a handful of diamonds intended to defray the unforeseen expenses of the expedition. After the supreme conflict some of her jewel-cases were found at Waterloo in the Emperor's carriages. She subsequently settled in Rome, and was reconciled to her husband, Prince Borghese, in whose arms she expired in Florence on June 9, 1825, at 3 A.M., begging that her face might be covered as soon as she was dead, and forbidding the surgeon's scalpel to desecrate her beautiful body.[1]

On March 5, Madame Mère despatched her furniture to Rome. In the second half of the month she left for Naples, to rejoin Pauline. From Naples she re-embarked for France, and on June 3 found her son once more actually upon the Throne in Paris. Less than a month after, at La Malmaison, she bade him an eternal farewell. Talma, who was present, in the uniform of the National Guard, saw two tears roll down the strong face of the mother, who in her subsequent retirement to Rome wore only mourning garments, meditating in her dreams the possibilities of arming a fleet and crossing the ocean, to deliver her martyred son. "Mother of all sorrows," her

[1] March. d'H., 170; Constant, I., 208; Larrey, II., 108, 129, 159, 297, 308, 309.

robust constitution enabled her to survive him, and she vainly implored the ashes of her dead from England, pleading "that hatred should not extend beyond the grave." Crippled by a fall in the garden of the Villa Borghese, and blind, "forgotten as it were, by death," her life was prolonged into another era, until she saw the day when the Emperor's statue was replaced upon the Column of the Grande Armée. On February 2, 1836, she gave up the ghost, after 85 full years, bequeathing her heart to her native town of Ajaccio.[1]

Comtesse Walewska was at Murat's Court, when the news of Napoleon's escape from the Island of Elba, sent by himself, arrived in the middle of a ball.[2] She hastened to Paris, and saw the coronation of her lover at the Elysée. "After the departure of the Emperor for St. Helena, she held herself free. Count Walewska had died in 1814. In 1816, she married a cousin of the Emperor, General d'Ornano, a former Colonel of the Dragoons of the Guard at Liège, where she had taken refuge." This marriage, which was communicated to him, was one of the crowning sorrows of the prisoner at Longwood.

[1] Larrey, II., 105, 111, 117, 123, 127, 130, 159, 266–7, 355, 359, 362, 373, 434, 484, 492; *Ile d'Elbe et Cent Jours*, 108; St. Helena Mem., May 19, 1816; *Memoires de Mlle. Cochelet* (Paris, 1838), III., 172. Madame Mère was 86 if we take her birthday as Aug. 24, 1749.

[2] The Emperor sent his forgiveness to Murat, imploring him to keep calm and commit no imprudence (St. Helena Mem., February 7, 1816; *Ile d'Elbe et Cent Jours*, 137). Murat, of course, went counter to this advice.

She whom he had loved so long, and who had so long been faithful to him, had given herself to another man! In 1817, she bore a child, and after returning to Paris in the same year, died there, on December 15, in her house in the Rue de la Victoire.[1]

Pretty Madame Bellina, who danced the fandango at the Mulini, was relegated to Peru by fate, where she conducted an important school for young ladies, at Lima, about 1840.[2]

Marshal Bertrand and his wife followed the Emperor to St. Helena, as well as his valet Marchand, the so-called 'mameluke' Ali, his comrade Noverraz, and an Elban servant, Gentilini.[3]

Drouot and Cambronne (the latter was picked up at Waterloo among the dead, and completely stripped by the pillagers, "naked," he said, "as the infant St. John"), escaped with their heads from the Court Martials, both being acquitted, inasmuch as they acted as the subjects of a foreign sovereign, and not as rebels against the authority of Louis XVIII. Drouot ended his days in retirement. Cambronne, who could not conceive of existence outside barracks and without uniform, begged to be re-instated in the Army, and took the oath of fidelity to the King, "for which," he said, "his past loyalty would be his guarantee." On April 24, 1820, he was appointed to the command of the 16th

1 Campbell, 157 (note); Marion, *Napoléon et les Femmes*, I., 230.
2 Pons de l'H., 155.
3 Mém. St. Hélène, December 15, 1815.

Military Division at Lille. On May 10 of the same year, he married an English "widow named Mary Osburn, a wealthy lady born at Glasgow." He died Vicomte and Chevalier of St. Louis, in the night of January 28-29, 1842.[1]

Major Mallet was killed at Waterloo.[2]

Pons de l'Hérault, commissioned by the Emperor after he landed, to go to Marseilles to sound Masséna and, if possible, to raise the fleet and the city at Toulon, came to grief from the outset of his mission, was imprisoned in the Château d'If, and only let out on April 11. He was promoted to be Préfet of the Rhone, and then, dreading the reprisals of the Bourbons, went into voluntary exile, whence he unsuccessfully addressed a triple petition to Marie Louise, the Emperor of Austria, and the Prince Regent of England, to the effect that he might be permitted to rejoin the "illustrious and unfortunate Napoleon" at St. Helena. Persecuted by the Austrian and French police, he remained for prolonged periods in Italy, and only returned to France in 1822. He was still kept under surveillance as a suspect. Louis Philippe's Government gave him the Préfecture of the Jura. At the end of six months, his strictness of character and conduct led to his dismissal. He became a Member of the Council of State after the Revolution of 1848, but his circumstances were once more reversed by the Coup d'État on

[1] Trial of Drouot and Cambronne; Brunschvigg, 157, 270, 272, 273, 283, 307.
[2] Peyrusse, 333.

December 2, at the age of 79. He held "that the Emperor was buried in his tomb," and protested energetically against "the violation of the Constitution, and the erection of illegal power." "Old Père Pons," as his friends called him, died in poverty, in 1858.[1]

The jovial treasurer, Peyrusse, held aloof during the Restoration, but after 1830 he was elected Mayor of his native town of Carcassonne, and Councillor-General of the Aude. Less rigid in his principles than Pons, he rallied to Prince Louis Napoleon and the Coup d'État. In 1853, he became Commander of the Légion d'Honneur, and only died in 1860, at the age of 84.[2]

The white charger Tauris carried the Emperor from Golfe Jouan to Paris. Napoleon mounted him in the Battle of Waterloo. Before leaving for St. Helena, the Emperor confided him at La Malmaison to the care of one of his grooms, M. de Montaran. As long as Tauris lived, M. de Montaran led him every morning to the Place Vendôme, and walked him round the column.[3]

* * * * *

Napoleon, King of Elba, reigned a little less than ten months. The island owed innumerable benefits to him. For several months, under his own supervision, he pursued, on a small scale and apparently trivial lines, the same labour of systematic organi-

[1] Mém. aux Puiss. All., 163–263, xxxiii.–xlviii. (Introduction); 278, 280, 281 (Appendix).

[2] Peyrusse (Biographical Notice, Introduction to the Mémorial et Archives de la Couronne).

[3] Vincent, 219.

sation and material progress that he had carried on for years with more complicated machinery within his vast empire.

He bequeathed a network of roads to a country where it was only possible to travel on donkey-back or mule before his time. He developed its resources according to the laws of modern political economy. He taught the peasants to clear the deserted territory, and to sow more corn as a provision against want, and left thousands of olive, orange, and mulberry trees from Italy on this once arid soil. He gave instruction to, and enforced the laws of hygiene upon, a people who wallowed in filth. He drained the fœtid swamps, the haunt of mosquitoes and fever, and forbade them to defile the wells. He sought out and cleared the springs, and dug cisterns for years of drought. He revived the commerce of the island, initiated improvements in the ports, and proposed to make Porto Ferraio a free harbour, to serve as a place of call and depot for the Levantine navigation. He made a point of taking half the expense in every detail of these matters upon his own shoulders. Often he paid for them entirely, notwithstanding the new subsidies. The municipal finances of Porto Ferraio exceeded the receipts, and if private individuals were ruinously lavish of their fêtes and parades in order to give him pleasure, and keep up the honour of their dignity, he repaid them royally.[1]

[1] Municipal Accounts of Porto Ferraio, 79; "Balance-sheet of 1814: Receipts, 64,954f. 15c.; Expenses, 62,285f. 94c.; Excess receipts, 2,668f. 21c."

After Campbell, Bruslart, Governor of Corsica, and the Grand Duke of Tuscany both attempted to lay hands on the island. The Governmental Junta resisted their pretensions.

General Dalesme was sent by the Emperor on June 6, with troops from Toulon, to resume his former military command at Porto Ferraio. But, on June 9, the Island of Elba and Principality of Piombino were restored by the Congress of Vienna to the Grand Duke of Tuscany. The island was blockaded by the English Squadron, and on July 29, a month after the Second Abdication, an Anglo-Tuscan fleet invited Dalesme to submit to the decision of the Congress. Dalesme signed an armistice, and requested orders from Paris.

The French Government declined to admit that there had been any question as to the Island of Elba. The island had been given to Napoleon; its fate was of no interest to France. Dalesme was authorised to do "what he judged desirable." Under these conditions there was nothing for it but to yield. By agreement with the Elban Council of Defence, however, he held out till September 2. Then, perceiving that he was finally abandoned by the Cabinet in Paris, he delivered up the place to the Tuscan troops, and re-embarked on September 6 for Toulon with the French garrison.[1]

And thus the Island of Elba was lost to France. The black years began again. 1815 was not at an end before the Barbary corsairs, seeing that "The

[1] Reg. de l'I. d'E., 267, 271, *et seq.* (Notes by L. G. Pélissier).

Great Lord of the Earth," the object of their fear and veneration, was no longer there, resumed their depredations. Eight hundred of them had to be repulsed, which led to fresh pillage and arson. 1816 was a year of starvation and misery. The harvest was swamped by floods of rain, typhus decimated the population, and the Grand Duke of Tuscany was obliged to send succour to the unfortunate island, which vainly implored Heaven to restore the happy era in which she was governed by the exiled Apollo. Prosperity was not restored till 1829.

From that date the history of Elba is merged in that of Italy. In 1848, patriotic committees were organised, and entered into relation with those upon the Peninsula for the furtherance of Italian unity. Garibaldi came to the island on a fishing-boat, in his flight, and was concealed there. On February 9, 1849, Rome proclaimed itself a Republic. Tuscany followed her example. The Grand Duke Leopold was deposed, and the tree of liberty was raised in Elba, only to be cut down some weeks later. It was not till 1860, after the final settlement of the Constitution of Italy, that the island found peace and rest from its numerous vicissitudes.

The population has been more than doubled in the last hundred years. It numbered 25,000 in the last census. Pianosa has been colonised. It supports 600 inhabitants, agriculturists and fishermen.

While they are loyal subjects to the House of

Savoy, the Elbans love France, and welcome any friendly overtures on her part. They fraternise with Corsica, their neighbour on the waves. Porto Ferraio and Bastia willingly clink glasses, and toast each other in cordial banquets.

They love to glorify the memory of the Emperor, year by year, in the funeral ceremony of May 5, as already described. The political passions which this Great Dead inspires in us, are non-existent in that remote island. He is respected because he was great, and because it is more difficult to rise above the common ruck of men than to criticise and judge those who have risen. He is honoured, too, in grateful remembrance of the good he did within his little kingdom, and for the place he has given it in history.[1]

After the Fall of the Second French Empire the rumour spread among the Elbans that the defeated hero of Sedan thought of retiring to their midst. Keen to show their undying veneration for the blood whence he was descended, the inhabitants of Porto Ferraio sent him an official Address by their Sindaco to assure him of the satisfaction this hope gave them.

Napoleon III. replied in the following letter:

WILHELMSHÖHE, *March* 10, 1871.

"MONSIEUR LE SYNDIC,

"I have received the address in which the inhabitants of Porto Ferraio proffer me the

[1] Benvenuto Giunti: *Il V Maggio*, 17.

Wilhelmshöhe, 10. Mars 1871

Monsieur le Syndic, J'ai reçu l'adresse par laquelle les habitants de Portoferrajo m'offrent l'hospitalité dans leur ville, pensant que j'avais choisi l'île d'Elbe pour y fixer ma résidence. Quoique cette nouvelle n'ait jamais eu aucun fondement je suis heureux du témoignage de sympathie qu'elle a provoqué et dont j'ai été vivement touché. Veuillez, Monsieur le Syndic, vous faire auprès de vos concitoyens l'interprète de mes remerciements et croire à mes sentiments.

Napoléon

AUTOGRAPH OF NAPOLEON III.

GENOESE TOWER AT PORTO FERRAIO.

hospitality of their city in the idea that I have chosen the Island of Elba for my residence. While there is no foundation for this rumour, I welcome the evidence of sympathy which it has elicited, and by which I have been greatly touched. I beg, Monsieur le Syndic, that you will convey my thanks to your fellow citizens, and assure them of my regard,

NAPOLEON."[1]

* * * * *

After his return to Paris, the Emperor made a gift of the Palace of the Mulini to the city of Porto Ferraio, to be preserved with its furniture and converted into a museum, the saloon to be used for fêtes. His books were to constitute a Public Library.

The Grand Duke of Tuscany, on repossessing himself of the Island of Elba, disregarded these arrangements. He confiscated the house, sold or broke up the furniture, and appropriated a portion of the books.

The Imperial Archives had been packed up in haste, and carried off by Marshal Bertrand and Peyrusse. Napoleon's signature at the foot of one of the Municipal Budgets, was the only thing left at the Hôtel de Ville in Porto Ferraio.

The Hôtel de Ville, as we have said, preserves the banner of the kingdom of Elba, a few chairs of the

[1] Original at the Municipio at Porto Ferraio.

period, which are battered and shaky and relegated to the loft, the sepia drawing by Mellini, chef-de-bataillon, which represents the nocturnal departure of February 26, and the residue of the books that belonged to the Emperor.[1]

In 1851, Prince Anatole Demidoff, who had allied himself to the Bonapartes by marrying Mathilde, daughter of Jérôme, acquired the house at San Martino, which had been unfurnished like the Mulini, and undertook to found a Napoleon Museum there for the preservation of whatever objects he was able to discover in the island, augmented by a very rich private collection, relating to the various epochs of the Emperor's career.[2]

In order to glorify the little house that had given shelter to the Great Emperor, Demidoff took advantage of the sloping ground to construct a large building (the façade of which was nearly 70 feet long, with imposing architecture, bearing eagles with outspread wings at the corners) below it, like a pedestal to its terraced roof and columns. Landslips, and the frequent subsidence of the foundations, prolonged the construction for eight years. It might have been better to preserve its original character, as a modest little house of countrified

1 *re* Authenticity of this banner, *see* Note 1, p. 270.

2 *See* p. 114. According to the catalogue of the Museo di San Martino, the dismantled house, when Demidoff took possession of it, contained only two busts of Elisa Bonaparte and her husband, two Sèvres vases, a central divan of mahogany covered with tapestry (bees and eagle) worked by Pauline Borghese, a marqueterie console with a white marble top, two plans of the domain, some architectural designs, and a design for the decorations in a public fête.

aspect, now known to us only from an old print, which has frequently been reproduced.[1]

Demidoff, too, erected the white marble shields and bas-reliefs, still to be seen among the flower-beds of the garden of the Mulini, and it was he who, to the joy of the Elbans, instituted the Funeral Ceremony of May 5. He, too, it was, who gave the ebony coffin, and the mask by Antommarchi, and who endowed the Beneficiary Church of the Miséricorde with a perpetual income of 500 francs a year, 100 francs of which were for the expenses of the ceremony, and 400 to be distributed in alms to the poor of Porto Ferraio.[2]

After his death, his nephew and heir, Paul Demidoff, dispersed the treasures contained in the Museo of San Martino. The sale took place at Florence, on March 15, 1880.

There were sold there, among the objects relating to the Emperor's stay in Elba, the cockade worn by Napoleon on the day of his arrival, for which he substituted the cockade of Elba, 290 francs; a lot of big and little cockades of the Sovereignty of the Island of Elba, 116 francs; a nécessaire for needlework, in malachite strewn with bees, which belonged to Princess Elisa, Duchess of Piombino, 330 francs; a leather cup, which Napoleon used for drinking in his rambles over the Island of Elba, and which he gave to his gardener, 10 francs; a pair of plated candlesticks, given to

[1] It may be seen in *Napoléon par l'Image* (A. Dayot, Paris, 1895).
[2] Benvenuto Giunti: *Il V Maggio*, 18.

the same, by the Emperor, 10 francs; the silver whistle of the boatswain's mate on the Imperial launch at Elba, 156 francs; a copy of the Emperor's banner at Elba, no price quoted.[1]

San Martino was subsequently sold to a wealthy Elban proprietor, Signor del Buono, who has turned out a number of heterogeneous objects that had accumulated in the house, and is engaged in re-constituting the museum.

He has placed in the Demidoff Gallery the superb mahogany bed which was sent to Madame Mère from Paris, and which she despatched after the Emperor's departure to Lucca, where it was probably used by Pauline, who often took the waters in that city during the last years of her life. Signor del Buono bought it at Lucca. The guéridon and coffee service in the Emperor's room above described, came from a family in Porto Ferraio.[2]

And it is among the private families that relics of the Imperial presence in Elba must be sought. I

[1] Catalogue of the sale at San Donato. The copy possessed by the Print Room of the Bibliothèque Nationale in Paris is marked with the sale prices written by hand. Can it be this copy of the Emperor's banner which has found its way back to the Hotel de Ville at Porto Ferraio, and is shown there to this day? Or was another copy made by Demidoff's orders and presented by him to the city along with the coffin and mask? This last suggestion is the most probable. It is hardly likely that the original can have survived.

[2] *Cf.* pp. 96 and 114. Madame Mère seems to have forwarded this bed to Lucca for her own use when she despatched the rest of her furniture to Rome (*see* p. 258). She intended in the first instance to go there on quitting Porto Ferraio, partly to take a course of baths, partly to be near Pauline, who had fallen ill at Viareggio (Letter from Cardinal Fesch to Caroline Murat, quoted by Larrey, II., 105).

have traced some of these, the authenticity of which appears to be indubitable.

Signora Traditi, granddaughter of the Mayor of Porto Ferraio, the Emperor's chamberlain, preserves and showed me the keys of the city, which her grandfather presented to Napoleon upon a silver tray, on May 4, 1814. She has also some armchairs which came, according to tradition, from the Mulini Palace, a much beautified miniature of the Emperor in the green coat of a trooper of the Guard, earrings, a pearl necklace, and a cameo which her grandmother received from Princess Borghese when the latter quitted the Island of Elba, and a fine carved ivory fan painted in the Chinese style, which Pauline sent from Rome five years later, to "kind Signora Traditi," in acknowledgment of a box of dried figs. The letter here reproduced accompanied the fan.[1]

She showed me another letter which the Grand Maréchal Bertrand wrote from Paris on March 24, 1815, to Signor Traditi, announcing the return of His Majesty to the Tuileries, and the present the Emperor was making to the city of Porto Ferraio of his full-length portrait, which is placed in the Assembly Hall at the Hôtel de Ville.[2]

[1] Pauline's letter: "Rome, February 15, 1820. It gave me great pleasure to receive the box of dried figs sent me by the kind Signora Traditi. I thank her much, and beg her to accept this little souvenir on my part, and to believe that I always think of her with pleasure. I hope she may care to have two fans from me. I beg her to convey my compliments to her husband, and to all in Porto Ferraio who remember me. Princess Pauline Borghese." The letter mentions two fans. One of these was subsequently lost.

[2] This portrait has disappeared. That which replaced it was presented by Prince Demidoff (*cf.* p. 9).

Signor Squarci, whose grandfather was surgeon to the military hospital of Porto Ferraio under Napoleon,[1] possesses the original of Note 13 of the Register of the Island of Elba, signed by the Emperor, which orders Drouot to form a company of gunners with the dismounted Polish Light Horse. In his cellars he has two or three dozen empty bottles from the Imperial cellars, stamped with N. surrounded by a laurel wreath, and his daughter, Signorina Squarci, dons the white satin gown which her great grandmother wore at the fêtes of the Mulini.

Signor Bigeschi, Sindaco of Porto Ferraio, whose great grandfather was one of the Governmental Junta in 1815, preserves among his papers the passport which the Pope gave Madame Mère when she went to Elba under the name of Madame de Pont.[2]

Thanks to the crystallisation of life in this little island, these various articles have never left the families who received them. These, and others, it is that might constitute a new museum of San Martino, and bring foreign visitors once more to Elba.

The theatre curtain, on which Napoleon is depicted in the guise of Apollo, has outlasted the use made of it by every company that passes through the island for a hundred years. But it is becoming more and more worn, and is a historical

[1] Pons de l'H., 347.
[2] *Cf.* p. 95.

Rome 15 fevrier 1820.

ho ricevuto, con piacere, la
scatola di frutte secche, che la
buona Madama Traditi mi ha
mandato. la ringrazio molto
e la prego di accettare questo
piccolo ricordo che gli mando
e crederle che sempre mi
ricordo di lei con piacere.
Spero che gli sarà agradevole
di avere due sventaglie di me.
prego di fare i miei complimenti
a suo marito, e a tutti quelli
di porto ferrajo, che si ricorda di
noi.

p.a paolina borghese

AUTOGRAPH OF PAULINE BORGHESE.

object that might with great advantage be transferred to the Demidoff Gallery.[1]

* * * * *

The Abbé Soldani, who was good enough to place himself at my service day by day, and to inscribe my name as an honorary member of the Confraternity of White Penitents (without any obligation to return to Paris in a cowl), took me one morning to the Church of the Most Venerable Confraternity of the Blessed Sacrament, where he served as priest, and showed me the treasures of the Sacristy, a Sacristy with shining cupboards and silent walls impregnated with an atmosphere of incense.

There he drew from a drawer an oval frame, of gilded wood, which encircled a *Pietà* of the Blessed Virgin holding upon her knees the body of her Son after the descent from the Cross. This picture was suspended, like a crucifix, at the head of the Emperor's bed, and he knelt before it night and morning, in the vague belief that fervent prayer to this divinity, Who seemed nearer to him than any other, might alter the decrees of destiny in his

[1] The enormous furnaces, recently set up at Porto Ferraio for the smelting of the iron from Rio Marina, and now in full work, will be the destruction of the old Island of Elba. Not only do they cloud the sky with their smoke, and bury the soil beneath the slag, already rising in mountains round them, but they will violate and imprison the murmuring springs of Maciana. The race of beautiful island women will disappear as the native blood mixes with an alien population. The streets of Porto Ferraio are sullied, prices are rising, the poor no longer know where to live, and the little capital where, formerly, everyone left his door open of a night, is now intimidated by burglars.

favour. And yet his own mother, whom he included in the superstitious adoration with which he prayed before this picture, unlike the Mother of Christ, was forbidden to hold his dead body in her embraces!

The Abbé assured me that this relic had been conveyed direct to its present sanctuary, and bought by a zealous Brother with his savings, to offer it to his church, to which the Emperor came on May 29, 1814, in great ceremony, with chamberlains and carriages, to hear the mass of San Cristino, as is attested by the dusty archives of the Chapter.[1]

The Abbé next drew from his cupboards a packet of stuffs sprinkled with camphor, and carefully wrapped up. These proved to be rich silk embroideries, with garlands of flowers in appliqué work. The gleaming colours were mellowed by age to a lovely softness. These, doubtless, came from the Piombino family, and had been the coverlet, curtains, and baldaquin of the Imperial bed in the Mulini Palace. They were subsequently acquired by the Church of the Blessed Sacrament, and the fabric of the coverlet had been cut and made over again, without touching the design, to drape the episcopal throne of the Bishop of Ajaccio, when he came to officiate in the Island of Elba.

The Abbé further invited me, before leaving, to pay a visit to his father, "who," he said in his

[1] Register of the Most Venerable Confraternity of the Blessed Sacrament at Porto Ferraro, 86. *Cf.* Pons de l'H., 227, 228.

quaint French jargon, which was better than my Italian, " was blind, and wished to see me."

He guided me to the first story of a house with a stone staircase and windows looking on to the magnificent bay, with its blue waves and green fishing-boats, on which I was to embark again the next morning. In a vast empty room, with a marble floor, a blind old man was seated upon an Empire sofa of mahogany and wicker-work, the medallions adorned with swans and lyres—another relic contemporaneous with the past, which had found harbour here.

"*Il Signor mio padre,*" said the Abbé.

The old man did not seem to hear us, for he was almost deaf as well as blind. A cloak with hanging sleeves was thrown over his shoulders, and he was warming his withered hands over a yellow earthenware pot in which burning cinders were consumed to ashes beneath a wire cover, so that he could not scorch himself. The primitive *brasero* was placed in front of him upon a stool, and he bent over it with limbs frozen by age. His sightless eyes were raised to the ceiling, to Heaven doubtless, for there is nothing between the blind and the object of his desires.

The Abbé touched him on the shoulder, and cried in his ear: " *Il Signor Francese.*"

He got up slowly (but with a rapid movement for his weakness), and his arms moved in the direction in which I was standing. I went towards him and took his hand in mine, and he asked, " Is it he?" I heard him repeating to himself: "French . . . The Emperor . . . My father . . . Waterloo." Then he began to talk volubly: "I am the son, *Signor*, of a Waterloo soldier. Napoleon! My father knew him when he was King of Elba. Eternal life to Napoleon! My father fought in his army, when he came from France, a General still, to deliver Italy. My father was at his side, at the Bridge of Lodi, as cavalry sergeant. The bullets rained in torrents on the regiment when they tried to cross the bridge, and the combatants all fell dead, or retired. Then my father saw the Emperor take the flag of the regiment, and plant it in the middle of the bridge, exclaiming "The bullet is not cast yet that will kill me." The Emperor was brave, he did not fear death. On the Island of Elba my father made part of the Emperor's Garde Mobile, and escorted him everywhere. The Emperor often spoke to him. He spoke to all alike, with no pride about him. My father was just married. The Emperor had promised to hold me in the church when I was christened. But when the time came the Emperor was no longer there. He left quite suddenly one day, and my father went with him. My father said: 'I should have followed him to the ends of the earth, and all the others would have been with me, because he was the Great Emperor.' He followed him as far as Waterloo. Then he came back. He was obliged to return on foot, as far as Piombino, without help, across

Germany, Switzerland, and Italy. That was four hundred leagues. He used to tell me all that when I was little, how the Emperor was dressed, what he said, and then how he had been defeated. Now the Emperor is dead, and my father is dead, too, and I am old in my turn, and have forgotten many of these things. But if the Emperor came back, I should go off with him, like my father. Long live the Emperor!"

The blind old man had become transfigured while he was speaking. His childhood seemed to surge up in him, with all these misty recollections of the Imperial epopee, related to him by the father who dandled him on his knee, the father who had returned on foot from Waterloo, had been raked with Wellington's cannon, and blackened by the guns of Mont Saint-Jean.

To me it was, indeed, one of the strangest experiences that can happen, to find myself suddenly confronted with this page of history, to be face to face with it, still living, and to be as it were in touch with it. I found myself in presence of the legendary fascination which the man with the little cocked hat wielded over all who came in contact with him, of the idolatrous admiration which these in their turn transmitted to their children. I understood, from this example, how men and nations become intoxicated with words and glory, and yield themselves wholly to those who know how to win them, following in their turn like sheep to the slaughter, to the mad carnage of the battlefield. Even I, whose every instinct was contrary, felt myself stirred in spite of my better judgment.

The blind old man sat down again exhausted. Tears streamed from his dead eyes. I went close to him, hoping to make him tell more, and give more exact recollections.

The Abbé, who could make himself better heard than I, explained my wishes. He remained pensive for some moments, and then began to laugh. "The Emperor was a sharp one! It was not easy to get the better of him. I remember, for my father often used to repeat this, that there was a little old woman in the next street to ours, called Battini. She lived in a room on the ground floor, where she worked all day at her spinning. One could see her through the window with her shuttle and threads.

"The Emperor never failed to look in when he passed that way. One day he stopped to talk to her. The Emperor was very generous. He always had gold pieces in his pocket, ready to bestow upon the poor. He came up to her with his generals, and said, 'My good woman, how much do you earn a day?' The little old woman (guessing his intentions) wanted to make herself out poorer than she was, so as to get larger alms. She looked very woe-begone, and replied, 'Alas! Your Majesty, only a few pence a day.' She was lying, *la Battini*, for she made much more. But the

Emperor knew the cost of things. He frowned, 'Only that, really? That shows you don't half work.' He turned away, and never looked at her again. She got nothing at all. It was quite right. No one could cheat the Emperor." And the old man added in a tone of conviction: "The Emperor could not bear falsehood."

Then he moved in his chair, and said something to the Abbé, who went to a desk at the far end of the room, and brought back a casket, which he put into his hands. The old man opened it carefully. He took out a gold key, and a flask of cut crystal. "This," he said, "is what the Emperor gave my father to keep in memory of him. My father always kept it, and so have I. I would not part with it for any money. There was also a copper lamp which my mother kept for a very long time. She used to put it in her window, when the Emperor returned late at night to the city. When the horses were galloping in the night out in the country, every one in the street the Emperor had to pass through in order to reach the Mulini lit one of these lamps in his window, which was always kept ready. For the road was very steep, and the horses often slipped upon the broken stones it was paved with. Some misfortune might have happened to the Emperor. The lamp has been worn out since, and I do not know what has become of it, but my mother showed it me when I was a lad."

The old man ceased to speak. I asked if there was nothing more he could tell me. He shook his head, and I saw that everything was getting confused again in his worn-out brain. He had entrusted the gold key and the crystal flask to my hands. I gave them back, and he put the two relics into their casket after kissing them. Keeping hold of my hands he carried them also to his lips, speaking in the flowery language of Italy: "He charges me to say," translated the Abbé, "that to have seen a compatriot of his Emperor will be the joy of his old age."

He still held my hand to his lips, and began to weep again. One of his tears fell, burning. He seemed unwilling to let me go, as though he feared to lose the distant past that I had awakened in him. I disengaged myself, almost by force, from his embrace, and left him in his darkness. He was put back on the mahogany couch with the sculptured swans. He pulled up his cloak, and took the little grated brasero between his legs, spreading his shaking hands above it again. I turned for the last time as I went out.

Next day I went back to the Continent. Returning subsequently to Paris, swallowed up as we all are by the devouring flood of our lives, I have never thought of the old blind man without emotion. He still lives in the time of Béranger, waiting peacefully for death amid his dreams of "the Great Emperor": while for us, those who vanished a year ago are already memories, the dead of twenty years have become a part of history, and those who went a century before are almost as remote as the Roman Cæsars and the Pharaohs of Egypt.

INDEX

INDEX

THE END

R. CLAY AND SONS, LTD., BREAD ST. HILL, E.C., AND BUNGAY, SUFFOLK.